C000046316

The Strategic Manager

The Strategic Manager provides a comprehensive, logical, and applied insight in strategic management. Unlike some more theory-heavy texts, this book focuses on how strategy works in everyday practice, taking readers' expectations and understanding beyond that of strategy as a matter of planning only. It enables the reader to learn and reflect upon their practical skills and knowledge, and critically evaluate the strategy process and their own strategic decision-making.

The book is based around six different strategy theories, individually presented and supplemented with useful lists of questions that encourage readers to become competent strategic thinkers. This third edition has been fully updated throughout, including fresh case studies and examples from across Asia, Africa, and South America that bridge theory with practice, new strategy practice boxes considering the importance of cooperation and strategic alliances, and reflective questions to aid understanding.

Essential reading for postgraduate students of strategic management, MBA students, and those in executive education, this text will also be a useful tool for reflective managers trying to develop a better understanding.

Online resources include chapter-by-chapter PowerPoint slides.

Harry Sminia is Professor of Strategic Management at the University of Strathclyde, UK.

The Strategic Manager

Understanding Strategy in Practice

Third Edition

Harry Sminia

Routledge
Taylor & Francis Group

LONDON AND NEW YORK

Third edition published 2022
by Routledge
2 Park Square, Milton Park, Abingdon, Oxon, OX14 4RN

and by Routledge
605 Third Avenue, New York, NY 10158

Routledge is an imprint of the Taylor & Francis Group, an informa business

© 2022 Harry Sminia

First edition published by Routledge 2015
Second edition published by Routledge 2018

British Library Cataloguing-in-Publication Data
A catalogue record for this book is available from the British Library

Library of Congress Cataloging-in-Publication Data
A catalog record for this book has been requested

ISBN: 978-0-367-46808-8 (hbk)
ISBN: 978-0-367-46806-4 (pbk)
ISBN: 978-1-003-03126-0 (ebk)

Typeset in Times New Roman
by Apex CoVantage, LLC

Access the Support Material: www.routledge.com/9780367468064

Contents

List of figures, tables, and boxes

Figures

Tables

Strategy practices

Illustrations

Exhibits

Preface

Back in 2013, I started writing the 1st edition of this book out of frustration. I found what was available in strategic management textbooks to be less and less relevant. Over the years, my teaching had moved away from presenting strategic management as an exercise of strategy formulation and strategy implementation because research into strategy process, strategy-as-practice, and my own experiences told me that this is not how strategy gets realized. Despite many firms, organizations, and managers devoting considerable time and energy to strategy formulation, the strategy that is eventually realized at best only partly reflects what had been intended originally. Yet the textbook orthodoxy continues to present strategic management in this overly ordered fashion, with chapters devoted to establishing the firm's objectives, doing an external analysis, doing an internal analysis, and formulating a competitive strategy, to finish with a chapter on how to then implement it. Subsequent editions of some textbooks have grown to contain hundreds of pages, but they all follow this basic template.

I was frustrated with this for two reasons. One, this is not how strategy and performance gets realized. Instead, it only helps to maintain this myth that strategic management should be this ordered process and that if you are unable to live up to these expectations, you are doing it wrong. Two, by grouping everything that has to do with the environment in one chapter and everything that has to do with the firm in another chapter, and so on, it prevents students from seeing how these ingredients of strategic thinking can be brought to bear upon each other. Since strategic management established itself as a distinctive management activity and a field of study, various different approaches have been put forward, but this is barely recognizable in most of the existing textbooks. The integrity of each distinguishable theoretical approach gets lost. As a consequence, students and managers are not shown how to put an argument together. What tends to happen is that when a strategic analysis is done, the result is nothing more than a collection of separate tools, often without any attempt being made explaining how it all fits together and leads to an overall conclusion. If the attempt is made, the reasoning tends to be disjointed and fragmented. Furthermore, it hides the richness of the field in that different approaches offer different ways in which a firm's situation can be appreciated.

So, I found myself in my teaching more and more at odds with what was available in the standard strategy textbooks. To remedy this, I started to write down what I was lecturing. And fortunately, Routledge in 2014 saw sufficient merit to offer me the opportunity to publish. Even more fortunately, the success of the 1st and 2nd editions led to the opportunity to publish this 3rd edition.

The 3rd edition still takes emergent strategy as its point of departure and fits elements of strategy formulation and implementation within it. In that sense, the strategy textbook orthodoxy is turned on its head. It presents strategic management as a real-time and ongoing activity. Strategy needs to be the subject of continuous questioning and problem-solving, which is aptly captured by the notion of 'wayfinding'. The world changes continuously. Consequently, a firm's strategic management has to constantly question what is going on and how it affects a firm's performance and future potential to perform. Strategic management requires managers to always be critical and self-reflective about how they go about and understand what is going on. To help achieve this, the book explicitly presents six different strategy theories, emphasizing their dissimilarity to fuel the debate. It is the quality of the argument and the inhibited exchange of views that I believe is pivotal for whether a firm will remain viable.

The difference between the 1st, the 2nd, and now the 3th edition is incremental. The cases at the end of each chapter have been updated or are replaced by more recent ones. Chapters have been added to and in parts are reformulated as a consequence of experience gained when teaching from the text and because strategic management research moves on. And I have added even more 'illustrations' – examples that explain bits of theory in more concrete terms.

The Strategic Manager reflects the experience of over 25 years in the field. During this time, students and colleagues have had to endure my attempts at designing strategy courses and classes that reflect how strategies actually get realized. Students at the University of Strathclyde Business School have been on the receiving end, as I used the 1st and 2nd editions to teach strategy in the Strathclyde MBA and various MSc courses. Their comments and reactions – negative and positive – helped to shape this book into what it is now.

I am indebted to the Strathclyde SAE teaching team and particularly Ron Bradfield, Alistair Gray, Anup Karath Nair, and Marisa Smith. I also want to mention the various local councillors in the Strathclyde International Centres in Bahrain, Greece, Malaysia, Oman, Singapore, and the United Arab Emirates (UAE), who over the years helped deliver strategy teaching to successive cohorts of MBA students. I am humbled by their appreciation of *The Strategic Manager* and their enthusiasm teaching from it.

There have been many more colleagues over the years – too many to mention – who I have worked with and from whom I have learned how strategic management can be understood and taught. I want to single out Frits Haselhoff, who set me on my way so many years ago. His voice is still present in what I do now. I also want to mention Andrew Pettigrew, whose ideas about strategy process still resonate with me, and Robert Chia, who introduced me to the notion of 'wayfinding' which is at the heart of this 3rd edition.

There are also a number of strategy practitioners who have shared their experiences with me. Their insights not only have been invaluable but also have been the inspiration to write this text. This is especially true for John Lever

Briggs. The many conversations I had with John about what it is really like to be a CEO have found their way into what I have written.

Terry Clague, Sinead Waldron for the 1st edition, Izzy Fitzharris for the 2nd edition, Emmie Shand for the 3rd edition, and undoubtedly various others at Routledge have been very helpful in getting this book out.

Finally, there is one person who deserves a very special mention, although she hates when I do this. Monique Röling has been there for me for the best part of my life.

Harry Sminia
Inverkip, Greenock, Renfrewshire, Scotland

CHAPTER 1

Strategic management basics

Strategic management is about making a firm or an organization perform and about maintaining the organization's or the firm's ability to perform (Sminia & de Rond, 2012). This book explains how to use strategy theory to evaluate whether the firm or organization will be performing, whether the firm or organization will maintain the ability to perform, and what a strategist can do about it.

Strategic management as wayfinding

Mintzberg (1987), very conveniently, came up with the five Ps of strategy. These Ps refer to the most commonly found definitions or usages of the term 'strategy' within management and organization speak. Strategy very often is seen as a plan: "some sort of consciously intended course of action" (p. 11). In some instances, strategy refers to a ploy: "a specific 'manoeuvre' intended to outwit an opponent or competitor" (p. 12). Describing what the strategic plan is about, strategy also is seen as a position: "a means of locating an organization in what organization theorists like to call an 'environment'" (p. 15). On occasion, the actual content of a plan reflects a particular and favoured way in which the organization's circumstances are interpreted rather than an impartial assessment of the situation. Others have advocated that the way forward should be expressed in terms of a vision. In either case, strategy has taken on the meaning of a perspective: "an ingrained way of perceiving the world" (p. 16). Another often found meaning of strategy beyond Mintzberg (1987) is strategy as a panacea: a solution to everything. To get you out of a tricky situation, you need a strategy. All of these definitions have in common that they look at strategy as just an intention, effectively downplaying the fact that a strategy should be realized to generate performance.

Practicing strategists very often see intentions never being realized. Most of what firms and organizations eventually achieve is due to interferences, happenings, and circumstances that have emerged, despite carefully formulated plans, as illustrated in Figure 1.1. This book focuses therefore on strategy as a pattern "in a stream of actions" and as "consistency in behaviour, whether or not intended" (Mintzberg, 1987, p. 12; Mintzberg & Waters, 1985). It takes strategy to

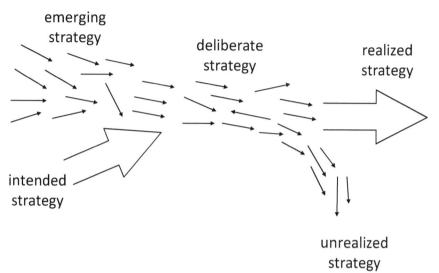

Figure 1.1
The strategy process

be a process: as something that strategists do, rather than what an organization has (Jarzabkowski, Balogun, & Seidl, 2007).

The emphasis in this book is less on doing a strategic analysis to formulate a plan or an intended strategy to then implement it. This is an overly stylized representation of the strategy process – found in many contemporary strategic management textbooks – and maybe something of a mirage. It has some – but limited – relevance for the actual practice of strategic management. Instead, the focus is more on realizing strategy and how to understand and manage the process by which this takes place. The starting point is how strategy is being practised – how it actually is being done.

In the real world, circumstances change constantly. Realizing performance, as well as maintaining the ability to perform, can be hampered or enhanced by what emerges all the time. Strategic management therefore requires to be done in a continuous fashion. It requires instant evaluation about what is going on and of the consequences this might have for the performance and viability of the firm or organization. It requires strategists to be able to act to move the firm or organization along, whenever this is required. You often cannot afford to sit down and carefully write down your strategic plan. This book explains how these instant judgements can be made using currently available strategy theories. It indicates what strategists can do to affect the course of the process by which performance is realized.

All of this does not necessarily mean that formulating an intended strategy and drafting a strategic plan is meaningless. It means that this should be seen as part of a larger process by which a strategy – as this pattern in a stream of activities – is realized. All in all, strategy as a process is elaborated here as wayfinding: a continuous questioning, analyzing, and problem-solving (Chia & Holt, 2009).

The practicality of strategy theory

> Nothing is so practical as a good theory.
>
> (Lewin, 1945; cited in: Van de Ven, 1989, p. 486)

Strategy theory provides two things. First, theory supplies a vocabulary to describe what is going on. Second, theory offers explanatory logics by which we can evaluate what is going on. A vocabulary to describe what is going on is useful because it provides a means to make sense of situations. Making sense of a situation by describing it in terms of a specific strategy theory is the first step in doing a strategic analysis. Strategy scholars have formulated theory to distinguish the wheat from the chaff; to see the wood for the trees; to focus on those things that need focusing on. This book provides an introduction to six strategy theories, with each theory providing a particular understanding of how firms and organizations can be made to perform.

Anyone who provides a description of a situation essentially engages in theorizing. Sense is made of a situation by abstracting from all the day-to-day experiences and observations and focusing on those parts that are seen as essential; maybe simplifying it into a short concise statement (Weick, 1989). Such a description is an interpretation of a situation, and the words chosen to communicate this interpretation are an act of abstraction, focus, and simplification. At the outset, anyone's interpretation can be just as valid as anybody else's. Strategy scholars engage in research to find out what theories might be the most worthwhile. These theories allow a strategist to construct an alternative interpretation that is bound to be different from the more intuitive first impression that everybody can come up with. In that way, strategy theory provides alternative points of view from what strategists might see by using their own instincts and presuppositions.

Strategy practice 1.1 What makes a SWOT analysis useful?

The SWOT (strengths, weaknesses, opportunities, and threats) analysis is arguably the most used and most popular analytical tool in the strategy field (Hodgkinson, Whittington, Johnson, & Schwarz, 2006). It is meant to provide an assessment of the environment in terms of opportunities and threats as well as an appreciation of the strengths and weaknesses of the firm. Its origin is credited to Albert Humphrey, who devised this 4×4 matrix while working for the Stanford Research institute in the 1960s. But on its own, it can be very misleading.

The problem is this. By itself there is little indication of when and why something needs to be qualified as a threat or an opportunity, or as a weakness or strength. Assigning something to either of these categories is purely arbitrary, unless . . .

The 'unless' is where additional theory has to come in. This should be theory allowing for an evaluation of the situation; telling the analyst when something has to be qualified as a threat, opportunity, weakness, or strength. It is only with the aid of strategy theory that employs a performance logic that a meaningful and sound SWOT analysis can be done. The theoretical approaches featuring in this book can serve this purpose.

A description is not an evaluation yet. For this, you need a reasoning by which a conclusion can be attached to the described situation. Some – but not all – theories allow the strategist to draw conclusions. This is the case when theory not only describes but also explains. Strategy theory is strategy theory because it attempts to explain performance. An explanation of performance indicates how a strategist can intervene in the course of events by which performance is realized. Two explanatory logics are common to all strategy theories. One of these logics is the process logic. It provides a particular take on how firms and organizations function in the wider environment and suggests what strategists can do to affect this. The other logic is the performance logic. It takes firm or organization performance as that what needs to be explained to suggest causes or reasons that provide an explanation for this success or failure.

The process logic

The way by which a firm or organization performs is a process. The way in which strategy theories understand this process allows us to distinguish between three process spheres (see Figure 1.2).

The sphere in which the other two spheres are embedded is the 'environmental survival process'. This refers to what takes place in the environment. The organization or firm participates in this sphere to function and survive. In a manner of speaking, you can zoom into the environmental survival process and focus on this smaller sphere that is the organization itself. The 'organizational strategy process' then comes into view. It is the process within the firm or organization that generates strategic intentions, deals with emerging issues, and realizes performance. What happens in this sphere determines how well a firm or organization is capable of dealing with what the environment throws at it. A strategist, in turn, has to function within this organizational strategy process. The 'actions of the individual strategist' refer to the individuals within the firm or organization – and more specifically, to what they do. This in turn affects how

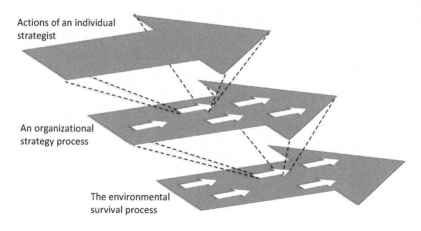

Actions of an individual
strategist

An organizational
strategy process

Figure 1.2
The process logic:
three zoom levels

The environmental
survival process

capable a firm or organization is and whether the firm or organization realizes its potential. Zooming into this third process sphere reveals the detailed activities of the individual strategists who are taking part in the organizational strategy process.

Every strategy theory has a specific take on who these strategists are and what they are expected to do. Ideally, whatever a strategist does should contribute to an organizational strategy process by which the firm or organization becomes a viable entity that can take part in the environmental survival process. You could say that the process logic refers to the management part in strategic management.

The earliest strategy theorists advocated an organizational strategy process that became known as strategic planning. The first strategy textbook portrayed the strategy process as consisting of two stages (Learned, Christensen, Andrews, & Guth, 1965). First, you formulate a strategy, and then you implement it. This quickly evolved into the idea that an organization should do strategic planning. Strategic planning, simply, is an organizational procedure that follows this formulation-implementation process logic. It is a framework by which a whole firm can engage in a basic strategic analysis. It is often set out as a carefully managed method by which a firm has to go through a number of successive steps. Ansoff (1965) was probably the first to develop a strategic planning methodology (see Figure 1.3). Many have followed in his footsteps; the vast majority of strategy textbooks are written around it, and they all incorporate the same basic template.

Following this basic template, strategic planning is supposed to start with top management deciding on a set of broad goals or objectives for the firm; maybe formulating a vision and a mission. These objectives are cast in terms of the kind of business the firm wants to be in and explicate which performance levels are expected. This is accompanied by an internal appraisal and an external appraisal – others would refer to this as the internal analysis and the external analysis. These appraisals intend to assess what the firm is capable off and what the environment

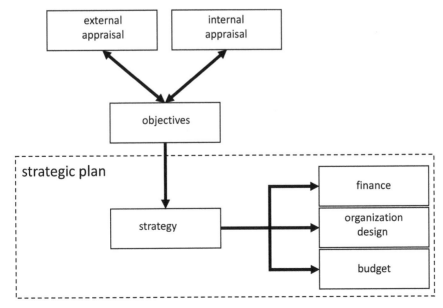

Figure 1.3
Strategic planning

looks like. Findings in one step will inform the other two. For instance, the business definition can be derived from the markets the firm intends to operate in.

All this information feeds into a strategic plan. The plan is formulated by stating what strategy the firm is going to pursue. It is also supposed to contain detailed statements about how resources will be allocated – normally by deciding on budgets, how the execution of the plan will be financed, and how everything will be organized. As soon this is decided on, it needs to be communicated to those who have to implement it. As soon as people have been told what to do, they then must be monitored by using something like a balanced scorecard (Kaplan & Norton, 1992). Many firms go through regular strategic planning or business planning cycles. Larger firms tend to have departments devoted to generating such a plan on an annual basis. Many people working in an organization find themselves monitored to determine whether what they do contributes to the organization's explicitly formulated strategy.

Strategic planning has its use, but its universal applicability is heavily disputed. For instance, Mintzberg and Ansoff entered into an intense debate about whether strategic planning has anything to do with strategic management at all (Ansoff, 1991, 1994; Mintzberg, 1990, 1991, 1994a, 1994b). As can be expected, Ansoff sees it as the cornerstone of strategic management. To Mintzberg, strategic planning is an oxymoron – a term that denies itself – because the flexibility inherent in strategy as dealing with an unknown future contradicts with the inflexibility of mapping the future out in a plan. This book sides more with Mintzberg than with Ansoff. Strategic planning can be useful, but its limitations need to be acknowledged, as well. The emergent nature of strategic management means that more often than not, a firm or organization cannot afford the luxury of limiting its strategic management to only going through an extensive strategic planning procedure.

Nevertheless, the expectation that strategic management should incorporate rational decision-making when this is appropriate remains. Many strategy theories are based on this notion. Consequently, these theories portray the strategist as a rational decision-maker. A strategist is seen as an information processor. The strategy theories that are built around rational decision-making are predominantly derived from economics (e.g. Barney, 1991; Porter, 1980; Rumelt, Schendel, & Teece, 1991). These specific strategy theories aim to explain firm performance on the basis of competitive advantage. The explanations provide a means to assess situations and to rationally pick a strategy that promises to yield the best results.

Some strategy scholars investigated how strategies are actually realized, and they draw a different picture (e.g. Johnson, 1987; Pettigrew, 1985; Quinn, 1980; Sminia, 1994). They overwhelmingly came across organizational strategy processes featuring continuous negotiating, people exercising power, and struggles with the prevailing organizational culture. Instead of taking their cues from economics, their strategy theories are derived from sociology and psychology. These scholars put question marks against the expectation that a strategist is a rational decision-maker and emphasize other qualities that the strategist should have.

Albeit, all strategy theories – explicitly or implicitly – share this basic idea that strategic management is the one process in which you can zoom in and out of these three process spheres. They all incorporate a specific take on how a firm or organization survives and is successful in the environment, how the strategy process inside the organization takes place, and what contributions an individual strategist makes. There are differences, however, with regard to how they think these process spheres are to be understood. This we can take to our advantage because the different takes on the same phenomenon provide us with a much more sophisticated understanding of what is going on. The six different theoretical approaches introduced in this book each understand the strategy process in their own specific way.

Illustration 1.1 Honda's deliberate or emergent strategy?

In the early 1970s, the then British government commissioned strategy consultants Boston Consulting Group (BCG) to write a report on the British motorcycling industry. It pinpointed the various reasons why a group of once proud and world-leading motorcycle manufacturers had gone into decline. The authors put particular emphasis on Honda and the way in which it conquered the US market at the expense of the British. "The basic philosophy of the Japanese manufacturers is that high volumes per model provide the potential for high productivity as a result of using capital intensive and highly automated techniques" (BCG report, quoted in Pascale, 1984). It reveals how the consultants' account focuses on explaining the Japanese mechanism of success. This mechanism allows you to become very efficient and simultaneously to drown out the competition and become the market leader. Of course, this does require a considerable investment up front in these "capital intensive and highly automated techniques". But if you have the money and the patience, this is how you do it. The report and subsequent cases used for teaching strategic management in many of the leading business schools in the world assumed that this was Honda's intended strategy. It was assumed that the people at Honda had worked this out and that they had been implementing this recipe for success.

Pascale (1984) went after the Honda executives concerned and asked them how they did it. They came up with a completely different story. Their inroads in the US started in 1958. They went on a reconnaissance mission and found out several things about the US motorcycle market. People in the US drive big cars. Motorcycles are bought by a small leather-clad subset of the US population. They are bought from a total of 3,000 dealers who were motorcycle enthusiasts first and business people second. Annual unit sales were 450,000, with 60,000 imported from Europe. On that basis, they decided without much analysis that it would be reasonable to go after 10% of the imported cycles. To compete with the Europeans, Honda would have to offer the 250cc and 350cc models.

They came back in 1959 but started small and set up base in Southern California. Because of all kinds of restrictions imposed by the Japanese government, they could only bring a limited number of cycles with them. They were able to convince 40 dealers to stock Hondas, and registered a few sales. Almost immediately, disaster struck and many of the bikes were returned – leaking oil and with failed clutches. Apparently, motorcyclists in the US ride their bikes much farther and much faster than those in Japan. While Honda technicians were frantically trying to resolve this, they were contacted by a Sears buyer. He had noticed the small 50cc Honda Supercubs they had been riding around on in Los Angeles to do errands. The Honda people had brought a few with them, but had not attempted to offer them for sale. They reckoned there would not be a market for them in the US, where everything was big and powerful. They first turned down the Sears buyer's requests. What would a 50cc moped do for the Honda brand while the market was in big bikes for macho motorcyclists? But with the big bikes breaking down and in desperation, they gave in. To their astonishment, there was a demand for motorcycles – not through motorcycle dealers, but through sporting goods retailers. This gave them their first foothold.

Honda subsequently moved the US motorcycle market away from the macho 'black leather jacket' customer on the back of the 'You Meet the Nicest People on a Honda' advertising campaign. The most junior Honda executive in the US pushed this through at the time, against the wishes of his superiors. Motorcycles became more of a leisure item and less of a mode of transport. By 1964, Honda market share in the US in lightweight motorcycles was 63%, compared with 4% for Harley-Davison and 11% for British manufacturers (as cited from a teaching case by Pascale, 1984).

So, if such a successful outcome is a matter of events that emerge and just happen, even against the initial judgement of those who were part of this process, what is the use of intended strategy? In a debate between four strategy scholars, Henry Mintzberg used the Honda case to make his point that strategic planning does more harm than good (Mintzberg, Pascale, Goold, & Rumelt, 1996). Instead, strategic management should embrace emergence and the process should be one of trial and error; of learning while you go along. Michael Goold (who was one of the authors of the BCG report and by then had moved on to become an academic at Ashridge Management Centre) argued there was still a place for planning, analysis and rational decision-making. To him, learning and emergent strategy does not preclude the possibility that there are explanations of firm performance like the one cited in the BCG report. His point is that such insights are worthwhile considering if you are interested in advising top management what to do (for a more extensive discussion, also see Mair, 1999).

The performance logic

If the process logic refers to the management part, then the performance logic refers to the strategy part in strategic management. It underpins all considerations with regard to strategy content. As was indicated earlier, an important part of strategy research tries to establish and validate what explains performance. Once you know about what explains success or failure of an organization or firm, you can understand the situation that you want to analyze in terms of this particular theory. Depending on your findings, you can draw conclusions with regard to whether the firm or organization is destined for failure or success.

Most strategy theories are derived from economics. The most common explanation of success among strategy theorists, therefore, is competitive advantage (see Figure 1.4). To many strategy scholars, competitiveness is at the heart of strategy content (Porter, 1980; Rumelt, Schendel, & Teece, 1994). Competitive advantage means that the firm somehow is better than its competitors. The majority of strategy theory tends to focus on the business firm and assesses

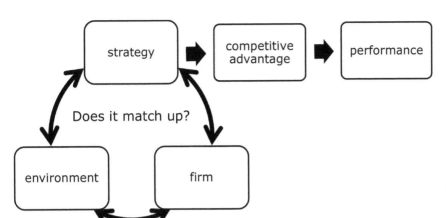

Figure 1.4
Performance logic
for business firms in
particular

performance in terms of one or more financial parameters. The assumption is that firms have to compete to remain viable and survive. The purpose of the firm is seen as generating a profit. In short, firm performance tends to be about the ability to outperform the competition.

Competitive advantage, in turn, is seen to be the consequence of the three main ingredients of strategic thinking. These three ingredients are: the environment, the firm, and the strategy the firm pursues. Furthermore, these three ingredients need to match up in some way for the firm to be competitive and successful. Yet it is with regard to these three ingredients that, again, there are profound differences between the various strategy theories currently in existence. This book will provide an in-depth look at four theoretical approaches developed to explain firm performance through competitive advantage. These are 'marketing-inspired strategic thinking', the 'industrial organization approach', the 'resource-based view', and 'agency theory and shareholder value'. These four approaches share a performance logic centring on competitive advantage. They differ with regard to how they describe the environment, the firm itself, and the strategies the firm can pursue.

It is difficult to deny that strategy theory is somewhat biased towards the business firm. There are, however, strategy theories that are equally applicable to both business firms and to non-profit and public sector organizations. Many organizations that are less bothered about competition still need to be concerned about their performance and about their continued ability to perform. Two of these theoretical approaches will be featured in this book. These are the 'stakeholder approach' and 'institutional theory'. Each approaches also has its specific take on the environment, the organization itself, and the strategies the organization realizes. Instead of centring on competitive advantage, these two approaches focus on legitimacy as the explanation of performance (see Figure 1.5). An organization's activities are legitimate if these activities are considered to be desirable, proper, and appropriate within a system of norms, values, beliefs, and definitions of the situation (Suchman, 1995). These two approaches also allow for a description of performance in other terms than just financial parameters.

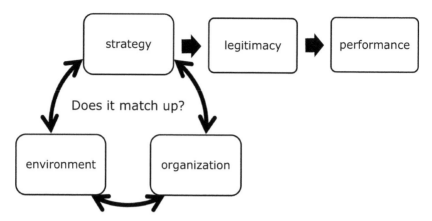

Figure 1.5
Performance logic
for organizations in
general

This does not necessarily mean that strategy theory centred on competitive advantage is useless for non-profit and public organizations. There are many occasions when these organizations find themselves competing for something. Most of the time, this is about securing scarce funds and resources. In these instances, the more business-like theories centring on competitive advantage are useful.

Each one of the six theoretical approaches provides a means to evaluate situations instantly, which is a requirement for the continuous character of strategic management as wayfinding. Yet the way they reason can lead to conclusions that can be profoundly different from each other.

Strategy practice 1.2 How useful is a PEST analysis?

Almost every strategy textbook features the PEST analysis (or PESTEL). It is normally the first thing in the chapter on the environment. Many management and business students never seem to progress beyond the PEST analysis. The assignments that they hand in tend to devote many pages to completing this analytical tool. This is a shame, because a PEST analysis has a very limited usefulness. It provides nothing more than a categorization. It tells a strategist to look at the environment and to decide whether something that is observed can be labelled as political, economic, social or technological. That is it. It does not tell the strategist anything beyond that. It does not give any indication of what to do or what is implied if something has been categorized as political, economic, social or technological. No further conclusions of any significance can be drawn. How useful is that?

Strategy as continuous questioning, analyzing, and problem-solving

There are very few certainties in strategic management. One of them is that there will never be a definitive answer or an infallible judgement on a situation. There are a couple of reasons for this. The first, obvious, one is that different strategy theories can provide different conclusions about the same situation. There is no way to definitely assess which theory will be the better one. This is inherent in what theory does. As was said previously, its advantage is in abstracting, focusing, and getting to the essence of a situation to be able to draw a conclusion. This is also its disadvantage, because each theory does this in a particular way, emphasizing one set of aspects while downplaying the rest. Strategy scholars do their best to get at the relevant things, and each scholar has an equally valid argument to back up the choices they make in their abstracting and focusing. Yet they have to make assumptions – and consequently, they reason in different ways.

These assumptions are necessary to provide a basis under their arguments. The nature of these assumptions is such that their validity can be neither investigated nor tested because they touch upon the very nature of empirical reality (ontology), upon what constitutes knowledge (epistemology), and upon how such knowledge is to be gathered (methodology) (if you are interested in this, see Burrell & Morgan, 1979; Morgan, 1980). So, this is one reason why strategy is a continuous questioning. It is a questioning fuelled by the different basic assumptions underpinning the various different theoretical approaches. The final chapter will come back to this to provide a little more insight how the six theories compare.

Another reason for continuous questioning, analyzing, and problem-solving is that the world moves on. Things happen all the time, and this urges the strategist to constantly reassess the situation. In fact, firms and organizations failing to see change as a permanent fixture of their existence will find that they are eventually overtaken by the course of events. This often leads to the demise of the firm or organization (Johnson, 1987; Pettigrew & Whipp, 1991). This is another scarce certainty of strategic management: there will always be change. It means that there is a constant need to revisit previous conclusions in the light of changing circumstances.

Firms and organizations – and their top management – do not like to appear to be continuously reassessing their strategy. Yet this questioning and inherent doubt tend to define the nature of the managerial job (Mintzberg, 1973; Watson, 1994). Chapter 7 on institutional theory will explain that there is an expectation in society for firms and organizations to have a strategy, or at least some idea of why they exist and where they are going – not because it is necessarily useful, but because it is seen as right and proper (DiMaggio & Powell, 1983; Meyer & Rowan, 1977). Top management teams are expected to be all-knowing, rational, and in control, even if experience tells them that this is impossible. For that reason, the official line of many firms and organizations is that they have decided on a strategy – about which they are in no doubt and which they are implementing without fail. Portraying themselves in that way is part of the requirement of legitimacy. Nevertheless, the actual experience at the top often does not reflect this ideal. On the contrary, those firms and organizations trying to live up to these expectations and organizing their strategic management for rationality and control often end up stifling the necessary critical attitude that allows for continuous questioning – and consequently, they lose touch with the many things that are going on (Chia & Holt, 2009; Johnson, 1988; Pettigrew, 1985). Strategic management as wayfinding recognizes this continues questioning, analyzing, and problem-solving as part and parcel of life at the top.

If you are cynically inclined, you may argue that not being able to provide definitive answers and questioning, and debating everything, makes strategic management a pretty useless affair. If you are unable to draw definitive conclusions, why bother? The counter-argument is that any assessment of the situation and its conclusions provide an educated guess that is preferable over sheer ignorance. There is merit in being informed by analysis and in debating partial and temporary truths. This is preferable to not knowing anything at all. Utilization of strategy theory will enhance the quality of the questioning and the quality of the analysis. Helping to improve the quality of the strategy process is the primary purpose of this book.

Doing strategic management as wayfinding

So how do you do it? There are two types of activities that a strategist should be able to do. A strategist should be able to act and make such contributions to the organizational strategy process that the firm or organization is able to function in the wider environmental survival process, and a strategist should be able to think and assess the situation so that the actions are well considered and have a chance of making the necessary contributions. This can be summed up as being able to answer two basic questions.

1 Are there any issues arising that might affect the future success and survival of the firm or organization?
2 If there are, what can you do about them?

Answering Question 1: strategic analysis

Strategic thinking is about continuous questioning and analysis. It is about asking and answering the first question. Here the performance logic comes in, and to utilize this performance logic, two ingredients should be combined. One ingredient is the strategy theory and the basic explanation of performance that it offers. The other ingredient is the empirical evidence – or data/information – about the firm or organization and the situation it is in. A strategic analysis needs to start with the theory and then bring in empirical evidence to describe the situation in terms of the theory. More specifically, the theory is used to generate even more specific and detailed questions so that data can be gathered to answer them.

Strategic analysis is not a matter of following a small number of easy steps which automatically lead to a conclusion. It is more of a puzzle, and its solution depends on the pieces that are available. Yet to do this continuously for a firm or organization that you are responsible for, you should already know about the environment the firm or organization is operating in, you should know about the firm or organization itself, and you should know about the strategy the firm or organization is realizing. You should be able to describe the situation you are in, in terms of the performance logics of the various available theoretical approaches. Every firm or organization effectively is realizing a strategy, whether it is articulated and consistent or not. There is an environment. The firm or organization is what it is. If you do not know about this, you cannot do wayfinding.

Strategic management as wayfinding is about dealing with a situation when it happens, or when you become aware that something might happen, or when you are wondering what will happen if you embark upon some initiative yourself. You basically try to assess how any of this will affect the firm's competitive advantage or the organization's legitimacy. Answering Question 1 is actually answering the very basic question whether the match between the strategy, the organization/firm, and the environment is or will be affected. If you find this is the case, there is an issue. Strategic analysis is about continuously asking questions, and this is the question to start with. If you know nothing about these three basic ingredients and whether they currently match up or not, it is impossible to think about how issues might affect an organization's or firm's future success, let alone doing something about them. If you know nothing, you need to get up to speed first.

Getting up to speed

You get up to speed when you become knowledgeable about the firm's or organization's environment, the firm or organization itself, and the strategy it realizes. Explaining how to do this at this stage will probably appear rather abstract, dull, and meaningless. It will become much clearer later on, when this is explained again in the context of a particular theoretical approach.

As was said previously, a theory provides two things: a vocabulary to describe the situation, and an explanatory logic that allows the strategist to evaluate the situation and draw a conclusion. At this stage, the explanatory logic to work with would be the performance logic. The theoretical vocabulary – the specific words, constructs, and variables that are part of the theory – indicate what questions there are to ask. Taking your cue from these questions, you can then look for data or empirical evidence to provide answers. In this way, you end up with a description of the situation for the investigated firm or organization in these specific theoretical terms. Each theory defines and describes the environment, the firm or organization, and strategy in a very specific way.

You can then draw your conclusion by answering the question whether the three ingredients of firm/organization, environment, and strategy match up. If they do, everything is fine (for the moment). If they do not, you have an issue on your hands and something should be done about it. It is simply a matter of finding out how the firm or organization fares in terms of a particular theory.

Such a very basic analysis can be the purpose of periodic strategy workshops or strategy evaluation exercises a top management team may engage in. This also covers much of the work of strategy consultants, as they are often commissioned to help firms or organizations to assess the situation. There will always be a problem of insufficient data. Only so much empirical evidence can be made available – even if a consultancy company is hired to do much of the legwork. This makes the puzzle such a challenge: working and drawing relevant conclusions within the existing data limitations.

Continuous questioning and analyzing

A strategist in charge of a firm or organization is actually supposed to know the situation the firm or organization is in. Managers are supposed to know the extent of the match or mismatch between the environment, the firm or organization, and its strategy, and they are expected to have ideas about how these three elements should be matched up. Simultaneously, the world moves on. The influence of governments and supra-governmental bodies varies over time. Local, regional, national, and global economies experience upturns and downturns. Societies change. Fashion changes. New technologies are developed, and others become obsolete. The availability of natural resources fluctuates. Natural disasters happen. Governments introduce new legislation all the time. And many more things happen and can be expected to happen.

Additionally, all kinds of individuals, organizations, and firms take initiatives to develop and change things. The firm or organization itself can become entrepreneurial by developing a new product/service bundle, moving into a new market or country, working on new technology, acquiring or merging with another firm, or finding a new way to do the same thing more effectively and efficiently. Evaluating how this may affect the firm or organization while all this is going on requires strategic management as wayfinding. It is the reason for continuous questioning, analyzing, and problem-solving.

The purpose of continuous questioning is to find out whether anything that crosses the path of a focal firm or organization, or any initiative the firm or organization may want to take, affects the competitive advantage or legitimacy of the firm or organization, either positively or negatively. It is about endlessly asking the question whether things still match up. Wayfinding is about questioning what is going on and analyzing whether it will affect the firm's performance levels and potential to perform, and whether something needs to be done about it. Strategic management as wayfinding should find out about possible changes to the three elements, to then trace their effects through possible changes in the way in which these three ingredients match up and affect competitive advantage or legitimacy, and eventually performance. Again, each theoretical approach provides a specific vocabulary to trace changes. It provides the language to formulate questions and find answers. This is what it is all about.

Answering Question 2: problem-solving and taking action

Strategic management is also about problem-solving and taking action. Or maybe about doing nothing and letting things develop naturally. Any action in essence is an intervention in a process that is currently happening. A strategy will be realized with the associated performance levels, whether a strategist does something or not, as is depicted in Figure 1.1. An intervention is necessary if an issue is seen to lead to an unwanted realized strategy, probably with the wrong or too low performance outcomes. There is a 'what?' question and a 'how?' question here. What can you do, and how do you do it?

With regard to the 'what?' question, the performance logic points the way. Each one of the six strategy theories provides the strategist with a range of options. These options can be found with regard to all three elements. In principle, a strategist can change the firm's or organization's strategy, change things about the firm or organization itself, or can even attempt to change (aspects of) the environment. Yet each one of the theoretical approaches is built on a specific understanding of what these three ingredients look like. Consequently, each approach puts forward particular recommendations to what there is to change, and consequently, what options exist and what recommendations can be made. Nevertheless, all options need to be scrutinized with regard how well they address the issue that has been identified. This is also part of wayfinding.

The 'how?' question is where the process logic comes into play. How to intervene and create a result depends on what process sphere you are talking about. But all three need to be considered. An intervention in the environmental survival process is about the firm manoeuvring in the world at large. An intervention in the organizational strategy process is about the strategist contributing to the questioning, analyzing and problem-solving and the functioning of the organization or firm. It is about how strategic management is done. An intervention at the level of the strategist is about you yourself and reflecting on your own actions, understandings and thoughts. Again, each of the six strategy theories has elaborated the strategy process in a particular way. This means that each approach has specific answers to the 'how?' question with regard to all three of the process spheres.

Nevertheless, there is one commonality. A process by which a strategy gets realized and by which performance actually is created is nothing more than a sequence of events (Pettigrew, 1990; Van de Ven & Poole, 1995). This means that any action or contribution made at all three levels adds events to the course of the process (Van de Ven & Sminia, 2012). The implication is that any answer to the 'how?' question takes on the general form of specifying what events to add to the sequence in the expectation that it changes the course of the process.

Strategy practice 1.3 Can you implement a strategy?

A common understanding in many strategy textbooks – and also among many managers – is that the 'what?' and 'how?' questions are a matter of strategy formulation and strategy implementation. You first decide on the 'what' by formulating your strategy. Once that is clear, you implement it and reap the results. But can you expect that there is a fail-safe method out there by which you can execute any strategy? Is it a matter of learning to apply an implementation tool?

Hrebiniak (2006) reports that implementation goes wrong for six reasons. A strategy does not happen when top management fails to overcome resistance, the formulated strategy is too vague, top management is not working according to an implementation guideline or model, there is poor communication, the strategy goes against the existing power structure, or when there is a lack of clarity about authority and responsibility. His remedy is to offer an implementation model that tells top management to derive local objectives from the overall strategy, and communicate these to middle managers, accompanied by a clear structure of incentives and controls to make sure that people are doing what they are supposed to do.

Balogun and Johnson (2005) arrive at a different conclusion. They find that different parts of the organization interpret what might be intended as clear strategy, objectives, incentives, and controls in all kinds of different ways, depending on how things are understood locally. Nobody at the top of any organization has enough local understanding to 'translate' anything formulated at the top in such a way that everybody everywhere in the organization understands it unequivocally. The local interpretations create their own dynamic, and people down in the organization adapt whatever is coming at them in a way that makes sense to them. The unintended outcomes that are thus generated are not necessarily worse than what was intended at the top; they are just different.

Business-level strategy and corporate-level strategy

For the sake of argument, strategy scholars have invented the notion of the strategic business unit (SBU). Most theories imagine that a business produces one single product/service bundle, which it tries to sell on a specific market. This is often referred to as a product/market combination. The SBU is the unit of analysis that has to have competitive advantage to perform well. Talking about strategy with regard to the SBU or business level is referred to as either competitive strategy or business-level strategy. The focus of any strategy theory dealing with the competitive strategy or business-level strategy problem is on finding ways how the SBU can compete better. How can the SBU outperform the competition?

Most of the time, real firms offer more than one product/service bundle. Strategy scholars then talk about multi-business firms. This is obvious for the large multi-national corporation (MNC) with a presence in many countries, offering a wide range of products and services, and consisting of various divisions and subsidiaries. It is also often the case for smaller firms, which have branched out over time into adjacent product/service bundles but are organized along functional lines. The multi-business firm creates an additional strategy problem. By definition, two or more businesses have been put together and are part of one firm, but each business has to compete in its own arena. The question then is whether an SBU would be a better competitor as part of the larger organization of which it is part, or on its own. Corporate strategy is about this.

Recognizable here again is the bias in strategy theory toward for-profit businesses, operating in an essentially competitive environment. However, the same distinction can be made for not-for-profit and public sector organizations. These types of organizations provide a specific public service or focus on a particular cause, and business-level strategy deals with the legitimacy of this public service or particular cause. This is the business-level strategy problem. Often, non-profit and public sector organizations find themselves engaged in more than one public service or cause. The question then becomes whether this public service is better provided as part of an organization that provides many services or whether this public service would benefit more from a single specialized organization. The same question can be asked with regard to championing a specific cause: is this better done as part of a multi-cause organization, or would a single-cause organization create better results?

Strategy theory will not make much sense without understanding the meaning of the notion of the SBU.

How to work the book?

This book aims to provide the reader with sufficient insight to 'practise' strategic management. One of the 'mantras' of strategic management is that there never is a 'right' answer. However, the expectation of many students is that there is. Most strategy textbooks are put together as if there is a single recipe – predominately derived from a strategic planning approach – by which you arrive at the appropriate strategy. This book's premise is to emphasize that there are profoundly different ways of doing strategic management which, when applied, lead to different answers. The reader is introduced to six different theoretical approaches. Each theoretical approach has its own chapter devoted to it. As was said earlier, these theoretical approaches are marketing-inspired strategic thinking (Chapter 2), the industrial organization approach (Chapter 3), the resource-based view (Chapter 4), agency theory and shareholder value (Chapter 5), the stakeholder approach and organizational politics (Chapter 6), and institutional theory and organizational culture (Chapter 7). Every chapter explains how an approach can be utilized to draw conclusions whether the firm or organization will perform, whether it will maintain the ability to perform, and what contributions a strategist can make

Each chapter has the same structure. First, the process logic of the theoretical approach is explained. This is followed by an explanation of the performance logic. Each chapter then has a section devoted to some additional features that come with each particular theoretical approach. These are further elaborations within the same basic argument that either have gained some prominence in the strategy field by themselves or provide a further understanding of what is typical about the approach. Some theories have more of these features than others. By this time, the specific theoretical vocabulary that characterizes this approach has been introduced.

Each chapter then moves on and explains how a strategist can apply this approach for the continuous questioning and analyzing that strategic management as wayfinding compels you to do. This leads to sets of questions by which a strategic analysis can be done. The next subsection is on problem-solving and taking action, making use of the process logic of the theoretical approach to discuss the various options that a theoretical approach throws up. A final section draws things together, extends some of the criticisms but also offers some thoughts on how to work with the differences that exist.

Each final section – on further questions and unresolved issues – maybe is the most important when it comes to wayfinding. It introduces the limitations of each theoretical approach, in a way setting the boundaries around an approach's usability. However, some of these limitations exist because of some very basic assumptions that have to be made. There are two aspects to these basic assumptions. First, these basic assumptions define the nature and type of theoretical approach. They are linked to core philosophical debates that can never be resolved. Second, these assumptions apply to all strategists, as well. Often involuntarily, each individual manager adopts a basic stance and attitude towards management – and the world in general – in terms of these basic assumptions. These assumptions should be at the heart of any manager's self-reflection.

A short final Chapter 8 wraps things up, dwelling on some of the similarities and key differences between each strategy theory, and providing some comments on the questions that remain unanswered. Moreover, this final chapter deals with this problem of abundance in strategic management: is there a way to use these many and often contradicting theoretical approaches alongside each other, or not?

Each chapter also features little interludes about specific strategic practices, like the ones earlier in this chapter on PEST analysis and doing a SWOT analysis. Strategic practices are ways of doing things that strategists draw on when they do strategic management (Whittington, 2006). Some are derived from and therefore are specific to a particular theoretical approach. Others are less specific but take on particular meaning within a theoretical approach. All strategic practice can be used and mis-used. Additionally, there are a number of illustrations like the one following about SKF: stories based on real events that aim to make the abstract theoretical terminology more tangible and concrete.

Finally, each chapter ends with a case. The case allows the reader to go through the sets of questions identified earlier in the chapter to effectively interrogate the situation and enter into the questioning, analyzing, and problem-solving that strategic management as wayfinding requires. The information provided in the case description is relatively raw. Part of the exercise is to find out what the evidence tells us, to then draw out and debate conclusions and recommendations.

Illustration 1.2 SKF has a strategic issue

SKF appears to have been confronted by an issue*. One of its larger US-based clients wants to organize a reverse auction. This client has asked its suppliers to bid for its business, with the lowest bidder getting the order.

SKF is one of the largest manufacturers of ball bearings in the world. Over 100 years old and originally from Sweden, it now has a worldwide market share of about 20%. It has organized itself into three divisions: Industrial, Automotive, and Service. The SKF Service Division serves this US-based client. The Service Division represents one-third of SKF sales. It provides replacement ball bearings and aftermarket services to manufacturing firms that operate machinery which contains ball bearings. A ball bearing is made up of small steel balls that are inserted into a bearing so that one object can rotate within another object. Every piece of machinery that has moving parts typically contains sets of ball bearings. SKF's strategy is based on providing durable solutions. It offers high-quality replacements and services, but typically charges higher prices. SKF's argument is that the quality of its hard-wearing ball bearings is worth the extra money because it makes machinery more efficient and reliable. Being asked now to compete on price is not something it is inclined to do. The question, of course, is: what should SKF do? Should it abandon its strategy and put in the lowest bid possible, or should it step away from it, accepting that the company will lose a big client but stay true to its strategy?

This issue will be examined in all subsequent chapters, examining the problem and making a recommendation utilizing the language and logic of each of the strategy theories.

* Value Selling at SKF Service, IMD-5–0751, 2009

CHAPTER 2

Marketing-inspired strategic thinking

The marketing concept provided a first rationale for doing strategic management. It directed strategists towards seeing the environment as filled with customers whose wants and needs should be fulfilled. They should then design a firm that is capable of pursuing a strategy aimed at satisfying these wants and needs.

The process logic of marketing-inspired strategic thinking

The marketing concept has not only spawned a distinct management function and the accompanying field of research; it also inspired a particular way of thinking within strategic management. Most of the earliest ideas about strategy and what a firm should do to remain viable have a distinctive marketing flavour. Marketing as a concept is defined by Kotler (1976, p. 14) as

> a management orientation that holds that the key task of the organization is to determine the needs, wants, and values of a target market and to adapt the organization to delivering the desired satisfactions more effectively and efficiently than its competitors.

The idea that firms can only be successful if they are able to fulfil customer needs has developed a specific vocabulary, as well as process and performance logics to do strategic management with (Biggadike, 1981; Hunt & Lambe, 2000).

From a marketing point of view, the environment thus consists of customers with wants and needs. These customers are taken to assemble into product markets on the basis of their specific demands. These can then be satisfied by the supply of a product that fulfils these demands. Firms compete with each other by offering goods and services which customers value enough that they want to buy them. Firms then have to ask the highest price that customers want to pay for these goods and services. The environmental survival process, therefore, is understood to be a process of competition for market share in product markets (see Figure 2.1).

Illustration 2.1 Restaurant customer types

A way to get to grips with product markets and market segments and the different customer preferences is to develop a typology based in what different customers want. For restaurants, such a typology could distinguish between the 'busy balancer', the 'food service hobbyist', the 'functional eater', the 'affluent socializer', the 'bargain hunter', the 'habitual mature', and the 'health enthusiast'*. The labels are neither here nor there. What matters are the different wants and needs that distinguish the different customer groups that these labels represent, and the observation that the 'food service hobbyist', the 'functional eater', and the 'busy balancer' apparently make up over 50% of the market. A 'food service hobbyist' goes out for a meal to socialize but does not want to pay too much. A 'functional eater' eats as cheaply as possible, mostly on the go. The 'busy balancer' is about making healthy choices when eating out.

Covid-19 has added another layer of customer wants to all of this. These include spaced-out tables, employees wearing masks, all common areas visibly wiped down regularly, extremely clean toilets, employees wearing gloves, sanitizing products provided to all customers, and smaller capacity**.

* www.restaurantbusinessonline.com/consumer-trends/7-key-consumer-types [accessed 24 November 2020]
** www.restaurantbusinessonline.com/consumer-trends/what-consumers-want-restaurants-now [accessed 24 November 2020]

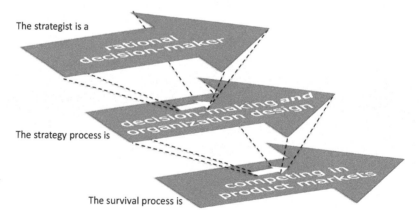

The strategist is a rational decision-maker

The strategy process is decision-making and organization design

The survival process is competing in product markets

Figure 2.1
The process logic for marketing-inspired strategic thinking

To deal effectively with customer wants and needs, and to be ahead of the competition, firms are urged to assess what these wants and needs are and formulate a strategy that tells the firm how to fulfil the customers' demands. This firm should then be designed in such a way that it is capable of delivering the appropriate goods and services. The strategic management task – in this classic approach – is seen as making planning and execution decisions to secure a highly performing firm (Christensen, Andrews, & Bower, 1973). The internal strategy process is very much associated with the highest echelons of the firm. Top managers take the strategic decisions and it is up to the people lower down in the hierarchy to act on them. These decisions should be about the firm's goals and objectives in terms of what product markets to serve, as well as the plans to attain them.

Only after these decisions are made and a strategy is formulated can it be implemented. Such implementation, in turn, requires managers to design an organizational structure and procedures that allow the firm to operate in the desired manner, to allocate resources to give people the means to do what they should do, and to secure the necessary finances for the firm to function, as well as putting in place a system of management control for top managers to check whether the firm remains on track. Ansoff (1965) developed this into an extensive organizational procedure and labelled this as 'strategic planning'.

From a wayfinding strategic management perspective, extensive planning exercises are less called for, as the world tends to be too complex for an all-encompassing plan (Mason & Mitroff, 1981) and things will change anyway (Mintzberg, 1990). What remains is the expectation that the firm's strategy process is about decision-making and organization design, about gathering and processing information on customers and product markets, and about redesigning organization structures and procedures that allow the firm to deliver on its strategy.

According to this process logic, there are only a limited number of strategists, and they are located at the very top of the firm. Top managers make the strategic decisions. Managers lower down in the hierarchy are there to act on them – although middle managers can become part of strategic decision-making activities when they are asked to provide input or elaborate on operational consequences detailing how the objectives and strategic responses formulated at the top should be implemented. Middle managers are also often asked to report on their progress as part of periodic management control procedures. The strategists at the very top of an organization are expected to process information, weighing various alternative ways forward against each other, and choose the one they see as the most appropriate. They are expected to act as rational decision-makers. Once they have made their decision, they communicate it down into the organization so that middle managers and employees know how they should do their jobs.

To sum up, a strategist's contribution to the eventual success of a firm is processing information in order to make rational strategic choices as part of an organizational process of decision-making and organizational design. The purpose is to compete for market share on product markets with other firms by fulfilling customer wants and needs better. If the strategist gets it wrong, according to this process logic, the firm will fail.

Illustration 2.2 Can there be too much competition?

This is some time ago, but in the late 19th century, there were two railway companies operating in the southeast of England (Bagwell, 1955). The London, Chatham & Dover Railway and the London & South Eastern Railway connected London with the county of Kent. The rivalry was intense. They opened up railway line after railway line. They also built a succession of new stations in London to be able deliver passengers ever closer to the city centre. Most of the larger towns – and many of the minor towns – in the southeast ended up with two stations with many lines running parallel. For instance, close to Chatham there were two bridges crossing the river Medway next to each other. Building railways incurs high fixed costs. The population numbers did not warrant the investments. Ironically, because both railway companies were so strapped of cash, they were barely able to maintain themselves. Consequently, they came to be known for their high fares and poor service. They also almost never returned a profit. The rivalry ended when they entered a working union in 1899, effectively working as one company from then on. They merged into the Southern Railway in 1923.

The performance logic of marketing-inspired strategic thinking

To make the right decisions, strategists should understand and utilize the particular performance logic of marketing-inspired strategic thinking. As was said, firm performance ultimately is explained by the extent to which a firm is capable of fulfilling customer wants and needs better than the competition. In other words, product market demand should be matched with the appropriate supply of products and services (Levitt, 1960). Marketing scholars also found that most product markets can be subdivided into market segments on the basis of more subtle differences with regard to what customers expect from a product. Firms consequently have to take this segmentation into account if they want to be successful (Biggadike, 1981).

Deciding which product markets or market segments to target is referred to as positioning. This is the way in which strategies tend to be formulated (Biggadike, 1981). The way to do the strategic positioning in this approach is to decide on a trade-off (Faulkner & Bowman, 1992) (see Figure 2.2). Any strategy here is a compromise between price and perceived customer value. A firm positions itself in a product market by offering a product or service that has some specific attributes that a customer values, for a price that they expect this customer is actually willing to pay for it. If a firm offers a simple product that only offers basic value to the customer at a low price, this firm effectively operates a 'no-frills' strategy. A firm employs a differentiation strategy when it offers something more specific and special, as customers are prepared to pay a higher price for it. Products or services that offer very bespoke value for a particular market segment is referred to as a niche, which tends to command premium prices – but only with those customers whose very particular wants and needs are being catered to. Any firm should avoid offering a product that nobody wants or asking a price that does not match what customers want to pay.

Only those abilities that are needed to deliver the value that fulfils customer needs are expressed in terms of key success factors (e.g. Hofer & Schendel, 1978) or critical success factors (e.g. Rockart, 1979). From a marketing point of view, success factors are those characteristics of the firm that enable it to pursue a competitive strategy in a product market. It is therefore at the heart of

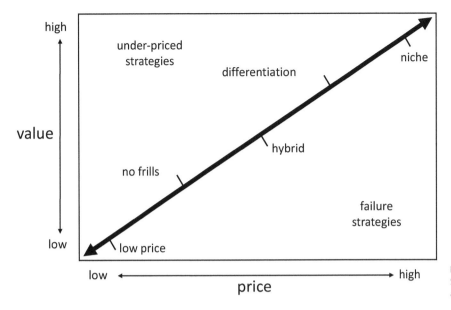

Figure 2.2
Strategic positioning
as a trade-off

competitive advantage. A firm has many abilities. An ability is 'key' or 'critical' for firm success when it is essential for offering a product or service with the right customer value at a cost that allows for a sufficiently high margin.

Based on the marketing concept, Abell (1980) argued that a business should be defined in terms of the customer wants and needs that are being satisfied, the product markets or market segments that are served, and the technologies that are utilized to serve these markets. This came to be known as the three-dimensional business definition. It also defines a firm's opportunity space in terms of customer wants and needs, and of the specific ways in which these can be met. Furthermore, this model is utilized to assess how competitors compare by finding out which needs and wants they serve, and what technologies they use.

The three elements of product markets (and market segmentation), positioning strategies in terms of the trade-off between perceived customer value and price, and the key or critical success factors, are all part of marketing-inspired strategic thinking (see Figure 2.3). The environment is a product market, consisting of customers with wants and needs. The firm is appreciated in terms of success factors that allow it to satisfy these wants and needs by way of a strategy that can be formulated as a trade-off between perceived customer value and price. Moreover, all three elements should fit together. A firm needs to have success factors that allow it to pursue such a positioning strategy that satisfies customers' wants and needs. If any of these three elements does not contribute to this fit, the firm is in trouble. At the heart of every decision that strategists may make on the basis of marketing-inspired strategic thinking, they need to address this question of 'fit'.

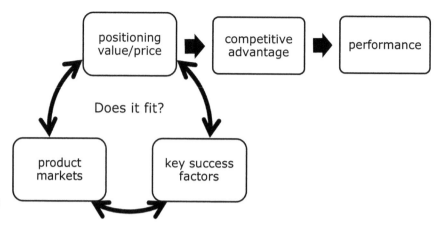

Figure 2.3
Marketing-inspired
strategic thinking

Illustration 2.3 Competition among car manufacturers

Allegedly, Henry Ford said that "you can have any car, as long as it is black". He was referring to the Model T, the first car manufactured in large quantities. Since then, car manufacturers have become so adept in designing and selling cars that many now have specific models for each segment they can distinguish. US drivers favour comfort and the cars manufactured for the US market have automatic gears and soft suspensions. European drivers like the frugality of diesel engines and prefer manual gearshifts to the extent that in many countries, diesel cars warrant a higher price than petrol cars. Looking at what can be observed on the streets, US car buyers like pickup trucks, SUVs, and MPVs. Chinese buyers prefer saloon cars. Europeans favour intermediate hatchbacks, while Brazil is a country for small hatchbacks. Within segments, manufacturers try to distinguish themselves even more, leading to specific success factors for different brands. Some try to appeal to the customer who sees a car as a status symbol, with the manufacturer concentrating on branding and snob appeal. To other customers, a car is just a mode of transport and an expense that has to be endured. The key success factor here is less about brand image but more about low price and the most efficient way to build and sell a car.

Segmentation in the market for cars has become so well established that it is even included in European Union decision-making in approving or rejecting proposed mergers. The document* that indicates approval for the merger between KIA and Hyundai in 1999 refers to no fewer than nine segments, referring to them with the letters A–F, S, M, and J. For instance, the B segment is small cars, the C segment is medium-sized cars, the D segment is large cars, the M segment is MPVs, and the J segment is SUVs. This categorization is commonly used throughout Europe.

A McKinsey** report on the future of the worldwide automotive industry distinguishes between a premium segment (10% of the market; highest prices and margins), a value segment (mid-price; 70% of the market), and an entry segment (least expensive; 20% of the market). They expect that it will become more difficult to differentiate premium cars from value cars, but that if this has to happen, it will have to be through car design features. They also expect the value segment to become even more competitive and efficiencies through scale are key, with globally operating volume firms having the best chances here. The entry segment is mostly relevant for emerging economies, and their rise will fuel growth in this segment. Low price – and therefore, low-cost production – are paramount here.

* Case No COMP/M.1406 – HYUNDAI/KIA, Regulation (EEC) No 4064/89, Merger procedure, (17 March 1999)
** McKinsey & Company, The road to 2020 and beyond: What's driving the global automotive industry? (August 2013)

Additional features

Understanding the environment as a 'product market' lies beneath a number of early strategy concepts. This has led to specific rationales that have found their use in strategy formulation. 'Economies of scale', the 'experience curve', the 'product life cycle', the 'Ansoff matrix', and the 'BCG growth share matrix' deserve mention. It also allowed for the distinction between business-level competitive strategy and multi-business corporate strategy. A more recent development within marketing-inspired strategic thinking is to think of product markets as being 'red oceans' characterized by cutthroat competition or newly developed and highly profitable 'blue oceans'.

The concept of 'economies of scale' refers to an insight from the field of micro-economics. It is based on the observation that the cost per unit is related to production volumes. Every organization that is in the business of making something has a particular level of production at which it operates at its highest efficiency. This insight is particularly useful for businesses with enormous fixed costs. These costs can be spread out over large production volumes so that their relative contribution to the overall costs per unit becomes minimized. Low costs can be a key success factors for firms that compete on price. A strategic lesson derived from this is that a firm, especially when it has high fixed costs, should be the largest producer in a product market. This would make it the most efficient producer, as the competitors very likely use similar production facilities and have high fixed costs, as well. Hence, the recommendation is that a strategy should aim for market leadership. The market leader is the firm with the largest market share, and therefore the largest production volume.

The 'experience curve' is a similar concept. It refers to another apparent insight from micro-economics that the longer a product is in production, the lower the cost per unit will be. In the course of time, firms tend to become more competent in what they are doing. Bruce Henderson, founder of BCG, realized that this effect offers possibilities for some strategic reasoning (Henderson, 1984). It means that firms that become market leaders will have gained the most experience and therefore will have the lowest costs. The market leader, by definition, has sold – and therefore produced – the most products. For that reason, it has gone faster down the experience curve and is consequently the most efficient (see Figure 2.4). It is easy to conclude that here, too, a firm's strategy should be directed at becoming the market leader to be able to out-compete any competitor.

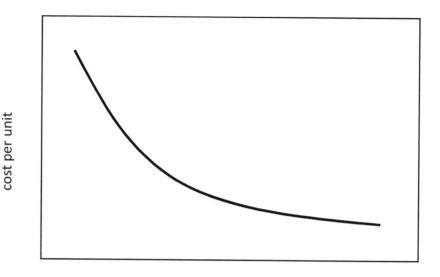

Figure 2.4
The experience
curve

total units produced over time

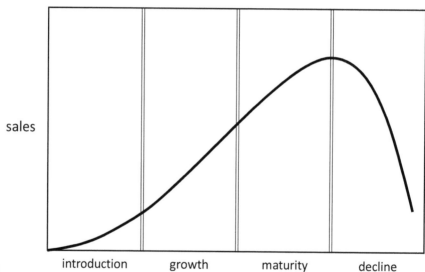

Figure 2.5
The product life cycle

The 'product life cycle' builds on a more general idea that everything goes through a process of birth, growth, maturity, and eventual decline. More specifically, this means that a product and its associated product market goes through these phases, as well (see Figure 2.5). Each phase should be managed in a specific manner. Theodore Levitt (1965) was first to coin this life cycle idea. It has since gained considerable traction (e.g. Day, 1981; Hofer, 1975).

The basic suggestion is that every stage creates its own specific form of competition. When a product is first introduced, the situation is very uncertain, and it is just a matter of sticking with it in the hope that customers will start liking it and the product will take off. The growth stage is expected to be a race for market share – cue the experience curve and economies of scale – with the market leader emerging as the winner. This phase also creates opportunities for differentiation, as customer demand tends to become more sophisticated. During the maturity phase, everything settles down and the competition moves to price, facilitated by decreasing cost bases of those few firms which have established themselves as the largest players. This also tends to open up possibilities for niche players who can serve segments that the big players find difficult to satisfy. The eventual decline means the end for most firms (unless they have developed a new product and can take part in another life cycle), with a few who are able to hang on serving limited demand that may continue to exist.

Illustration 2.4 Xiaomi's smartphones and the product life cycle

Xiaomi is one of the major smartphone companies in China. However, market research firm IDC* reported that Xiaomi's market share fell by nearly 40% in 2016. The firm grew market share by offering first-time buyers phones with some high-end features for a relatively low price. Smartphone penetration in China has reached 75%. Consequently, the majority of smartphone sales have become replacements. With this, Chinese customers' preferences have changed. Many now favour mid-price phones that are innovative but less gimmicky. The fall in Xiaomi's market share can be attributed to the firm's offerings not moving along with the product life cycle as the Chinese smartphone marker went from the growth phase into the maturity phase.

* Xiaomi: Show me again, *The Economist*, 3 September 2016 (provided by Anup Karath Nair)

Apart from thinking about how to compete in a product market, marketing-inspired strategic thinking also leads to a vocabulary to describe the various ways in which a firm can develop itself either within a specific product market or across a range of product markets. Igor Ansoff (1965) came up with the 'Ansoff matrix', summarizing the ways in which a firm can seek to grow its business in terms of just four growth vectors. Market penetration means that a firm seeks to gain market share with its existing product in the product market it already serves. Market development means that it takes its existing product to a new product market to create additional turnover. Product development means that the firm creates a new product for the market it already serves to grow in that way. Diversification means that the firm branches out by creating a new product for a new market. These four growth vectors are purely descriptive and do not indicate by themselves what the most sensible course of action would be.

Corporate strategy and the multi-business firm

The growth vectors from Ansoff's (1965) matrix suggest that firms can end up serving more than one product market. If this is the case, we are talking about a multi-business firm. It means that the strategic management of this firm not only has to deal with the business level or competitive strategy question of how it is going to compete in every single product market. The multi-business firm also has to think about how it is going to be able to keep it all together. The corporate strategy question needs to be answered, too. Does keeping all of these businesses together in one firm make each separate business a better competitor, or are they getting in each other's way?

From a marketing perspective, there are two ways to justify the multi-business firm. One way refers to sharing; the other way makes use of portfolio thinking. A multi-business firm is justified when some sharing is taking place, allowing for lower costs or for utilizing the same success factors to serve more than one product market. Ansoff (1965) labelled the advantages that come with sharing as synergy. Making two different products, each for its own distinct product market, in the same production facility can create synergy, if it contributes to economies of scale or experience, or if the second product utilizes spare capacity. Similarly, using existing marketing channels for additional products can also create synergy. It spreads fixed costs over additional volumes. However, it will create extra coordination costs.

Illustration 2.5 Synergy in VAG*

In 2018, VAG's Porsche subsidiary built 253,000 cars. This only accounted for 10% of VAG's revenues, but contributed 30% of the profits. In contrast, the Audi subsidiary made just a little more profit but did that with 1,500,000 cars. Porsche's margin is €16,250 per car, while Audi's is €3,200; cars sold under the VW brand only have a €960 margin. Some VAG shareholders think Porsche would be better off as a stand-alone business. Equity research firm Evercore ISI thinks floating Porsche would yield €150 billion. However, Porsche makes use of common VAG technology. The Porsche Cayenne SUV uses the same platform as the VW Touareg and the Audi Q7. Porsche and Audi will also use the same platform for future battery-powered models. The question is whether Porsche could continue to be successful if it were detached from VAG.

* Porsche is small but highly lucrative, The Economist, 12 September 2019 (provided by Anup Karath Nair)

Portfolio thinking imagines the multi-business firm as a portfolio of activities. The most famous portfolio-based theoretical tool is the BCG 'growth share matrix' (Henderson, 1984). These tools follow a similar logic of categorizing business on the basis of various marketing-based variables to make an assessment of the portfolio as a whole. The BCG 'growth share matrix' uses two variables – market growth and relative market share – to characterize each business in a multi-business firm as a 'question mark', a 'star', a 'cash cow', or a 'dog' (see Figure 2.6).

There are suggestions at competitive strategy level with regard to treating each one of these types of businesses differently, yet the BCG matrix's most important usage is at the corporate strategy level. What you are looking for is balance in the portfolio. You want each of the four types of business to be represented,

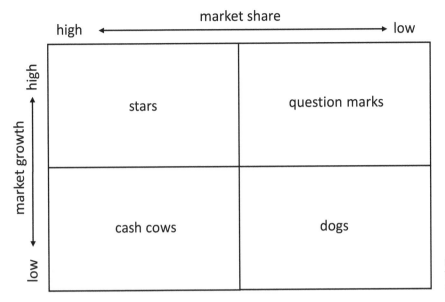

market share

Figure 2.6
The BCG growth share matrix

especially when you take the product life cycle into account (Barksdale & Harris, 1982). Every business is expected to go through this cycle, effectively starting as a 'question mark' to subsequently developing into a 'star', transitioning into a 'cash cow', and finally ending up as a 'dog'. You need the cash cows to generate the money that you require to grow the market for a question mark and to increase market share for a star. A dog can be maintained as long as it generates cash and helps to prop up the stars and question marks. An unbalanced portfolio will mean that this little motor of successive businesses eventually will stall.

Illustration 2.6 IKEA in Sweden, the UK, and China

IKEA sells furniture in 37 countries. The firm is often perceived to be a global retailer, offering the same concept – flat-packed furniture at a reasonable price, which customers have to put together themselves – in the same way: big out-of-town stores you drive to in your car to get the flat-packed furniture you want out of the warehouse yourself. However, IKEA operates more as a multi-business firm with adaptations to its concept tailored to the demands of different countries. There are differences in the way they operate in Sweden, the UK, and China (Burt, Johansson, & Thelander, 2011).

In all three countries, IKEA operates under the same brand name; 95% of the product range is the same across the world. This is where synergy can be found. However, in Sweden, IKEA is a mature brand, the company having been founded there in 1958. The typical IKEA customer is a 20–49-year-old woman with children, but increasingly the 55+ age group becomes attracted to the stores. IKEA is known for low prices and delivering value for money. Swedes are accustomed to 'do-it-yourself' (DIY) work in and around the house. They have fully accepted that IKEA's low prices mean that you have to assemble the furniture yourself. Because IKEA is long established and very well known, with every Swedish home having a piece of IKEA furniture inside it, it is relaunching itself and trying to make itself new and exciting again.

IKEA has been present in the UK since 1987. The typical UK customer is a 25–45-year-old middle-class woman with her family. The British do not mind DIY and are therefore not averse to home assembly. They also realize that the low price point has to come with certain compromises. IKEA markets itself as being different – i.e. not British – to the British customer, as that is what is valued the most about their offerings.

IKEA entered China in 1998. The typical Chinese customer is 25–35 years old, lives in an urban environment, and typically does not drive a car. IKEA stores therefore tend to be located close to public transport facilities. The Chinese are also alien to DIY. Combined with IKEA's brand perception as an exclusive Western retailer for the Chinese higher middle-class, and with a price level that is relatively high for Chinese standards, their way of operating does not naturally fit with the Chinese market. Chinese customers do not understand why you have to put this relatively expensive furniture together yourself. Instead of as a low-price furniture retailer, IKEA presents itself more in terms of interior design, offering smart solutions for the relatively small apartments in Chinese cities. On the one hand, IKEA is trying to educate Chinese customers on the merits of self-assembly. On the other hand, in some stores, IKEA has also started to offer a delivery and assembly service which is included in the price.

In terms of the product life cycle, you could argue that in Sweden, IKEA is edging between maturity and decline. In the UK, IKEA has matured, while in China, it is maybe on the brink of the growth phase.

Business development from red oceans to blue oceans

Ansoff's (1965) growth vectors, combined with the product life cycle, urges firms to continuously develop new business, as mature product markets will suffer from cutthroat competition on price and eventually die out. Kim and Mauborgne (2004) refer to such a situation as a 'red ocean'. A 'red ocean' is a product market or market segment that lacks further growth and where firms are left to compete for market share with highly commoditized products. The way to escape such a situation is to find a 'blue ocean': an as-yet-unknown product market or market segment where firms have not ventured yet. The main thrust of finding a blue ocean is value pioneering. Value pioneering is a deliberate attempt to develop a new value proposition that is different from how customers perceive the current offerings. This includes stepping away from some product/service aspects that are taken for granted to develop and emphasize alternative product/service aspects that have not been considered and offered previously. In this way, it is believed that a firm can find new demand for a previously non-existing product or service.

Illustration 2.7 Casella Wines' Yellowtail blue ocean strategy

Casella Wines was a small Australian winery which was looking at entering the US wine market (Kim & Mauborgne, 2005). Wine traditionally was associated and appreciated as a complicated product that required knowledge and a dissenting taste to be appreciated. That is how wine drinkers in the US valued wines, and that is how wine companies marketed their products, with sales price matched to prestige and how exquisite the wine tastes. Yet margins were thin, with a few very large wine companies competing for market share. A large proportion of the US population was not interested in drinking wine because of the complicated nature of the product. Canella Wines targeted the non-wine drinkers with its Yellowtail brand. For this, the company de-emphasized the reasons for subtle taste differences by which traditional wineries were competing with each other like vintage, grape types, soil differences, etc. Instead, they positioned Yellowtail wines as easy and fun to drink. As a consequence, Casella's Yellowtail did not appeal to existing wine drinkers. Instead, it tapped into the non-wine drinkers who started to drink Yellowtail wine in large quantities.

Doing marketing-inspired strategic management

From a strategic management as wayfinding perspective, the question that continuously should be asked is whether there still is a fit between the strategy (in terms of the trade-off between price and value) and product market demand, i.e. the wants and needs of the customers, and whether the firm's success factors are still in place. Anything that happens that disturbs this fit should be qualified as a strategic issue and action should be taken. Therefore, from a marketing point of view, the two questions to ask and answer are as follow.

1　Are there any issues that jeopardize the fit between the product market (market segment) the firm serves, the positioning strategy it realizes, and the success factors the firm has?
2　If there are, what can you do about them?

Answering Question 1: strategic analysis

The purpose of a strategic analysis is to find out whether something that is happening, or which is about to happen, will jeopardize the fit. Doing a strategic analysis is about asking the right questions and finding answers. The things that trigger the need to analyze can come from anywhere. There might be something happening in the environment: a move from a competitor, an innovation, new legislation, a takeover threat, an economic upturn or downturn, or something else. The need to do an analysis can also come from internal reasons: the idea to make a competitive move, an innovation the firm is working on, the opportunity to do an acquisition or a merger, or something else. The purpose of a strategic analysis is to assess what is going on, and to decide whether it warrants action. To be able to do this, the strategist needs to know about the firm's current success factors, the customer wants and needs, and what strategy the firm is realizing. If this knowledge is lacking, you need to get up to speed first.

Getting up to speed

If, for some reason, the strategist does not know about the firm's strategy, its success factors, or customer wants and needs, then the performance logic tells what information should be gathered and how all this information should be evaluated. There is a very specific set of questions to answer. Exhibits 2.1, 2.2, and 2.3 provide the key questions for the external and the internal appraisal, and about the positioning strategy the firm is realizing.

The core question for any marketing-inspired strategic analysis refers to what the relevant product market is. Any answer should be based on customer wants and needs. A very common pitfall is to define the market in terms of a product: the market for product A or service B. Instead the wants and needs that characterize a distinguishable group of customers should be assessed. The market should then be defined in terms of these wants and needs. Another common pitfall is to describe the market or a market segment in terms of customer characteristics or 'demographics', such as the demand from young people or old people or the market for people who commute to work by car. These demographics and characteristics are just indicators for distinct product markets or market segments. They can be used as indicators because they coincide with specific wants and needs. Knowing that someone is old by itself does not tell you what that person's needs and wants are. Knowing that specific wants and needs coincide with the age of the customers who display these wants and needs allows you to describe them on the basis of these or other demographics.

Exhibit 2.1 Marketing-inspired external appraisal questions

- Who are the customers, and what wants and needs do they have?

    - This defines the product market the firm wants to serve

- Are there any market segments in this product market?

    - This tells us what segments there are to target

- Who are the competitors, what is their strategy, and how well are they able to compete?

    - This tells us how we compare

- What stage in the product life cycle are we in?

    - This tells us to expect market growth or decline, and what competition to expect

---

Exhibit 2.2 Marketing-inspired internal appraisal questions

- What are the products that we have on offer?
- What is it about our offerings that is valued by our customers?
- What is it about what we do that creates this value?

    - These answers tell us about our success factors

- How efficient are we in making our products?
- Is there an experience curve effect?
- Are there economies of scale?

  - These answers tell us about our margin

Exhibit 2.3 Marketing-inspired positioning questions

- What are the qualities of our products?
- Does the customer perceive these qualities as providing value?
- At what price level do we offer our products for sale?

  - These answers tell us where we are with the positioning strategy in terms of the trade-off between value and price

---

Whether the firm is a multi-business firm or a single business firm should be considered as well. The questions in Exhibits 2.1, 2.2, and 2.3 refer to the single business firm competing in one market or market segment. It is about competitive strategy. If the firm consists of more than one business, we should think corporate strategy. This means two things. First, the competitive strategy analysis has to be performed for every SBU that can be distinguished. An SBU refers to a product/market combination a firm is active in. Second, an additional analysis at the level of corporate strategy should be performed, as well. This corporate-level strategy has to engage with questions with regard to synergy between the SBUs, as well as whether there is a balance in the BCG matrix (see Exhibit 2.4).

Exhibit 2.4 Marketing-inspired corporate strategy questions

- Do different SBUs share facilities so that they become better competitors?
- Do different SBUs benefit from economies of scale?

  - These answers tell us about synergy

- What is the level of market growth for each SBU?
- What is the market share of each SBU?
- How much cash flow does each SBU generate?

  - These answers allow us to fill out the BCG matrix and tell us about the balance in the portfolio

---

Strategy practice 2.1 A marketing-inspired SWOT analysis

The purpose of a SWOT analysis is to find out about threats and opportunities in the environment and about strengths and weaknesses with regard to the firm. But what makes an opportunity an opportunity, a threat a threat, a strength a strength, and a weakness a weakness? Marketing-inspired strategic thinking may be of help here.

The environment is about product markets. Opportunities are product markets or market segments that are untapped, and where the firm's success factors are particularly promising for meeting this existing but as-yet-unsatisfied demand. These success factors obviously represent a firm's strength.

If a competitor can wade in on the firm's market and can do that because it is better equipped to cater to the customers' demands, this obviously is a threat. The apparently not-so-successful factors of the focal firm have become weaknesses.

Anything that can happen to a firm that has an effect with regard to the 'fit' between a firm's success factors, product markets and segments, and positioning strategy – either positively or negatively – can be described as having consequences in terms of the firm's strengths, weaknesses, opportunities, and threats in the environment.

At the level of corporate strategy, a similar argument can be developed. However, this has to concentrate on questions of 'synergy' and 'balance' in the portfolio.

Getting up to speed's main purpose is to get ready for the continuous questioning and analysis that is required for wayfinding. However, it can happen that getting up to speed uncovers issues by itself when a lack of fit, synergy, or balance becomes apparent. This, of course, requires that action has to be taken.

Continuous questioning and analyzing

For wayfinding from a marketing-inspired point of view, the strategist should have a comprehensive understanding of the firm's strategic situation. On the basis of this, the strategist knows what customers want and need. The strategist knows what product markets and market segments are out there, about the various ways in which customer satisfaction can be created, and whether the firm is able to do this better or worse than the competition. The strategist also knows what strategy the firm is realizing. Also, if this concerns a multi-business firm, the strategist is supposed to know about the synergy that may exist and whether there is balance in the portfolio.

Exhibit 2.5 lists a range of questions by which impending developments can be traced. By searching for answers, the strategist is able to analyze and evaluate whether something that happens may endanger a firm's competitive advantage and associated performance. It does if it threatens to mess up the 'fit' between the strategy, the environment, and the firm. This fit can become unstuck in all kinds of ways, depending on what it is that is happening; or, in corporate strategy terms, the synergy between SBUs or the balance in the portfolio may be threatened.

These questions cover changes to the circumstances under which the firm is operating. The continuous questioning and analysis should concentrate on whether the changes that are happening or could happen are severe enough that it warrants a reaction. If it does not, the firm can continue to function as it currently does. If change could mean that this 'fit' between the strategy, the environment, and the firm itself is in danger of disappearing, the firm is about to lose its competitive advantage and its performance is in peril. Such an assessment calls for an intervention. Action needs to be taken to pre-empt what will happen and to restore fit. At the corporate strategy level, the questioning needs to focus on synergy and balance in the portfolio. It does not necessarily have to be bad news. Change might also strengthen the fit, the synergy, or the balance, adding to the firm's competitive advantage and promising increased performance.

Exhibit 2.5 Marketing-inspired continuous questioning

Competitive strategy:
- Is there change to who the customers are, and what wants and needs they have?
- Is there change to how the product market is segmented?
- Is there change to who the competitors are, what their realized strategy is, or how well they are able to compete?
- Has the product life cycle moved on a stage? Does maturity mean the situation has become a 'red ocean'?
- Is there change in what it is about our offerings, which is especially valued by our customers?
- Is there a change in the price level at which we offer our products for sale?
- Is there change in how efficient we are in making our products?
- Does any of this mean that the 'fit' between the chosen strategy, the state of the product market, and the firm's success factors is affected?

Corporate strategy:
- Is there change in the synergy between the SBUs?
- Is there change in the balance in the portfolio?
- Does any of this means that the SBUs are better competitors if they operate on their own and not as part of a multi-business firm?

Strategy practice 2.2 A marketing-inspired strategy workshop

Top management teams periodically book themselves into a nice retreat over a weekend to discuss how they or the firm is doing. This is an ideal opportunity to do some questioning and analysis. Quite often, an external consultant facilitates the workshop and is asked to design a programme for the workshop and to suggest topics for discussion.

Marketing-inspired strategic thinking is very much suited to inform a consultant about how the workshop may be put together. The consultant can have the management team discuss the product markets that the firm is targeting, what the status of the success factors is, and whether the firm's positioning strategy is still suitable. Overall, the consultant can have the top management team spending the weekend evaluating the question of 'fit'. Or if they are responsible for a multi-business firm, they can focus on the questions of 'synergy' and 'balance' in the portfolio.

Alternatively, the reason why the workshop is organized may be because something alarming has happened recently and the top management team members need to put their heads together to think about how to respond. Again, marketing-inspired strategic thinking can inform the content and nature of the discussion. The question of 'fit' and the effect this alarming incident might have can be the focus of the discussions. The response should be aimed at restoring fit if this is found to be threatened.

Strategy practice 2.3 Internationalization from a marketing-inspired viewpoint

The idea that the world is globalizing has gained much traction over the last couple of years, which in turn is seen to have a considerable impact on business. From a marketing-inspired point of view, Levitt (1983) has argued that customer wants and needs are converging around the world. This means that successful firms have to have a 'global strategy', targeting customers around the world in the same way and benefitting from the economies of scale and the experience curve that comes with being the worldwide market leader. A global firm effectively is a worldwide operating single business.

To Bartlett and Ghoshal (1992), there are at least three more ways of operating strategically across a number of countries. The 'international strategy' is also highly centralized, but operates as a multi-business firm. Instead of offering everybody everywhere the same product or service while concentrating on cost efficiency as the key success factor, the aim is to maximize synergy among the various businesses across countries yet offering differentiated products or services for each country. The 'multi-national strategy' is a highly decentralized multi-business firm that is highly adaptive to local markets' wants and needs. The 'transnational strategy' is a combination of the other two. The aim is to benefit from synergies while being adaptive to local circumstances.

Answering Question 2: problem-solving and taking action

Problem-solving and taking action utilizes the process logic (see Figure 2.1). Options need to be considered about 'what' to do and 'how' to do it. The first process sphere to consider is what to change about the way in which the firm competes in the product market(s). At the level of competitive strategy, the options of what to do can be derived from all three elements of the firm's strategy, the environment in which it competes, and the characteristics of the firm itself. With regard to the strategy, a firm can move up and down the trade-off between price and value, and decide to reposition anywhere along it. It can also do value pioneering for developing a 'blue ocean'. With regard to the success factors, the decision can be made to develop them further. The firm can be reorganized or redesigned to lower costs or to improve on the delivery of the value proposition of the products and services that are on offer, or the firm can change the value proposition completely. With regard to the environment, the firm can abandon its current product market and position itself in another existing market, or it can try to find a 'blue ocean': a completely new market. Yet every option needs to be assessed in terms of its potential to restore fit.

The Ansoff matrix (1965) describes four ways to develop a firm's competitive position (see Figure 2.6). Market penetration means staying in the current market but improving the firm's value proposition to gain market share. If there are economies of scale and an experience curve to benefit from, market leadership is the outcome to aim for. Product development is the other means by which a firm can improve its position in its current market. By concentrating on improving what is on offer, a firm can advance its value proposition in this way. Market development is entering a new market with the current product. This can mean going into markets where the firm's product happens to satisfy a different set of customer wants and needs. It could also mean going into new geographical areas, which includes going abroad and internationalizing. If the aim is to find a completely new market that nobody has entered yet, this becomes a 'blue ocean' strategy (Kim & Mauborgne, 2004). Diversification is a combination of entering new markets with newly developed products.

Market development and diversification will change the firm from single business into multi-business. If the firm is already active in a range of product markets and there are issues with synergy or balance in the portfolio, regaining synergy or rebalancing the portfolio is what should be aimed for. Adding or losing business units through mergers, acquisitions, and divestments can do this (Schoenberg, 2003). A merger or an acquisition is a way to enter a new market and to diversify. Together with divestment, they change the shape and the size of a portfolio, and therefore can rebalance it. Synergy is also a motive for mergers and acquisitions to take place. A lack of synergy is a reason to divide multi-business firms up into independently owned and operating business units.

Strategy practice 2.4 Formulating a strategic business plan using marketing-inspired strategic thinking

There are many occasions when a strategy needs to be formulated from scratch. This is what the early strategy scholars concentrated on, and marketing-inspired strategic thinking, which they adopted, is suited to do the job. What is advocated is to do an environmental analysis first. Find out about the wants and needs of customers in the market that you want to target, then pick a strategy in terms of value and price that fits best with market demand. When this choice has been made, the firm needs to be kitted out. List the various activities, technologies, human resource necessities, and the financial and capital needs that are required to have the firm up and running and delivering on its competitive strategy. Finally, do the maths. Check if the expected sales volumes and turnover allow for a sufficient margin, bearing in mind the running costs as well as a sufficient return on the initial investment needing to be covered. If the numbers do not add up, start again or abandon the plan.

In the organizational strategy process sphere, what is supposed to take place is an ordered discussion among the top managers of the firm – maybe with the help of specialized staff members or external consultants – to assess the situation and to weigh the various alternative options. Some have argued that the whole organization should become customer-driven or market-driven, with every decision made aimed at satisfying customer needs (Day, 1994). The quality of the strategy process in this approach is primarily determined by the accuracy by which data/information is gathered and scrutinized. The expectation is that the content of the information will tell the decision-makers what the best option is. Individual strategists are assumed to act as rational decision-makers. The organizational strategy process is expected to take on the form of top managers checking on each other and the quality of the data in order to collectively make the right decisions for the firm.

As soon as a decision has been made, the strategy process is expected to move into implementation mode. This involves (re-)designing the organization structure to enable it to deliver on the newly formulated strategy, to communicate with people, and to instruct them and explain what they are expected to do. Additionally, budgets are to be allocated and a management control system has to be put in by which spending can be checked and progress can be tracked.

Illustration 2.8 SKF from a marketing-inspired point of view

Should SKF* compete on price and put in the lowest bid possible to retain a big US-based client, or should it step away and persist with its high-quality strategy?

The US-based client is a customer with wants and needs*. Apparently, its need is cheap ball bearings. Stepping back, the first thing to consider is what market and market segments there are that can be served with replacement ball bearings and services. The problem suggests that there are at least two segments: one group of customers wants reliability and does not mind paying for it. Another segment is less bothered about reliability and does not need over-specified, expensive ball bearings. SKF Services' positioning strategy is one of differentiation. SKF targets the high-quality segment. To serve these more demanding customers, it not only fabricates high-quality bearings; it has also equipped members of its sales force with a computer-based sales tool with which they can quantify and demonstrate the value that their products bring to the customer. This piece of software allows sales representatives to demonstrate how using more reliable and hard-wearing ball bearings will save clients money in the long run. This combination of marketing ploy and product quality has been SKF's success factor. Its main competitors in the US are US-based Timken, Germany's Schaeffler, and Japan's NSK, with respective US market shares of 30%, 8–10%, and 5–7%. SKF comes in as second with 12–13% market share. Newer low-price rivals are appearing from Eastern Europe and China. However, SKF is the most capable ball bearing manufacturer. So, on the face of it, there is a fit between SKF's success factors, positioning strategy, and customer demands. One client moving from one segment to another does not necessarily indicate that SKF needs to change its strategy and take part in the reverse auction. Therefore, there does not seem to be much cause for further discussion.

However, there are things to consider and keep an eye on. For instance, what is the relative size of the two market segments? If the high-quality segment is relatively small and primarily served by SKF, one big customer's change of mind can have a big impact. Is this just one client changing the nature of its demand, or is there is a larger trend of clients wanting to downgrade which would change the conclusion entirely? This refers to possible developments going into the future and indicates the continuous need for questioning, analysis, and reconsideration.

* Value Selling at SKF Service, IMD-5-0751, 2009

Criticisms and unaddressed questions

There is an emphasis in marketing-inspired strategic management on formulating an intended strategy at the expense of actually realizing the strategy. The theories and tools aim to help a strategist to formulate a strategy, but tell little about how to realize what is formulated. Consequently, there is a tendency to remain stuck in the formulation phase. The expression of 'paralysis by analysis' (Lenz & Lyles, 1985) is one way of criticizing this mode of strategizing.

Realizing a strategy is taken to be a matter of strategy implementation. Implementation is a subject that has seen far less interest from marketing-inspired strategy scholars. It simply is seen as executing the plan: a matter for middle management to get on with. When a new plan requires that elements of the firm should be changed, another plan should be drawn up by which the reorganization will be accomplished. However, planned organizational change is seen as falling more within the realm of the field of organizational behaviour and therefore as not something strategy scholars should be too concerned about. The question, of course, is whether this is wise.

Furthermore, the notion of rational decision-making as a representation of managerial work has been heavily criticized. The basic thought behind emphasizing decisions as the focus for strategic management is that you become compelled to think before you act. This sounds sensible, but putting this into practice means that many strategic decisions never get implemented (Kiechel III, 1982, 1984). One reason for this to happen is that there simply is too much going on (Mintzberg, Raisinghani, & Théorêt, 1976). By the time a decision is made, so much has happened that the decision is obsolete before it has had a chance to be acted upon. Or circumstances and planning assumptions have altered since the intention was formulated, prompting all kinds of improvizations and workarounds that never were part of the plan.

Moreover, to see management work primarily as decision-making tends to separate thinking from acting. The thinkers of the firm, doing the decision-making, very often have little contact with the do-ers, or the people who have to implement the plan. Some concluded that it is not decision-making or the decisions that are wrong, but that it is strategy implementation that is seen as the enduring problem (Noble, 1999; Whipp, 2003). Alternatively, decision-making and planning is seen as just a 'theoretical exercise' with outcomes that will never work in 'practice'. As was explained earlier, this is bitterly debated among various prominent strategy scholars (Ansoff, 1991; Mintzberg, 1990, 1991; Mintzberg et al., 1996).

Marketing-inspired strategic thinking is not helped, either, by this approach's inherent static character. The analyses this approach provide basically are snapshots, descriptions of situations at a particular moment in time (Pettigrew, Woodman, & Cameron, 2001). With a concept like the product life cycle, there is recognition that things change over time; that product markets and the products that are traded on them have a limited life span. Market dynamics are also present in Ansoff's (1965) matrix and Kim and Mauborgne's (2004) 'blue oceans' as firms can develop new products and go after new markets. However, the nature of the change that is incorporated into marketing-inspired strategic thinking is predictable variability, like for instance with the product life cycle or with seasonal fluctuations in demand.

There is, however, little explanation about more fundamental and unpredictable change and how this takes place. What makes customers change their tastes? At a very basic level, people may have a number of prime needs (Maslow, 1943), but how these prime needs manifest themselves and translate into ever-changing customer preferences is not covered by marketing-inspired strategic thinking. Marketing-inspired strategic thinking can only start when customer wants and needs are sufficiently clear so that these customers can be asked about their preferences. Even 'blue ocean' thinking is based on finding new markets by thinking creatively about people's unsatisfied but already existing wants and needs. Only if wants and needs are knowable can firms start considering ways to satisfy them. The question remains unanswered what to do in situations when customers are unsure about what they might need or could want. Therefore, there is little on offer with regard to firms taking their destiny in their own hands to pro-actively be strategic about needs and wants that might or might not develop in the future.

It is important to recognize that this way of doing strategic management comes with very specific basic assumptions about the information that is used to formulate a strategy, as well as about the way in which management is supposed to work (Haselhoff, 1977; Sminia, 1994). The information that informs the analysis and on which strategic decisions are based is expected to correspond to an objectively knowable business reality out there. This business reality is taken to consist of product markets, positioning strategies, and success factors. Gathering information is believed to be a matter of probing what is out there. Managers, analysts, and consultants process information that they believe is true in that it corresponds with this objectively existing business reality out there, depending on how well they have done their research.

This assumption of a knowable reality, existing independently of the observer, and about which objective knowledge can be gathered, is heavily debated in the philosophy of science and even within the realm of management and organization theory (e.g. Burrell & Morgan, 1979; Smircich & Stubbart, 1985). This is the objectivism–subjectivism debate. On the face of it, taking an objectivist stance is nothing more than an assumption. Whether such a business reality out there actually exists can never be empirically verified, as the idea that it is verifiable is based on the assumption that there is an objective reality out there. Furthermore, top management is taken to consist of impartial information processors and decision-makers whose judgements are unclouded by biases and personal preferences. A subjectivist position maintains that information is always biased – that whatever the information is that people work with, it is the result of a very personal and unique interpretation of the situation.

The extent to which these basic assumptions are justified should always be questioned. More fundamentally, the assumption of objectivism, both in terms of an objectively knowable business reality as well as top management as impartial information processors and infallible implementers, on the one hand, is necessary for marketing-inspired strategic thinking to be feasible. On the other hand, these assumptions are just that: beliefs about the nature of business reality that can never be verified. The question can never be answered whether there is such a thing as an objectively knowable business reality out there, which allows impartial managers to make unbiased strategic decisions that are then simply implemented at their will.

Exhibit 2.6 Marketing-inspired reflective questions

- In the performance logic, how does marketing-inspired strategic thinking understand the environment, the strategy, and the firm?
- What in marketing-strategic thinking is the key question that a strategist should always be worried about and serves as the 'starter' question for a strategic analysis?
- From a marketing-inspired point of view, what are firms competing for?
- Why do economies of scale and the experience curve urge a firm to go for market leadership?
- With the product life cycle, how is the situation for a firm different for each life cycle phase?
- Which four growth vectors does Ansoff (1965) distinguish in his matrix?
- What is the difference between competitive/business-level strategy and corporate strategy?
- How does synergy and the BCG matrix justify the multi-business firm?
- What is the difference between 'blue ocean' and 'red ocean'?
- From a marketing-inspired point of view, what can a firm do if it has to deal with a strategic issue?
- In the process logic, how are the environmental survival process and the organizational strategy process understood, and how is a strategist expected to contribute?
- Why is marketing-inspired strategic thinking considered to be objectivistic?

Case 2.1

Miele

For 2019, the Miele Group reported a turnover of €34.16 billion, a 1.5% increase compared to 2018.[1] It announced that a new washing machine plant in Ksawerów, Poland, would become operational in 2020, adding to the other two washing machine plants in Uničow (Czech Republic) and Gütersloh (Germany) where it is also headquartered. Apart from these three plants, Miele has seven more production facilities in Germany, two in Italy, and one each in Austria and in Romania, and a joint venture in South Korea.[2] Miele categorizes its product ranges as baking and steam cooking, hobs and combisets, cooker hoods, coffee machines, refrigerators, freezers and wine units, dishwashers, washing machines, tumble dryers, rotary ironers, vacuum cleaners, cleaning products, and accessories. There is also a professional range. Miele sells and is represented in 74 countries.

Miele & Cie. KG is a family-owned business that markets its product ranges on the basis of durability, performance, ease of use, energy efficiency, design, and service.[3] A total of €1.2 billion of Miele's 2019 turnover was in Germany,[4] where Miele washing machines are priced between €1,109 and €2,095, while the cheapest machine overall sells for €289.[5] Miele dishwashers are offered for between €973 and €1,219, while the cheapest dishwasher can be had for €252.[6] When you look at what is on offer with the major retailers in Europe or the US, washing machines tend to be fully automatic. In India, a choice is given between fully automatic and half-automatic.[7] Fully automatic machines wash and spin in one cycle. Half-automatics require some handling along the way. Fully automatic machines tend to be more expensive than half-automatic. The cheapest washing machine in India is priced at Rs5,290.[8] A Miele vacuum cleaner retails at Rs14,238.[9]

Market research firm Dunn & Bradstreet lists SEB SA, Whirlpool Corporation, and AB Electrolux as Miele's main competitors.[10] In contrast to Miele, Electrolux and Whirlpool offer appliances under different brand names in different countries and segments. Electrolux's main brands are AEG, Electrolux, and Frigidaire.[11] Apart from the Whirlpool brand, Whirlpool Corp. also uses KitchenAid as a global brand but retains Maytag, Brastemp, Consul, Hotpoint, Indesit, and Bauknecht in different countries and across different price points.[12] Whirlpool and Electrolux are multi-national companies, headquartered in Sweden and the US, respectively, but having concentrated production in a few large plants that basically make the same appliances as cheaply as possible, which are then labelled differently. SEB SA is a French firm but operates worldwide, concentrating on smaller kitchen appliances with 22 different brands.[13]

Other firms that have offerings similar to Miele are BSH, Haier, and LG Electronics. German firm BSH Hausgeräte uses Bosch, Siemens, Gaggenau, and Neff as more global brands while retaining local brands like Thermador, Pitsos, and Zelmer.[14] Haier is a more recent arrival. Originally known as the Qingdao Refrigerator Industry, the company transformed into a major appliance manufacturer after it started exporting its products to the US in 1999.[15] Since then, Haier has expanded across the world and has reached position 68 in the top 100 most valuable brands list, with none of the other major appliance firms being mentioned.[16] LG Electronics is part of the larger South Korean LG Corporation. LG Electronics is involved in business-to-consumer (B2C) activities in home appliances, TVs, and mobile communication, and business-to-business (B2B) activities including air conditioners and car parts.[17] Haier prides itself as being the leading 'Internet of Things' firm, embracing smart applications for its products. In the US, smart Haier washing machines are priced between $1,200 and $1,300, while LG smart ones sell between $800 and $1,300.[18] With regard to the move towards smart technology, management consulting form PwC makes a point about embedded software becoming more important for appliance makers but questions how system integration is going to be provided.[19] The question is whether it will be appliance manufactures or the likes of Apple and Google which will provide this system integration. As it happens, Miele has just opened a new 'digital hub' in Amsterdam in The Netherlands.[20] Customers in Germany care more about ease of use than their dishwashers being smart.[21] Germany has also seen a small decline in household appliance sales because of a decrease in the number of households.

In the US, there is an increasing interest in energy efficiency and low water consumption, as well as design and colour.[22] In India, people in rural areas more and more are buying their first washing machines, while people in urban areas are now looking at replacements and upgrades.[23] In the UK, washing machines are mostly bought when the existing one breaks down – and depending on the availability of disposable income, price is a large factor in the buying decision.[24] It has long been acknowledged that household appliances and washing machines in particular are not built to last anymore.[25] This is largely due to price competition that forced manufacturers to save costs on materials and build quality, and to concentrate manufacturing in large facilities that produce the same basic appliances that are then branded and marketed differently to different segments and countries. Electrolux has a manufacturing strategy based on modularization to increase production efficiency.[26] Whirlpool has been forced to recall large numbers of fridges, tumble dryers, and washing machines because they pose a fire risk.[27]

Notes

1 Miele press release No.68/2019, 27 August 2019
2 www.miele.com/en/com/index.htm [accessed 18 August 2020]
3 www.miele.com/en/com/about-us-2065.htm [accessed 18 August 2020]
4 Miele press release No.68/2019, 27 August 2019
5 https://tests-waschmaschine.de [accessed 18 August 2020]
6 https://reoverview.de/geschirrspueler/ [accessed 18 August 2020]
7 India Washing Machine Outlook, 2022, February 2017
8 www.pricekart.com/appliances/washing-machines [accessed 18 August 2020]
9 www.pricekart.com/appliances/home-appliances/vacuum-cleaners/miele-classic-c1-45-litre-vacuum-cleaner-270074 [accessed 18 August 2020]
10 www.dnb.com/business-directory/company-profiles.miele__cie_kg.1ea218c9b885d54c4c6a7ae495736169.html#competitors [accessed 18 August 2020]
11 AB Electrolux 2019 annual report
12 Whirlpool Corporation 2019 annual report
13 www.groupeseb.com/en/our-brands [accessed 19 August 2020]
14 www.bsh-group.com/brands/appliance-brands [accessed 19 August 2020]
15 www.haier.com/global/about-haier/history/?spm=net.31999_pc.footer_141718_20200720.2 [accessed 19 August 2020]
16 www.brandz.com/brands [accessed 19 August 2020]
17 www.lgcorp.com/about/companies [accessed 19 August 2020]
18 www.lowes.com [accessed 19 August 2020]
19 www.pwc.co.uk/industries/power-utilities/insights/energy2020/connected-home/appliances.html [accessed 19 August 2020]
20 www.miele-x.com [accessed 19 August 2020]
21 Euromonitor, Dishwashers in Germany, December 2019
22 Euromonitor, Home Laundry Appliances in the US, January 2020
23 Euromonitor, Home Laundry Appliances in India, January 2020

24 Mintel Report on "How greater optimism about finances will affect spending on the home", 22 April 2016

25 www.bbc.co.uk/news/business-27253103 [accessed 23 December 2016)]

26 AB Electrolux 2019 annual report

27 www.ft.com/content/3c62ec68-20e6-11ea-b8a1-584213ee7b2b [accessed 17 August 2020]

CHAPTER 3

The industrial organization approach

The industrial organization way of strategic thinking initially directs us to the industry in which a firm competes. It lets us consider the industry forces that are at play there to evaluate whether the firm is capable of a suitable response. Incorporating more recent developments in how business is taking shape, the notion of industry is losing its relevance and is increasingly being replaced with the notion of ecosystem, recognizing that firm performance not only depends on how a firm competes but also on how it cooperates. Nevertheless, the industrial organization approach is credited as the first systematically thought-through treatment of strategy content.

The process logic of the industrial organization approach

Originally, the industrial organization approach states that firms compete in industries. "Although the relevant environment is very broad, encompassing social as well as economic forces, the key aspect of the firm's environment is the industry or industries in which it competes" (Porter, 1980, p. 3). An industry is "a group of firms producing products that are close substitutes for each other" (p. 5). The core of the early industrial organization approach is found in two books Michael Porter published in 1980 and in 1985, respectively. The 1980 book introduced the five forces framework and the generic strategies. The 1985 book added the value chain and the value system. More recently, the value system idea has developed into the notion of ecosystem, recognizing the relevance of complementarity and cooperation in addition to competition (Brandenburger & Nalebuff, 1996; Jacobides, Cennamo, & Gawer, 2018). An ecosystem refers to "groups of firms that produce products or services that together comprise a coherent solution" (Hannah & Eisenhardt, 2018, p. 3164). Ecosystem – rather than industry – will be the focus of this chapter.

This approach owes a lot to Michael Porter, who very cleverly took the industrial organization subfield in economics and made it relevant for strategic management (Porter, 1981). Industrial organization economists try to find out why one industry apparently performs better than another industry. Their explanatory framework puts forward that the performance of an industry is determined by the conduct of all the firms operating in this industry. They continue to argue that the conduct of a firm, in turn, can be explained by the industry structure. Because firms are assumed to act rationally and given that the industry structure is the same for every firm that competes in this industry, these firms are all expected to arrive at the same decisions and consequently conduct themselves in the same way. This suggests that the industry structure determines industry performance. Industrial organization economists then try to explain performance differences between industries on the basis of differences in how these industries are structured. This explanatory framework became known as the Bain/Mason paradigm, named after two prominent industrial organization economists.

Because a strategy scholar is interested in explaining performance differences between firms rather than industries, Porter lifted the assumption that all firms will conduct themselves in the same manner because they face the same circumstances. Instead, he argued that firms can and will act differently within a given industry structure. They will have different strategies. However, not every strategy will create the same level of firm performance. He put forward that there are only three generic strategies – cost leadership, differentiation, focus – that create, as he put it, "a superior return on investment for the firm" (Porter, 1980, p. 34). Each one of these three strategies deals in a particular way with the structure of the industry in which a firm has to compete. Each one of these three strategies encompasses competitive advantage in a different way. Porter understands the environmental survival process to be a process of competition in an industry. This is competition about value appropriation – about how much money each firm is able to appropriate from the price at which a product sells, bearing in mind that all firms that are involved in making this product add some value and need to be paid. This is where the industrial organization process logic starts to become very different from marketing-inspired strategic thinking.

Illustration 3.1 ASML's position in the semiconductor ecosystem*

ASML is the sole provider of photolithographic machines based on EUV technology. EUV means 'extreme ultraviolet'. These machines are used to make integrated circuits or micro-chips. It is a kind of printing technique at an ultra-small scale. ASML supplies the only machine that goes down to the frequency of ultraviolet light with a wavelength of just 13.5 nanometres (a nanometre is a billionth of a metre). This allows chip manufacturers like Intel, Samsung, and TSMC to put increasingly more components on their micro-chips, making these increasingly more powerful. ASML competitors like Canon and Nikon have not mastered this technique as yet. As a consequence, ASML's revenues grew 8% in 2019, despite a slump in the semiconductor business, indicating its ability to appropriate value. The company has 100% of the EUV business and 85% of the total chip machine market. However, ASML relies on Carl Zeiss and its optical systems to direct the ultraviolet light in the printing process, on VDL and its robotic arms to feed the waivers into the machine, and on Cymer to provide the ultraviolet light source. The research that was needed to develop the EUV technology took 20 years and was partly financed by Intel, Samsung, and TSMC.

* How ASML became chipmaking's biggest monopoly, *The Economist*, 29 February 2020 (provided by Anup Karath Nair); https://nos.nl/artikel/2319764-hoe-asml-een-grote-gok-waagde-en-daarmee-monopolist-werd.html [accessed 24 November 2020]

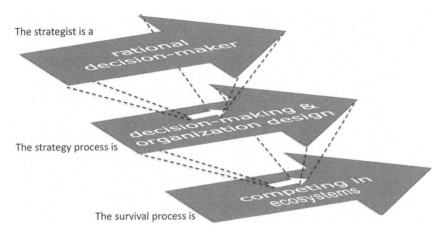

The strategist is a *rational decision-maker*

The strategy process is *decision-making & organization design*

The survival process is *competing in ecosystems*

Figure 3.1
The process logic
for industrial
organization

Brandenburger and Nalebuff (1996) were among the first to recognize that firms not only compete but also have complementary relationships. If a user of your product values your product more because they can use it in combination with another product made by another firm compared to using your product on its own, that other firm is your complementor. It might be the case that your offering needs complementary products or services to be useable at all. Users look at the whole product-service bundle rather than the individual products and services that make it up. This other firm and the complementary product might be from a completely different industry. To make this work for both firms, often some form of cooperation is required. However, with regard to the combined value of the whole product-service bundle, the issue still is present of value appropriation and how much money each firm will get when a user has to buy both products to get some use out of them. Such a situation that is marked by both competition and cooperation is labelled as 'coopetition' (Bengtsson & Kock, 2000).

It also meant that the notion of industry is being replaced by the notion of ecosystem, as complementary products represent different industries (Teece, 2010). Such a coherent solution tends to take on the form of a bundle of products and services (Sminia, Ates, Paton, & Smith, 2019). Within ecosystems, a balance needs to be found between cooperation to add value and competition to appropriate value.

Illustration 3.2 Coopetition turning to conflict: Apple and Epic

An example of complementarity exists in the Apple ecosystem. Mac computers, iPads, and iPhones need apps to make them useful. Although some apps are provided by Apple, there are many more that are developed and sold by others, albeit through the Apple App Store. Apple insists that it needs to approve any app and also takes a 30% cut out of each app sale, yet Apple depends on all these third-party apps to maintain its position among rivals like Google and Microsoft.

Game developer Epic tried to circumvent Apple's App Store – or at least its payment structure – by adding an in-app payment system*. As a consequence, Apple stopped distributing Epic's popular Fortnite game. Epic then sued Apple for violating antitrust laws and Apple sued Epic back for lost App Store fees and a court order to stop the in-app payment system.

* www.reuters.com/article/us-apple-epic-games-idUKKBN25Z30E [accessed 24 November 2020]

The other two process spheres are identical to marketing-inspired strategic thinking. Porter and others in this approach also take it that there are only a limited number of strategists located at the top of the firm and that they are engaged in rational decision-making. And here too the organizational strategy process is one of choice and design. The difference is that the information that is being gathered and processed has to be about the ecosystem and how best to compete and cooperate within it, so the vocabulary and the performance logic that should be employed are different from marketing-inspired strategic thinking.

The performance logic of the industrial organization approach

The reasoning originally started with the industry – or more specifically, the industry structure. Porter (1980) defined the industry structure as consisting of five different forces: the threat of new entrants, the threat of substitutes, the bargaining power of suppliers, the bargaining power of buyers, and the rivalry between competitors. The stronger a force, the more difficult it is for a focal firm to realize high performance. The reason is that each one of the forces sucks money out of the focal firm or it puts a ceiling on the price at which a product can be sold. This is referred to as the problem of value appropriation, of how much money a focal firm gets for its contribution to the whole product-service bundle. With the notion of industry being replaced by ecosystem, we effectively have to add a sixth force, the bargaining power of complementors (Brandenburger & Nalebuff, 1996) (see Figure 3.2).

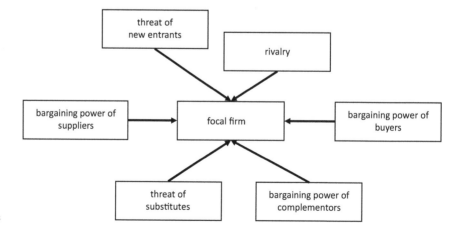

Figure 3.2
The six forces

Intense rivalry means that a firm has to put more effort into maintaining market share and there is a downward pressure on sales prices. High bargaining power of suppliers means that they are able to negotiate high prices for what they supply. High buyer bargaining power means that the firm has to give large discounts when it tries to sell their products or services. The bargaining power of complementors means that another product or service in the overall product-service bundle is more essential for the ecosystem value proposition than that what the focal firm contributes. A high threat of new entrants means that outside firms can enter easily as soon as the ecosystem becomes more profitable. This threat puts downward pressure on the price level. A high threat of substitutes means that there is a limit to the price at which the product of the focal firm can be sold, as substitutes are readily available. A substitute product is a different product that provides the same value. A rival product is the same product as what is produced by the focal firm, but offered by a competitor. The combined strengths of all six forces determine how attractive the ecosystem is to operate in. Which of the forces is the strongest indicates what the strategist should focus on when formulating a business-level strategy (see Figure 3.2).

Illustration 3.3 Entry barriers for COMAC*

The state-owned Commercial Aircraft Corporation of China (COMAC) has ambitious plans to supply planes to the booming Chinese airlines. Chinese airlines currently equip themselves with Boeing or Airbus planes. To cater to the growing appetite for air travel in China, Boeing estimated that China will need to buy another 6,810 passenger planes over the next 20 years. To get a piece of this pie, COMAC has developed the ARJ21 regional jet. Eight entered service with Chengdu Airlines in June 2016, eight years behind the initial scheduled introduction. COMAC is also busy developing the C919 as a competitor to the Boeing 737 and Airbus A320, aiming to have it ready to enter operation in 2022**.

COMAC built a factory and offices in Shanghai, employing more than 50,000 workers, in just over two years. However, developing a commercial airliner that has the same reliability and economy of Airbus and Boeing has proven to be difficult. COMAC had to deal with dodgy wiring, cracks in the wings, and faulty doors when developing the ARJ21. The plane also had difficulty coping with rain. COMAC is now taking its time designing the C919, but experts say that by the time they have this one ready, the technology will have moved on and the offerings of Airbus and Boeing will be so much better.

* China's big aerospace ambitions are delayed, *The Economist*, 5 November 2016 (provided by Anup Karath Nair).
** https://www.chinadaily.com.cn/a/202103/02/WS603d8fb2a31024ad0baac01e.html [accessed 22 March 2021].

To counter these six forces and improve their value appropriation, firms in an ecosystem need to choose how they want to compete and cooperate. With regard to cooperation, there is a choice with regard to the role a firm wants to play in the ecosystem. A firm has a choice of being a supplier, a complementor, or a platform leader (Adner & Kapoor, 2010; Gawer, 2014). The supplier role means that a firm concentrates on providing a subassembly or part of a product or service that goes into a larger product or service offering. The complementor role means that a firm concentrates on providing a product or service that complements other products and services, with all these different but complementary products and services comprising the overall ecosystem's product-service bundle. Some ecosystems feature a platform leader, and a firm can choose to opt for that role. Platform leaders appear if an ecosystem is characterized by a specific proprietary technology or product-service bundle design of which the platform leader takes charge and, by implication, has a key role in organizing the ecosystem.

Illustration 3.4 Google and the Android ecosystem

Google acquired a firm by the name of Android in 2005*. Android as a firm was in the process of developing an operating system (OS) for digital cameras. As cameras more and more were being incorporated into mobile phones, the scope of the project moved with it. Google launched Android as a mobile phone OS in 2008.

Android is now administered by the Open Handset Alliance**. The alliance has many members, including mobile operators, handset manufacturers, semiconductor companies, software companies, and commercialization companies. Android in effect has become a standard by which various devices can link up and create a functionality that exceeds each individual component, product, or service, extending into phones, tablets, TVs, cars, and numerous other 'smart' devices.

Although the source code of the Android OS is open source, its usefulness only appears in combination with a number of proprietary Google apps. This makes Samsung so dependent on Google that it favours Android for its devices rather than its own Tizen OS***. Google, in effect, is the platform leader of the Android ecosystem

*   www.androidauthority.com/google-android-acquisition-884194/ [accessed 24 November 2020]
**   www.openhandsetalliance.com/oha_overview.html [accessed 24 November 2020]
*** www.ibtimes.com/samsung-renews-relationship-google-android-launch-gear-live-1618028 [accessed 24 November 2020]

With regard to how a firm competes, it has to make two choices. The first choice concerns the question whether a firm wants to compete on cost or on value. This choice is based on Porter's assumption that every industry is characterized by what can be referred to as the 'standard product'. This applies to ecosystems, as well. The standard product has to have the minimally required attributes that an end user is willing to pay for, and which makes it eligible to be included in the ecosystem's product-service bundle. These minimally required attributes indicate basic value that corresponds with the basic sales price level for this contribution. Standard does not necessarily mean simple, as end user expectations can be quite sophisticated, depending on what they are used to and have learned to expect. Any product below end user expectations will not be sold.

One option available to a firm here is to become the most efficient producer of what it is that the firm contributes to the product-service bundle. This is the strategy of cost leadership. The cost leader is the firm that has the highest profit margin among those firms which supply this contribution to the bundle. This contribution necessarily is priced at this basic level that reflects what end users are willing to pay for it as part of the bundle. Consequently, there can only be one cost leader for this product (see Figure 3.3).

Competing on cost is completely different from competing on price. The cost leader does not want the price level at which the standard product is sold to erode, nor would any other firm who is competing in this ecosystem, as it only leads to diminishing margins – and consequently, lower profits for everybody. Competing on cost means that you try to be the most efficient producer and maintain the price level at which the standard product is sold. Porter (1980) adamantly urges firms never to compete on price because it makes everybody (apart from end users) worse off.

Those firms which are less efficient than the cost leader can compete on value. "Value is what buyers are willing to pay" (Porter, 1985, p. 3). To increase the price buyers are willing to pay, you have to offer a product or service to the bundle with extra features which, when compared to the basic offering, will appeal more to end users. Not every feature will do. They have to represent enhanced value in the eyes of the people who buy the bundle. If this value is added at a cost lower than the extra margin that is made on the enhanced product because of the higher price end users are willing to pay for it, then the firm has a higher than average performance.

The other choice with regard to how to compete concerns the question how the firm wants to compete on value. A firm can go either ecosystem-wide or

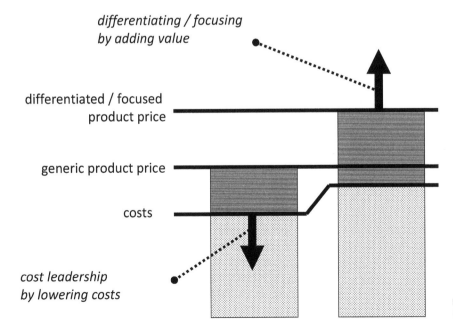

Figure 3.3
Price, costs, and value

targeting a specific element in the overall ecosystem product-service bundle (Hannah & Eisenhardt, 2018). Translating Porter's generic strategies to ecosystems, a firm specializing in a specific element of the ecosystem product-service bundle would be opting for a focus strategy. A firm that spreads out over various elements of the product-service bundle would be opting for a differentiation strategy. Both strategies require an enhanced value proposition compared to the basic product offered by the cost leader. In his 1980 book, Porter presented just these three competitive generic strategies. In his 1985 book, he made a distinction between a cost focus strategy and a differentiation focus strategy, with the cost focus strategy being the cost leader for a specific element, while differentiation focus refers to a differentiation strategy with regard to this specific element.

Porter (1980) argues that every firm has to stick to one of his competitive generic strategies to shield themselves from the forces. This particularly applies to the choice between competing on cost or competing on value. Bearing in mind that there is only one cost leader, all the other firms should have a credible and different value proposition by which they can make enough money to withstand the 'money sucking' tendencies and 'price ceiling' effects of the forces. Essentially, the answer to what strategy to pursue is a multiple choice question, with the competitive generic strategies of cost leadership, differentiation, and focus (either cost focus or differentiation focus) as the options to choose from. Porter also described a strategy that every firm should avoid. This is the stuck-in-the-middle strategy. Porter argues that any firm that is trying to do more than one competitive generic strategy simultaneously is outcompeted and outperformed by firms that keep to one of the competitive generic strategies.

If the competitive generic strategies are about competing for value appropriation, cooperation strategy is about how to safeguard the overall added value of an ecosystem's product-service bundle. This is about how all firms in an ecosystem coordinate their activities to ensure that the whole bundle is sufficiently valued by end users. Between the two extremes of relying on arms-length market exchange relationships and of complete integration of an ecosystem into one firm, there are many hybrid forms. These hybrids vary between temporary consortia, strategic alliances, certification and standard-setting schemes, preferred supplier arrangements, dedicated outsourcing relationships, and subcontracting (Sydow, Schüssler, & Müller-Seitz, 2016). Each comes with various advantages and disadvantages, which apply differently depending on the situation. They are also inherently unstable because of tensions arising from the coopetition they have to accommodate. Competition and cooperation are based on contradicting logics of interaction, with competition informed by self-interest and cooperation based on mutual interest (Bengtsson & Kock, 2000). As yet, ecosystems researchers have not come up with specific ways to deal with these tensions, apart from the broad indication that firms have to keep in mind that their performance eventually depends on the performance of the ecosystem as a whole (Kapoor, 2018). Besides, any cooperative arrangement that might need to be present to enhance the overall ecosystem value proposition will put limitations on how aggressive a firm can be in appropriating value.

To assess whether a firm is able to pursue one of the competitive generic strategies, Porter (1985) came up with the notion of the value chain. Continuing along the same lines of his 1980 book, a firm is taken to add value at a certain cost. The 1985 book adds the idea that a firm can be subdivided into separate value activities. To Porter, there are nine separate value activities. The primary activities are inbound logistics, operations, outbound logistics, marketing and sales, and service. The support activities are firm infrastructure, human resource management, technology development, and procurement. The primary activities are physically involved in creating the product and service and getting it to the end user. The support activities, as the term suggests, allow the primary activities to take place. There is a bit of a bias to manufacturing firms in this model, but distinguishing between separate value activities is relevant for all kind of firms.

By elaborating on a firm as a combination of value activities, Porter makes it possible to look inside the firm and to evaluate the extent to which each activity contributes to the value proposition represented by the competitive generic strategy the firm pursues. Given the specific added value that the firm claims to produce, the question can be asked which value activity, or specific combination of activities, is responsible for that. The additional question should be asked at what cost this value is produced. If the costs exceed the price at which the product can be sold, there effectively is no margin and no profit to be made. Hence, Figure 3.4 is labelled as a firm's value (and costs) chain.

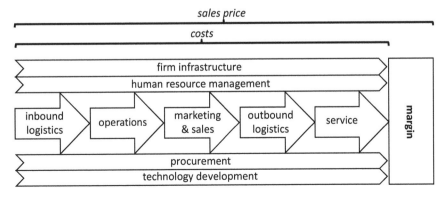

Figure 3.4
A firm's value (and costs) chain

To Porter (1985), the forces combined with the value chain make a value system. Moving from value system to ecosystem by adding the sixth force, a firm finds itself positioned among suppliers, buyers, complementors, firms that can enter the ecosystem, firms that offer substitutes, and rival firms making the same contribution to the ecosystem, with each of these firms having its own specific value chain (see Figure 3.5). Whether a firm performs depends on how its value chain compares with all the other value chains around it, and each value chain of these surrounding firms determines the relative strength of the force with which each surrounding firm is associated. It is up to the focal firm to position itself adequately within an ecosystem by choosing a specific cooperative role and opting for a suitable competitive generic strategy to be able to perform and survive. One important realization to make here is that a firm not only competes with its rivals. The firm also competes with suppliers, buyers, complementors, firms that provide substitute products, and firms which can easily enter the industry. They compete with each other about value appropriation, or how much of a margin is created and how much of this margin each firm is able to retain.

To sum up, the performance logic of the modern industrial organization approach covers the three ingredients of the environment, the firm, and strategy in a very specific manner (see Figure 3.6). The environment is seen as an ecosystem that is further described in terms of the six forces. The firm is appreciated as a value chain. Strategy is further specified by way of the three roles of supplier, complementor, or platform leader, and the competitive generic strategies, with the strategy embodying competitive advantage. This enhanced Porter framework allows the strategist to evaluate a situation because of a requirement of fit. All three ingredients should fit together. A firm should have a value chain that allows it to pursue the cooperative role and competitive generic strategy that, in turn, deals with the strength of the forces, as they exist in the industry in which the firm has to compete. If any of these three elements does not contribute to this fit, the firm is in trouble.

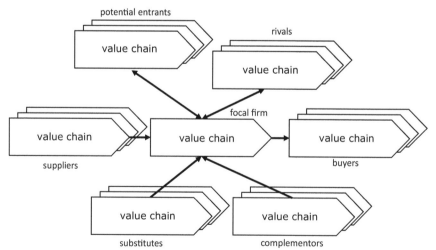

Figure 3.5
The value system

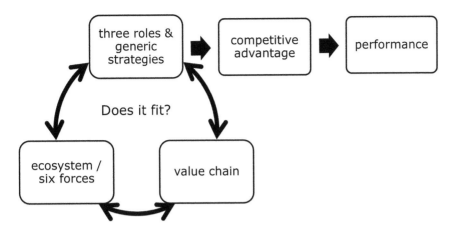

Does it fit?

Figure 3.6
The industrial
organization approach

Illustration 3.6 Automotive ecosystems

The automotive industry has developed into an ecosystem of global proportions (Sturgeon, Van Biesebroeck, & Gereffi, 2008). A modern car consists of many parts and subassemblies. Car production and sales require many suppliers, subcontractors, and complementors which together offer a product-service bundle. There are the major car manufacturers which are involved in the branding, engineering, design, and final assembly of a range of models. Many manufacturers have a worldwide presence. However, they rely on advertising agencies and sometimes outside marketing specialists to help them with their branding. In the early stages of car design and engineering, independent specialist design and engineering firms are often involved. Car sales tend to be done by independently owned dealerships, and even car assembly is sometimes outsourced to subcontractors which build and manage assembly plants. When a new model has reached the stage that a decision needs to be made about where it will be produced, the car manufacturer's plant where the previous model was assembled often not only finds it has to compete with the possibility of constructing a new greenfield plant somewhere else; it also finds that it has to tender for a new contract alongside outside firms which specialize in car assembly and act as subcontractors for various different car companies.

A car consists of many different parts involving a wide range of suppliers, with companies specializing in specific subassemblies having their own network of suppliers, as well. There are engines, transmissions, shock absorbers, car seats, electronic motor management systems, wire looms, body panels, interior trim, tyres, paint, etc. There are also equipment manufacturers which provide the robotics and tools with which the assembly and manufacturing plants are kitted out. Sometimes, a major car manufacturer develops and builds its own engines and transmissions. Sometimes, they source it from other car manufacturers or specialized firms. A more recent development is that platforms, chassis designs, and drive trains are not only shared across models from the same manufacturer but also across different manufacturers. Many of the other parts and subassemblies are made by specialist suppliers, sometimes tied into some form of exclusivity with one car manufacturer, but often supplying many different manufacturers. Moreover, the product-service bundle more and more has morphed from owning and driving a car into car mobility. This then also includes finance and insurance services, and extended warranty and car maintenance arrangements. Fleet managers also are looking to include fuel deals in their product-service bundles.

They all compete with each other for margin. Imagine that a car can be sold for a maximum of £20,000. What all these firms are competing for is how much of this £20,000 comes to them. This is determined by the value – as perceived by the end user – that their involvement or specific part adds to the final product. If it is the after-sales service that nails a sale, car dealerships have the upper hand. If it is the branding, the car manufacturer will be the most powerful player, although they might depend too much on an outside advertising agency. Or is it a specific part or subassembly like the engine or the sound system that sets the car apart in the eyes of the end user? Is it the build quality, the finance deal, or the insurance quote? Depending on how crucial your cooperative role is in producing value, you will get a larger proportion of this £20,000. If you are unable to compete on value for your share of the £20,000, you will have to make your margin by lowering your costs.

Doing industrial organization approach strategic management

From a strategic management as wayfinding perspective, the question that continuously should be asked is whether there still is a fit between the firm's realized strategy (in terms of the firm's cooperative role and the competitive generic strategies) and the ecosystem in which the firm competes and cooperates, and whether the firm has a value chain that allows the firm to position itself in this way. Anything that happens that disturbs this fit should be qualified as a strategic issue, and action should be taken. Therefore, from an industrial organization point of view, the two questions to ask and answer are:

1 Are there any issues that jeopardize the fit between the ecosystem in which the firm operates, which of the cooperative roles and competitive generic strategies it realizes, and the firm's value chain?
2 If there are, what can you do about them?

Answering Question 1: strategic analysis

Of course, if you find that the firm is 'stuck in the middle' in that it has not committed to one of the competitive generic strategies, you have already found an issue. To draw this conclusion, or any other one concerning the level of fit, you need to know about whether and which cooperative role and competitive generic strategy a firm is realizing, how this compares with the ecosystem, and what value at which costs the firm adds in terms of its own value chain. If you do not know, you have to get 'up to speed' first.

Getting up to speed

The industrial organization approach is designed to be used as part of a strategic decision-making exercise (see the Introduction in Porter, 1980). The 1980 book covers the external appraisal and the choice of strategy. This has since been enhanced by moving away from industry in favour of ecosystem. The 1985 book adds the internal appraisal. Obviously, the external appraisal needs to be done by looking at the ecosystem the firm operates in, and the internal appraisal should assess the firm in terms of the value chain.

The vocabulary and performance logic of the industrial organization approach tells us which information should be gathered and how it should be evaluated. However, before you can start, two initial questions need to be answered first before any analysis can be done: one is about the ecosystem, and the other one is about end user value. The first initial question refers to the external appraisal, the second one to the internal appraisal.

Exhibit 3.1 Industrial organization external appraisal questions

- Which ecosystem is the firm operating in?
- Are there any cooperative arrangements that the firm has to engage in, and if so, how do these arrangements shape how the firm can compete?
- Who are direct rivals to the firm?
- How many are there?
- What do their value chains look like?

    - This tells us about the strength of the rivalry force

- Who are suppliers to the firm?
- How many are there?
- What do their value chains look like?

    - This tells us about the supplier power force

- Who are buyers from the firm?
- How many are there?
- What do their value chains look like?

    - This tells us about the buyer power force

- Who are complementors to the firm?
- How many are there?
- What do their value chains look like?

    - This tells us about the complementor power force

- Who offers substitute products?
- How many are there?
- What does their value chain look like?

    - This tells us about the threat from substitutes

- How easy is it to set up a similar business?
- What would their value chains look like?

    - This tells us about the threat of entry

First of all, the ecosystem that is analyzed should be defined. This is not a trivial matter, for two reasons. One, if it is not clear what is actually being analyzed, any result is meaningless. Two, ecosystem definitions are not clear-cut. As was said previously, in abstract terms, an ecosystem refers to "groups of firms that produce products or services that together comprise a coherent solution" (Hannah & Eisenhardt, 2018, p. 3164). The problem is that what this solution is, is not always clear-cut. This has its effect on what you will have to take into account when it comes to assessing the six forces. For instance, when a narrow ecosystem definition is the basis for analysis, certain firms will end up being part of the substitutes threat, which with a more encompassing definition would be considered rivals, or, with a very narrow definition, would not be considered at all. Who are the buyers, suppliers, or complementors would vary with the ecosystem definition, as well. If in doubt, you can always do the analysis more than once; based on different – say a narrow and a broad – ecosystem definitions.

Illustration 3.7 Industry classification and ecosystems

To measure economic activity, governments and their statistical offices have produced classification schemes by which they are able to slot firms into industries. The US Standard Industrial Classification (SIC) framework has been much utilized in research and has recently been replaced by the North American Industry Classification System (NICS). The UK has the United Kingdom Standard Industrial Classification of Economic Activities (UKSIC), and other countries and bodies like the UN and the EU have thing similar things. These schemes provide descriptions and codes of categories of business activity. Because economic data are gathered using these codes, they are being used extensively for the purpose of research. However, industry qualification schemes increasingly are becoming obsolete, as ecosystems tell us that business activity more and more extends across industries.

Second, it should be established what it is that the end user values about the product-service bundle, the solution that is being offered by the ecosystem, and what price level is attached to it. This 'value' is connected to certain attributes of the product-service bundle. Only once you know what these attributes are, are you are able to find out who in the ecosystem is responsible for them. It allows the strategist to evaluate the firm's value chain and to compare it with all value chains of the other players in the ecosystem. Knowing about the price level that is achieved with an ecosystem will tell you which margins to expect and how these relate to the costs that are associated with the firm's value chain, as well as all other value chains in the wider ecosystem. So, a strategist should find out what the end user appreciates about the product-service bundle and how much this end user is prepared to pay for it. There are bound to be ranges of bundles with different value propositions and price levels, catering to specific end users, offering the ecosystem a choice to go for specific solutions.

Once these two initial questions have been answered about ecosystem definition and about end user value, the more specific questions in the external and internal appraisals – and what strategy the firm is realizing – can be tackled (see Exhibits 3.1, 3.2 and 3.3).

Exhibit 3.2 Industrial organization internal appraisal questions

- What do end users value about the product-service bundle that defines the ecosystem?
- Are there different product-service bundles that provide more specific solutions to end users?
- Does any or a combination of value activities in the firm add this value to the overall value of the product-service bundle?
- How efficient is the firm in executing value activities in its value chain?

Exhibit 3.3 Industrial organization positioning questions

- Is the firm acting as a supplier, a complementor, or a platform leader?
  - This answer tells us which cooperative role the firm is taking on
- Does the firm compete on cost or on value?
- Does the firm compete ecosystem-wide, or does it concentrate on a specific element of the product-service bundle?
  - These two answers tell us whether the firm's strategy needs to be described as cost leadership, differentiation, cost focus, differentiation focus, or stuck in the middle

Strategy practice 3.1 An industrial organization SWOT analysis

The purpose of a SWOT analysis is to find out about threats and opportunities in the environment and about strengths and weaknesses with regard to the firm. But what makes an opportunity an opportunity, a threat a threat, a strength a strength, and a weakness a weakness? The industrial organization approach may be of help here.

The environment is about the ecosystem. Opportunities are ecosystems that are attractive and where the firm's value chain is particularly promising for developing a strong position. A firm's value chain that adds the value that matters for end users obviously represents a firm's strength.

If one or more of the six forces becomes stronger, this clearly is a threat and the apparently not-so-strong value chain of the focal firm becomes a weakness.

Anything can happen to a firm that has an effect with regard to the 'fit' between a firm's value chain, ecosystem, and a firm's cooperative role and competitive generic strategy, either positively or negatively, and can be described as having consequences in terms of the firm's strengths, weaknesses, opportunities, and threats in the environment.

The information gathered as a consequence of the internal and external appraisal and the assessment of firm's strategy should be collated and evaluated. Here, the performance logic comes in. The strategy should fit both the ecosystem – appreciated as comprising of six forces, and the firm's value chain. A cooperative role and one of the competitive generic strategies should be chosen.

As was said earlier, being stuck in the middle is always a cause for concern. The best fit is a situation where the firm takes advantage of its value chain with the appropriate cooperative role and competitive generic strategy in light of all the value chains that surround the firm in the ecosystem in which it operates.

Continuous questioning and analyzing

Once the strategist knows about the ecosystem the firm is operating in and about the firm's value chain and how it compares with the value chains in the wider ecosystem regarding delivering the value that end users want, and if the strategist knows the relative efficiency of all value chains and what specific cooperative role and competitive generic strategy the firm is realizing – in effect, if a comprehensive understanding of the firm's strategic position is in place – then the strategist is able to evaluate and debate anything that is happening and decide whether countermeasures are in order.

Exhibit 3.4 Industrial organization continuous questioning

- Is there change to the strength of the rivalry force?
- Is there change to the strength of the supplier force?
- Is there change to the strength of the buyer force?
- Is there change to the strength of the complementor force?
- Is there change to the threat of substitutes?
- Is there change to the threat of entry or mobility?
- Is there change to any of the cooperative arrangements that are in place, and if so, does this affect the way in which the firm can compete?
- Is there change to what end users value about the product and the price they are prepared to pay?
- Is there change to the firm's ability to add value?
- Is there change to the firm's efficiency in adding value?
- Does any of this mean that the 'fit' between the chosen cooperative role and competitive generic strategy, the state of the ecosystem, and the firm's value chain is affected?

Exhibit 3.4 provides a range of questions that fuels the discussion. The overall worry should be focused on the question of fit between the firm's strategy, its value chain, and the ecosystem in which the firm operates. Whether this fit is threatened or maybe strengthened on the basis of the changes that are happening should be the focus of the continuous questioning and analyzing among top managers. These changes can happen in the ecosystem if firms associated with any of the forces innovate, merge, or move forward or backward in the system. In short, firms can do things that make the associated force stronger (or weaker). It could also be a change in legislation, economic upturns or downturns, or natural disasters that can affect the strength of the forces. Change can also concern the cooperative arrangements that exist, and new ones can be established or existing ones can break down. These arrangements are inherently unstable because of the coopetition. Changes can also originate from inside the firm. It can have found a way to become more efficient. It can have come across an improved value proposition. There can even be change in what end users actually value.

Strategy practice 3.2 An industrial organization strategy workshop

Top management teams periodically book themselves into a nice retreat over a weekend to discuss how they or the firm is doing. This is an ideal opportunity to do some deliberate questioning and analysis. Quite often, an external consultant facilitates the workshop. The consultant is asked to design a programme for the workshop and to suggest topics for discussion.

The industrial organization approach is very much suited to inform a consultant about how the workshop may be put together. The consultant can have the management team discuss the forces and cooperative arrangements in the ecosystem that the firm operates in, what the firm's value chain looks like, and whether the firm's cooperative role and competitive generic strategy is still suitable. Overall, the consultant can have the top management team spending the weekend evaluating the question of 'fit'.

Alternatively, the reason why the workshop is organized may be because something alarming has happened recently and the top management team members need to put their heads together to think about how to respond. Again, the industrial organization approach can inform the content and nature of the discussion. The question of 'fit' and the effect this alarming incident may have can be the focus of the discussion. The response should be aimed at restoring fit if this is found to be in jeopardy.

Strategy practice 3.3 Internationalization from an industrial organization viewpoint

Porter (1986) reckons that industries vary from multi-domestic to global. This applies to ecosystems, as well. In a multi-domestic ecosystem, competition and cooperation in one country is independent from competition and cooperation in another country, with each country having its own six forces and cooperative arrangements. A firm operating internationally in a multi-domestic ecosystem effectively is a multi-business firm. A global ecosystem means that there is one globally organized system in which every firm has to operate. An effect of globalization is that multi-domestic ecosystems morph into global ecosystems.

Answering Question 2: problem-solving and taking action

Questioning and analysis applies the performance logic of a theoretical approach. Taking action utilizes the process logic. This is about what a strategist can and should contribute to the firm's strategy process so that eventually the firm remains successful as it operates in the ecosystem. There is a 'what' to do and a 'how' to do it. With regard to the job of the strategist, the expectation is that this is a matter of information gathering and processing about the situation at hand, to contribute to an ordered and organized firm-sphere strategy formulation and implementation process that aims to deal with the issue that has been identified.

To remain viable in an ecosystem characterized by coopetition, there are a number of options available with regard to 'what' to do, which aim to reinstate the 'fit' between the strategy, the ecosystem, and the firm's value chain. The strategist can choose to work on all three of these ingredients. Switching between cooperative roles and competitive generic strategies, improving the value chain, or entering or leaving an ecosystem are all alternatives to consider. With regard to the 'how' to do it, Porter (1980) suggests that there are three courses of action that a firm can embark upon. These are vertical integration, capacity expansion, and entry into new business. These options mostly concern a firm's value appropriation. A firm can also take initiatives to improve the overall value proposition of the ecosystem's product-service bundle, but this would require changes to the cooperative arrangements in the ecosystem.

Vertical integration means that the firm takes activities in-house that are done by either suppliers (backward integration) or buyers (forward integration). From an ecosystem point of view, complementors can also be acquired (sideways integration). These activities then effectively become part of the firm's value chain. This can make a firm more cost efficient – adding to the cost leadership side of the firm's strategic position, or it can boost the ability of the firm to add value – adding to the differentiation or focus side of the firm's strategic ability. Alternatively, the firm has a choice to develop these additional value activities internally by investing in supplementary production facilities and know-how. The alternative is to enter into a merger or acquire a supplier, buyer, or complementor firm and add the additional capability in that way.

Strategy practice 3.4 Formulating a strategic business plan using the industrial organization approach

The industrial organization approach is also very well suited to formulate a strategic business plan. Again, the environmental analysis comes first. Start with defining the ecosystem the firm wants to operate in. Then find out about the strength of the six forces, preferably by investigating the value chains of all the firms that can be associated with each of the forces. Also look out for cooperative arrangements that need to be taken into account. The next thing to do is to assess the value chain of the firm for which the plan is formulated. To be able to do this, you first need to find out about what exactly end users value about the product-service bundle or solution that defines the ecosystem. Once the picture is complete, on the basis of the strength of the six forces and existing cooperative arrangements, the firm wants to position itself in the ecosystem on the basis of the firm's own value chain and what value the firm actually is adding by picking a cooperative role and a competitive generic strategy. This, effectively, is the formulated strategy. Finally, do the maths. Check if the expected price and cost levels allow for a positive margin. If the numbers do not add up, start again or abandon the plan.

Capacity expansion is another way of becoming a more prominent player in the ecosystem. In an ecosystem with a growing demand, it is an obvious choice to grow with the expanding demand and even to try to grow faster than the ecosystem growth rate to get a bigger slice of an increasing pie. By adding capacity faster, the firm can become more efficient than the competition and improve its margin alongside growing its turnover. The experience curve from marketing-inspired strategic thinking applies here, as well.

In a mature ecosystem with limited growth, adding capacity only makes sense when it allows the firm to increase its turnover at the expense of the competition. This is very often not a viable opportunity. In these kinds of situations, the ecosystem sees a lot of consolidation activity. Firms merge with each other to create larger firms in order to dominate the ecosystem or to prevent being dominated by such newly created combinations. This is effectively a change to the cooperative arrangements in the ecosystem.

Alternatively, and especially if a firm gets crowded out, it can decide to leave the ecosystem and start up somewhere else. The firm then has to enter another ecosystem. To do that, it has to overcome both exit barriers and entry barriers. Exit barriers prevent a firm from changing the nature of its business. These can be specific assets and know-how that cannot be deployed elsewhere or a lack of knowledge about alterative business opportunities. The ecosystem the firm likes to move into should be attractive, i.e. the strength of the six forces should be low. Yet ironically, a high entry barrier makes an ecosystem attractive but also difficult to enter.

If the firm moves into another ecosystem while remaining active in the ecosystem it already is part of, this is a diversification move. This could be warranted if its existing abilities give a competitive advantage in both the new ecosystem and in the old one. The notion of synergy from marketing-inspired strategic thinking applies here, too.

Illustration 3.8 Consolidation in steel

In January 2008, the Indian company Tata Steel acquired the Anglo-Dutch steelmaker Corus for $12.1 billion*. Tata had beaten CSN of Brazil in a bidding war. Tata, as the 56th largest steel company in the world, combined with eighth largest Corus to create the fifth largest firm. The takeover of Acelor by Mittal had created the largest steel company in the world less than a year before. Corus, in turn, was the result of the 1999 merger between the Dutch firm Hoogovens and British Steel.

Steel is used in many product-service bundles and therefore as a product appears in many ecosystems. Although steel comes in grades and qualities, it is a relatively undifferentiated product. Its production requires capital-intensive plants and facilities. The demand for steel is tied into the economic tides. If the economy goes up, the demand for steel goes up, and steel firms do well. If the economy goes down, overcapacity ensues, and the less efficient plants suffer the most. Entry is an onerous affair. It takes 5–6 years to build a new steel plant at a cost of about $1,200 or $1,300 per tonne production capacity. The price at which a tonne of hot rolled coil steel – an accepted reference point in the industry – was sold in 2007 was $550, but was expected to go down to $450 in the following year.

Buyers of raw steel tend to be big companies themselves, like for instance car manufacturers. To withstand these pressures, especially in times of overcapacity, the size of a steel company matters, as well. Tata's production costs in 2007 were $150 per tonne because of its access to cheap Indian coal and iron ore; the industry average was $330. Corus made it for $540 per tonne, mainly as a consequence of high material costs.

Corus was looking for a partner after surviving a few loss-making years and wanted to move up from a European producer to become part of a global steel company. Its management's aim was to get access to both emerging economies and to cheaper raw materials. Merging with either CSN or Tata would have solved both problems. Tata was looking to expand its production capacity without having to resort to building new facilities. Combined, they think they are better equipped to pursue a low-cost strategy in an ecosystem with strong forces and in which differentiation opportunities are limited.

* BBC News, 31 January 2007, http://news.bbc.co.uk/1/hi/business/6069492.stm [accessed 21 January 2014]; Wharton, 8 February 2007, http://knowledge.wharton.upenn.edu/article/did-tata-steel-overheat-in-its-zeal-to-win-corus/ [accessed 21 January 2014]; Forbes, 22 October 2006, www.forbes.com/2006/10/22/tata-corus-mna-biz-cx_rd_1022corus.html [accessed 21 January 2010].

In addition to Porter's (1980) suggestion and apart from the three forms of integration distinguished previously, there are other modes of cooperation (Sydow et al., 2016). This would be cooperation that is aimed more at improving the overall value proposition of the ecosystem rather than improving an individual firm's value appropriation. Integration to improve coordination is at one end of the scale. Adjusting price levels upwards or downwards in arms-length market exchange relationships is at the other end of the scale. In between, there is a range of options that firms can move between, or they can change the conditions of specific cooperative arrangements that they are already part of. These options include temporary consortia, strategic alliances, certification and standard-setting schemes, preferred supplier arrangements, dedicated outsourcing relationships, and subcontracting.

Illustration 3.9 SKF from an industrial organization point of view

Should SKF* compete on price and put in the lowest bid possible to retain a big US-based client, or should it step away and persist with its high-quality strategy?

Ball bearings are used almost everywhere where there are moving parts, and they therefore are part of many product-service bundles and the associated ecosystems. Yet the supply of ball bearings is fairly global and dominated by a few big players like SKF, Timken, Schaeffler, and NSK. There are low-end mostly local offerings by Chinese and Eastern European firms, and a more high-end well-established offering as provided by SKF. A low-quality producer cannot suddenly become high quality. The other way around, SKF cannot simply abandon its more costly but sophisticated production process to become a low-cost ball bearing manufacturer. So SKF is mostly competing with the aforementioned other four, which combined serve 59% of worldwide ball bearing needs. The ball bearing business is fairly mature, with total sales going up and down with world GDP and business cycles. The market is carved up between the big players with the rivalry force therefore not overwhelmingly strong as yet.

In the US, SKF sells through distributors: independent companies which act as a kind of wholesaler for end user firms. This is a common practice in the ball bearing business. It was through a distributor that the US-based client communicated its intention to hold a reverse auction. The distributor firms have gone through a cycle of consolidation. End user firms have been piling pressure on distributors, with ever more aggressive procurement tactics being deployed. A common expectation is that with every new contract, there will be a 5% discount on the previous agreed contract price. The distributors and their suppliers, including SKF, have largely absorbed this. Some larger end users are dispensing with distributers altogether and are starting to negotiate directly with ball bearing manufacturers. The buyer force therefore is pretty strong. If distributers become less prevalent, the whole ecosystem possibly becomes subjected to change.

SKF's value activities are strong when it comes to service, marketing, and operations. Its service offering positions SKF more as a complementor than a supplier, especially if this develops into selling packages that include ball bearing servicing contracts rather than just ball bearings. This is where SKF can build on its reputation of high-quality ball bearings. In this way, SKF does not sell ball bearings. It sells solutions that make end user machinery more reliable and efficient. This has been something that end users value – and SKF solutions have always allowed for premium pricing, and therefore relatively high margins. The competitive generic strategy of focused differentiation best describes how SKF is positioned in all the ecosystems where ball bearings are used, as SKF offers high value but concentrates on a specific contribution in various ecosystems.

The US-based client's invitation to participate in a reverse auction is another manifestation of the strong buyer force. Ball bearing manufacturer margins are under pressure, even though SKF's are relatively high. With a number of big players being put under the same pressure, mutual rivalry might go up, as well. Whether SKF is sufficiently shielded from this depends on the relative importance end users place on low price or on high value. Obviously, they are pressuring ball bearing manufacturers into accepting a lower price while retaining value. Should SKF give in and participate in the auction? Porter does say that you should never compete on price. But this looks like the price level for the ball bearings in general is coming down. End users, distributors, and ball bearing manufacturers are competing for margin in ecosystems, and it looks like the pressure is becoming too big to withstand it for much longer. This is not just about one end user, but more of a general trend in the ecosystem. For SKF to remain in business, it looks like it has to accept the squeeze and get used to continuing to offer the same product at a lower price. To be able to do that, it has to work on its value chain to become more efficient in offering the same product.

* Value Selling at SKF Service, IMD-5–0751, 2009.

Criticisms and unanswered questions

Much of the criticism that is levied against marketing-inspired strategic thinking also applies to the industrial organization approach. The emphasis on intended strategy and rational decision-making comes at the expense of consideration with regard to how to actually realize the strategy. The industrial organization approach is also essentially static, providing snapshots of the firm's environment, abilities, and strategy. It also requires the same basic underlying assumptions regarding a real business reality out there about which objective information can be gathered to base decisions upon, and about unbiased and all-powerful top management taking charge of the firm. This theoretical approach leans towards objectivism.

The static character of the industrial organization approach worried Porter, as well (Porter, 1991). If you read his 1980 and 1985 books carefully, you find him urging strategists not to take the status quo as a given but to actively try to change industry structures and value systems to their advantage. The same argument applies to ecosystems, as well, with ecosystem innovation drawing considerable researcher interest, as yet only resulting in the recognition that innovation means that forces and cooperative arrangements will be disturbed, but also that for innovation to succeed, a collective effort is required (Adner & Kapoor, 2010; Wareham, Fox, & Cano Giner, 2014). The only suggestion as to how to strategically deal with this is a belief that ecosystems can be purposefully designed and redesigned (Jacobides, 2019; Kapoor, 2018).

Drawing on the product life cycle concept, Porter does suggest that industries are subject to a life cycle (Porter, 1980). The argument has been made for ecosystems, as well (Moore, 1993). To him, the early days of any industry are best described as 'emergent'. In an emergent industry, things are ambiguous. It is not clear yet what product defines the industry, nor who the rivals are, or any other players in the system. End users are unsure, as well, about what they value and whether they like the product at all. In such a situation, it is not very meaningful to formulate a competitive strategy in terms of the generic strategies, although it is a situation of enormous potential for when the industry does settle down.

As soon as things get settled, the industry becomes 'mature'. This is a situation with a value system of vested interest, with clear definitions of products and product categories, as well as clear ideas among end users about what they expect from a product. This is the situation to which the theoretical language of the industrial organization approach tends to apply the best. The expectation is that the industry eventually winds down and becomes 'declining'. Some firms are able to hang on, while others decide to opt out or are forced out by bankruptcy as a consequence of decreasing demand. Porter (1980) refers to industries that never get settled down as 'fragmented'.

While recognizing that industries change and evolve, he provides little guidance about how this happens, let alone suggests strategies of how firms can have an active role in this. His work does not deal with questions about how industry structures change or how the forces become stronger or weaker. He came as far as suggesting that industries take shape within the context of particular countries (Porter, 1990), and offers this as a first step in the explanation (Porter, 1991), yet he also recognizes that his analysis of the competitive advantage of nations still is essentially static, as well, and that it does not deal with the process by which it actually happens.

All of this applies to ecosystem thinking, as well. Adding the complementor force, recognizing the need for cooperation, and going from products to product-service bundles does not make the industrial organization approach less static. Ironically, the instability that comes with coopetition makes the ecosystem more prone to change.

Exhibit 3.5 Industrial organization reflective questions

· In the performance logic, how does the industrial organization approach understand the environment, the strategy, and the firm?
· What in the industrial organization approach is the key question that a strategist should always be worried about and serves as the 'starter' question for a strategic analysis?
· From an industrial organization point of view, what are firms competing for?
· From an industrial organization point of view, why is there a need for firms to cooperate?
· What is coopetition, and why is it inherently unstable?
· What defines an ecosystem?
· Which forces are present in an ecosystem, and what do these forces do to a firm?
· What cooperative roles are available for a firm in an ecosystem?
· Which competitive generic strategies can a firm choose from, and how do these represent competitive advantage?
· Why should you never compete on price?
· What is a value chain, and why do you need to assess value added and costs?
· From an industrial organization point of view, what can a firm do if it has to deal with a strategic issue?
· What different ways are there for a firm to cooperate?
· In the process logic, how are the environmental survival process and the organizational strategy process understood, and how is a strategist expected to contribute?
· Why is the industrial organization approach considered to be objectivistic?

Case 3.1

Spotify

On the occasion in 2016 of music streams becoming included in making up the music charts in the UK alongside downloads and physical record sales, founder and CEO of Spotify, Daniel Ek, told artists to stop the fight against streaming.[1] At the time, artists like Taylor Swift, Garth Brooks, and The Beatles refused to have their music streamed.[2] However, a search on the Spotify web player revealed that their music has become available since.

Spotify is a music streaming service by which you can listen to music using your computer, your tablet, or your smartphone. Increasingly, high fidelity equipment manufacturers like Cambridge Audio and Naim offer streamers with Spotify Connect,[3] an app that links your Spotify account with your music device.[4] Spotify Connect is also available for smart speakers, including Google Home and Amazon Echo, smart watches, game consoles, car audio, and Apple TV.

Using Spotify, you can listen to music for free – but then you will have to endure ads – or you can take out a subscription, which also gives you a somewhat improved sound quality, although you can buy software that claims to block ads.[5] Monthly rates in the US vary between $9.99 for an individual, $12.99 for a duo, $14.99 for a family of six, and $4.99 for a student.[6] Apple, Google, Amazon, Napster, Deezer, Pandora, Idagio, Qobuz, and Tidal are also available.[7] Apple, Google, and Amazon offer packages that include TV and film, with Amazon also adding its streaming services to the larger Amazon Prime package. Idagio specializes in classical music, while Qobuz and Tidal offer the highest audio quality. In the US, Apple Music offers the same subscriptions for the same price as Spotify, but students get Apple TV included while others have to pay an additional $4.99.[8] A Qobuz streaming plan starts at $14.99 per month.[9]

Spotify was launched in 2008 and is based in Sweden. It claims to have 138 million subscribers in 92 countries who can pick from 60 million different tracks.[10] Despite having never returned a profit, it is considered a sound investment opportunity, but not as good as Apple.[11] It is seen as comparable to other high-growth software companies in that it has low gross margins.[12] Spotify has started to get into exclusive deals with prominent podcasters and has bought a few podcast companies, as well. Spotify and China-based Tencent Music own 10% stakes in each other.[13]

Spotify offers a range of free services for music artists for them to improve their music and to develop their fanbases.[14] For a music artist to get their music on Spotify, they are told to find themselves a distributor or record label, which can handle licencing deals and distribution, and who will collect royalties on the artist's behalf. It is estimated that Spotify pays artists between $0.003 and $0.005 per stream[15]; it depends on the region where the music is played and whether it is played through a free or a subscription account. Streams from the US pay more than streams from India, as do subscription streams compared to free streams. For example, an Australian band received $4,955.90 for 1,023,501 streams, while classical violinist Tasmin Little received $15.67 for between 5 million and 6 million streams.

Spotify's organizational structure appears to be rather functional, with accounting, HR, research and development (R&D), legal, content, and sales departments.[16] The company has also been put forward as a prime example of a balanced organization between employee autonomy and employee accountability, with at least engineering and R&D organized around 'squads, tribes, chapters, and guilds'.[17] A squad is a fairly autonomous co-located interdisciplinary group of eight people who are responsible for a specific aspect of Spotify's product offering throughout its life cycle. A chapter's leader is a formal manager of a category of employees. Spotify's organizational structure is effectively a matrix. This is claimed to drive agility and innovation,[18] but is also criticized for driving up costs.[19]

US-based ad agency RSM Marketing claims that advertising on Spotify is a good cross-platform and cross-device marketing tool; it is ideally suited to reach millennials, does not suffer from marketing fatigue and ad-blindness, and preserves retention and awareness over long buying cycles.[20]

Notes

1 www.bbc.co.uk/newsbeat/article/27918765/spotify-founder-daniel-ek-dont-fight-against-streaming [accessed 4 September 2020]

2 www.rollingstone.com/music/music-news/islands-in-the-stream-the-10-biggest-holdouts-in-digital-music-232923/ [accessed 4 September 2020]

3 www.whathifi.com/best-buys/streaming/best-music-streamers [accessed 4 September 2020]

4 https://spotify-everywhere.com [accessed 4 September 2020]

5 www.audfree.com/spotify/block-ads-on-spotify.html [accessed 4 September 2020]

6 www.spotify.com/us/promo/endofsummer/?checkout=false [accessed 4 September 2020]

7 www.zdnet.com/article/best-music-services/ [accessed 4 September 2020]

8 www.apple.com/apple-music/ [accessed 4 September 2020]

9 www.qobuz.com/us-en/music/streaming/offers [accessed 4 September 2020]

10 https://newsroom.spotify.com/company-info/ [accessed 4 September 2020]

11 www.fool.com/investing/2020/08/31/better-buy-spotify-vs-apple/ [accessed 4 September 2020]

12 www.fool.com/investing/2020/08/20/where-will-spotify-be-in-5-years/ [accessed 4 September 2020]

13 www.fool.com/investing/2020/06/20/forget-tencent-music-spotify-is-a-better-streaming.aspx [accessed 4 September 2020]

14 https://artists.spotify.com/?ref=logo [accessed 4 September 2020]

15 www.digitalmusicnews.com/2020/08/17/how-much-does-spotify-pay-per-stream-latest/ [accessed 4 September 2020]

16 www.theofficialboard.com/org-chart/spotify [accessed 4 September 2020]

17 Mankins, M., & Garton, E. (2017). *Time, Talent, Energy: Overcome Organizational Drag and Release Your Team's Productive Power*. Cambridge, MA: Harvard Business Review Press.

18 Kniberg, H., & Ivarsson, A. (2012). Scaling Agile @ Spotify. Retrieved from https://creativeheldstab.com/wp-content/uploads/2014/09/scaling-agile-spotify-11.pdf

19 Davis, S. M., & Lawrence, P. R. (1978). Problems of matrix organizations. *Harvard Business Review, 56*(May–June), 131–142.

20 https://howtoadvertiseonspotify.com [accessed 4 September 2020]

CHAPTER 4

The resource-based view

The resource-based view takes the firm itself as the starting point for strategic thinking. It has branched out into a static resource-based view and a dynamic resource-based view. While the static resource-based view complements marketing-inspired strategic thinking and the industrial organization approach, the dynamic resource-based view was intentionally pitted against these two theoretical approaches.

The origin of the resource-based view is traced back to the economist Edith Penrose (1959), but not until a paper by Birger Wernerfelt (1984) was published was the relevance of her work for strategy theory recognized. The resource-based view starts with the economist's definition of the firm as a production function in which the output of a firm is determined by what is put in. These inputs are described in terms of production factors like land, capital, and labour. These production factors are also referred to as resources. If there are performance differences between firms, so the reasoning continues, it is due to differences between the resources available to the firm. Hence, the notion of firm heterogeneity – differences between firms in terms of their resource bases – became the pivot on which the resource-based view explanation of why firms vary with regard to their performance turned.

Furthermore, they came up with two reasons why firm heterogeneity exists (Barney, 1991; Peteraf, 1993; Peteraf & Barney, 2003). One reason is imperfect factor markets (Barney, 1986). The other reason is resource accumulation within the firm (Dierickx & Cool, 1989). The factor market argument developed into a more static resource-based view and the resource accumulation argument was at the heart of a more dynamic resource-based view (Maritan & Peteraf, 2011).

The process logic of the static resource-based view

Economists imagine that resources are traded on factor markets. These factor markets are purely theoretical constructs and should not be confused with procurement and the product markets where firms source their supplies. Economists like to think that firms are submitted to the market mechanism. A perfect market means that supply and demand balance out at an equilibrium price (see Figure 4.1). The reason for this is perfect information about costs and benefits among the various buyers and sellers.

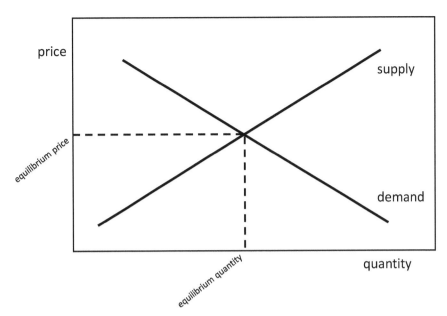

price

supply

equilibrium price

demand

equilibrium quantity

quantity

Figure 4.1
A perfect market

Nevertheless, this argument creates a conundrum. If the resources that a firm needs to make a product are imagined to be traded in perfect factor markets, then it would be impossible for a firm to make a profit. The reason is that the moment a firm makes a profit from a resource, other firms, because of perfect information, would know about this. Everybody would want to buy this resource to make a profit, too. Increasing demand would make the price for this resource go up. This will go on until the price that has to be paid for this resource will equal the money that can be made from the output for which this resource is used. This is the equilibrium price, and at this price, nobody is able to make a profit. At the equilibrium point, the costs to acquire the resource would equal the amount of money you can make with it. If a firm is able to make a profit, then there should be a factor market where the market mechanism does not work (Barney, 1986). This is referred to as an imperfect factor market.

So, the environmental survival process that forms the basis of the static resource-based view is competition in factor markets (see Figure 4.2). The crucial question is whether a factor market for a particular resource is perfect or imperfect. Only when a factor market is imperfect does it hold the promise of sustainable competitive advantage for the firm that possesses this resource, because this resource – when deployed – allows you to make a profit. This notion of sustainability adds to the previous theoretical approaches of marketing-inspired strategic thinking and the industrial organization approach. Sustainable means that this competitive advantage will last over a certain period of time. The resource that underpins this advantage is not widely available, which makes it difficult for other firms to catch up quickly.

Barney (1991) presented this insight for the benefit of doing a strategic analysis, arguing that the strategists should consider the resource base of the

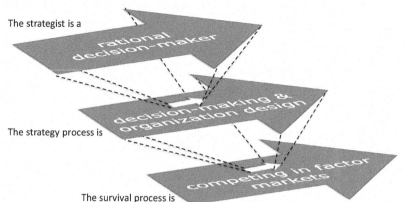

The strategist is a

rational decision-maker

The strategy process is

decision-making & organization design

The survival process is

competing in factor markets

Figure 4.2
The process logic for
the static resource-
based view

firm with special emphasis on finding out about the sustainability of a firm's competitive advantage; hence, the continuation of seeing the organizational strategy process as strategic planning, and the strategists' contribution in terms of rational decision-making (see Figure 4.2).

The performance logic of the static resource-based view

Barney (1991) also came up with four criteria that a resource should fulfil to allow a firm to have sustainable competitive advantage and make a profit. These are known as the VRIN criteria. A resource should be valuable; that is: it should be useable for the implementation of a competitive strategy. A resource should be rare: it should not be so common that everybody can lay their hands on it. A resource should be inimitable: it should not be easy to create the same resource from scratch. Finally, a resource should be non-substitutable: there should not be another resource readily available with which this competitive strategy can also be implemented. If a resource fulfils these four criteria, the firm has a sustainable competitive advantage. A firm's performance is based on its competitive advantage, which it has when it possesses resources that are valuable, rare, inimitable, and non-substitutable (VRIN). For this reason, factor markets has been put in grey italics in Figure 4.3 because finding that a resource is VRIN automatically means that the associated factor market is imperfect.

However, there is an important caveat here, especially in light of the existence of both the static and the dynamic resource-based view. In the static resource-based view, VRIN resources only represent 'current' competitive advantage. Furthermore, the strategy that the firm pursues should exploit this particular resource in order to create performance (March, 1991). This is the requirement of fit (see Figure 4.3).

The reasoning is simple enough. The difficulty lies in defining and identifying the resources that may fulfil these criteria. One problem is that as soon as this information about a resource becomes available, it makes the factor market more perfect and therefore erodes the possibility of competitive advantage

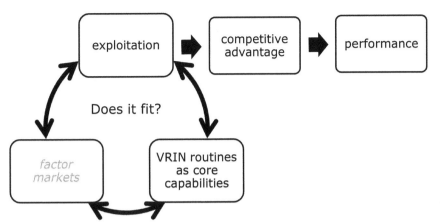

Figure 4.3
The static resource-
based view

(Kraaijenbrink, Spender, & Groen, 2010). Another problem is that the easily identifiable resources are less likely to fulfil the VRIN criteria. One rule of thumb is that if a resource is tradable, it would not be a source of competitive advantage (Mahoney & Pandian, 1992). If a resource can be identified with a particular procurement market where a firm can source it as a supply, the rarity criterion is not fulfilled.

To get to grips with this notion of resource in the resource-based view, various strategy scholars have come up with their own extended vocabulary and associated but complicated definitions. To provide a few examples: Grant (1991) distinguished between resources as "inputs into the production process – they are the basic unit of analysis" (p. 118) and capabilities as "the capacity for a team of resources to perform some task or activity" (p. 119). To Amit and Schoemaker (1993), resources are "stocks of available factors that are owned or controlled by the firm" (pp. 34–35). Capabilities are "a firm's capacity to deploy resources" (p. 35), while strategic assets are "the set of difficult to trade and imitate, scarce, appropriable and specialized resources and capabilities" (p. 36). Teece, Pisano, and Shuen (1997, p. 516) distinguish between factors of production as the "'undifferentiated' inputs available in disaggregate form in factor markets", resources as the "firm-specific assets that are difficult if not impossible to imitate", organizational routines or competences as the "firm-specific assets . . . assembled in integrated clusters spanning individuals and groups so that they enable distinctive activities to be performed", and core competences as the "competences that define a firm's fundamental business".

A common thread can be teased out here. The term 'resource' is too coarse. If there are production factors that fulfil the VRIN criteria, they can be found among the 'capabilities' or 'competences' of a firm. These capabilities tend to be combinations of more basic resources that combine into routines (Ackermann & Eden, 2011), with a routine understood as an assembly of a people's skills and motivations, as well as a firm's basic physical, financial, knowledge, cultural, marketing, and organizational resources. A 'routine' is a regular and predictable behavioural pattern in a firm (Nelson & Winter, 1982), which makes particular use

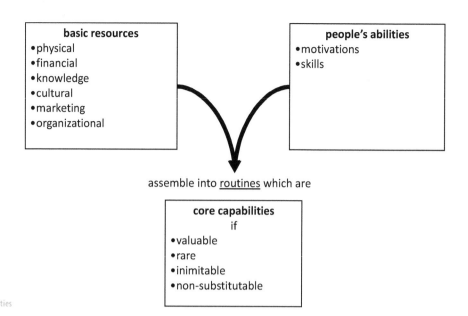

Figure 4.4
Core capabilities

of people's abilities and these more basic resources. It rarely is just one routine that fulfils the VRIN criteria. More often, it is a combination of routines that is the source of competitive advantage (see Figure 4.4). The capability that routines that fulfil the VRIN criteria represent is labelled as 'core' (see Figure 4.4). Static resource-based view strategic thinking concentrates on identifying these VRIN routines by probing the existence of core capabilities.

Illustration 4.1 The core capability of Rolex

Rolex has a history that goes back to 1905.* It is now a premium Swiss watchmaker. Rolex watches hold their value so well that they tend to resell at a higher price than they were originally bought for. Rolex watches are made in Switzerland at sites in Bienne and Geneva. The company is fully integrated. It manufactures every one of the over 200 bits and parts of the watch itself. Highly skilled craftsmen put each watch together by hand. Rolex claims to be the inventor of the wristwatch. It was the first to make the wristwatch waterproof, the first to integrate the day – date in the movement, and the first to perfect a self-winding movement to become mass producible.

   Both Rolex's manufacturing and marketing routines can be claimed as core capabilities. State-of-the-art facilities, a culture of Swiss watchmaking, and the employees' unique skills back up the daily routines of the Rolex watchmakers. Although the patent on the 'perpetual movement' ran out in 1948, new inventions like the 'blue parachrom hairspring' take their place. Rolex marketing trades on this exclusivity, the quality of the Rolex mechanical movements, and the firm's history.

   It is the combination of these routines – with each one an assembly of the various Rolex resources – and the individual abilities of Rolex employees that constitutes core capability. The high prices a Rolex watch commands as part of a highly focused competitive strategy indicates their value. Relatively scarce ingredients are put together in a very rare combination of ability. A history of more than 100 years is difficult to imitate, let alone putting together an organization and facilities that produce 750,000 high-quality mechanical movements, as well as highly prized and carefully designed watch cases, annually. There are cheaper and even more accurate substitutes available utilizing quartz technology, but that does not have the same cachet as the Rolex movement.

* www.rolex.com [accessed 27 January 2014]; What Makes Rolex Tick? by David Liebeskind, http://w4.stern.nyu.edu/sternbusiness/fall_winter_2004/rolex.html [accessed 27 January 2014]; RolexMagazine.com, http://rolexblog.blogspot.co.uk/2012/10/inside-rolex-rolex-manufacturing.html [accessed 27 January 2014]

The process logic of the dynamic resource-based view

The dynamic resource-based view is based on the other reason for firm heterogeneity. Firms differ because of unique trajectories of resource accumulation that occur within the confines of a firm (Dierickx & Cool, 1989). The argument here is that firms develop routines from scratch, which are not offered for sale because the firm does not want to – as they are at the core of what allows the firm to out-compete the competition – or they cannot be offered for sale because they are essentially non-transferable. Routines by which a firm can out-compete the competition tend to be unique, as these have been developed over time. It is impossible to package such capabilities and transfer them to other settings. Quite often, the firm itself does not really know how this unique package came together in the first place, and is therefore not able to purposefully recreate it when asked. This is referred to as causal ambiguity (Reed & DeFillippi, 1990). In these instances, a routine is not transferable and therefore unique to a particular firm.

This argument of development and change is at the heart of the criticism that the dynamic resource-based view has mounted against marketing-inspired strategic thinking and against the original industrial organization approach as devised by Porter (Hamel & Prahalad, 1994). These two approaches take the environment – the product market or the industry – as their starting point. The argument against this is that the environment is deemed too volatile to base a strategy on. By the time the wants and needs of the customers or the strength of the forces are assessed, everything has changed. Furthermore, even core capabilities do not stay VRIN forever. It is only a matter of time before competitors catch up. The environment, so the reasoning goes, is characterized by hyper-competition (D'Aveni, 1994), with firms engaging in quick one-upmanship to outwit each another. As a basis for strategic management, something is needed that has more of a continuous presence in such an ever-changing world. The thing having a more continuous presence is the firm's resource base.

The process logic of the dynamic resource-based view is therefore a profound departure from the previous theoretical approaches (see Figure 4.5). The environmental survival process is characterized as dealing with volatility. The way to do this is to continuously develop new routines and routine combinations, which underpin a succession of subsequent competitive advantages. The starting point here is that any competitive advantage is only temporarily and

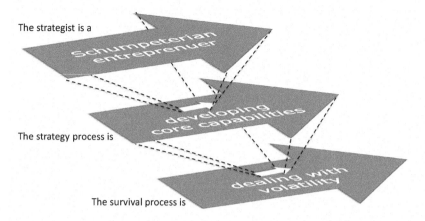

The strategist is a

Schumpeterian entrepreneur

developing core capabilities

The strategy process is

Figure 4.5
The process logic for
the dynamic resource-
based view

dealing with volatility

The survival process is

that a firm has to reinvent itself over and over again. The strategist is expected
to be a Schumpeterian entrepreneur (Hitt, Ireland, Camp, & Sexton, 2001).
Joseph Schumpeter was an early Austrian economist who described economic
development as creative destruction, driven by entrepreneurs who come up
with *neue Kombinationen*: new combinations of resources that allow new and
previously unknown economic activity (Schumpeter, 1934). Unfortunately, the
dynamic resource-based view has not yet developed the fail-safe formula of how
to be an ever-successful entrepreneur, if it ever will.

The performance logic of the dynamic resource-based view

The continuity in the firm's resource base that allows dealing with environmental
volatility is labelled as dynamic capability (Helfat et al., 2007; Teece et al.,
1997). It is a process of deliberate resource accumulation (Dierickx & Cool,
1989). The identification of dynamic capability in a firm is even more difficult
than identifying VRIN routines and core capability in the static resource-based
view. To a large extent, the jury is still out whether this actually can be done.
Nevertheless, there are two schools of thought here. One school elaborates
dynamic capability as an attribute of a firm. A firm either has dynamic capability
or it does not have it. The other school associates dynamic capability with specific
and identifiable routines that a firm has or does not have available. Dynamic
capability routines are taken to be a specific subset of routines that create and
change VRIN routines.

Eisenhardt and Martin (2000) proposed to understand dynamic capability as
specific identifiable routines that create and change VRIN routines. They suggest
that activities like R&D, product development, entering strategic alliances, and
how a firm does its strategic management exemplify dynamic capability. These are
examples of a whole range of activities in which a firm can engage, which purpose
is to adapt to changing circumstances or to create new possibilities. It is the
occurrence of these kinds of activities that indicates whether dynamic capability is
present.

Unfortunately, whether these activities actually create innovations and change is always an assessment after the fact. Past success is not necessarily an indicator of future performance. The degree to which a firm is actively engaged in adapting to or even creating new futures is taken as an estimate for dynamic capability. However, because the future tends to be uncertain and ambiguous, a fail-safe method to assess whether a firm's dynamic capability always gets it right still needs to be developed. The question can be asked – as with Schumpeterian entrepreneurship in general – whether that would be possible at all.

Illustration 4.2 Acquisitions as a dynamic capability routine at Cisco Systems

For a period of time, Cisco Systems acquired technology start-ups as a matter of routine (Goldblatt, 1999). Cisco makes the equipment on which the Internet runs. To keep abreast of new technological developments and when it found itself unable to develop a technology in-house, Cisco would look around Silicon Valley and buy the firm that was in the process of developing it. Up to 1999, Cisco had spent $18.8 billion on acquisitions. It bought and absorbed ten companies in 1998 alone. It has dedicated people to look out for eligible firms, to negotiate the takeover, and to subsequently integrate the acquired firm into the Cisco organization. They have done this so many times that they can strike a deal in days and integrate the newly acquired firm in months, without much upset to them or to the acquired firm.

Hamel and Prahalad's (1994) 'core competence' is an example of dynamic capability seen as a firm attribute. It is a concept specifically targeted at the level of corporate strategy as they see it as a feature of a multi-business firm. Core competence refers to a basic understanding about how to combine and coordinate diverse capabilities and technologies. To them, a product is just a temporary manifestation and a consequence of a translation of a firm's core competences into something that fulfils customer wants and needs while these exist for a limited period of time. They picture a firm as a tree with the core competences as the roots from which core products sprout as trunks, branching out into SBUs, with the products as the leaves (see Figure 4.6). Products, like the leaves, come and go with the seasons while the roots and the trunk are more permanent fixtures that live on. A multi-business firm should have a small number of core competences and associated core products, where SBUs can tap into to remain viable in an ever-changing world. The competitive strategy at the SBU level is about exploiting existing products and of finding new applications of core products, which cater to changing customer demands.

Illustration 4.3 The core competence of Honda

Honda was showcased as a firm that is organized around core competence (Prahalad & Hamel, 1990). The actual core competences that form the basis of Honda's success are combustion engineering and robotics. This translates into the combustion engine and manufacturing robots as core products. Its line of businesses, ranging from cars, motorcycles, power generators, lawnmowers, outboard marine engines, and snow blowers. All these products feature a combustion engine and are manufactured to a very high standard with the aid of robots.

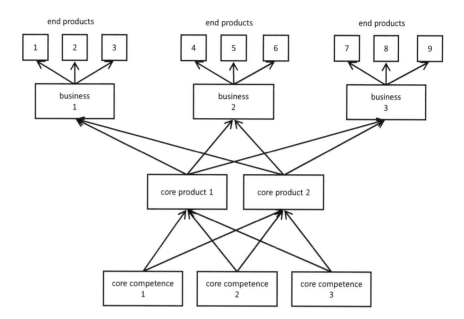

Figure 4.6
Core competence

Corporate strategy for the multi-business firm is about maintaining – and more importantly, developing – core competences through strategic intent by stretch and leverage. Strategic intent refers to an ambition about what the firm will be about in the future, not what the firm currently is. It is not based on the current set of routines that make up the firm, but on capabilities that still need to be developed. This, in the eyes of Hamel and Prahalad (1994), creates a situation of stretch, of reaching beyond the horizon to achieve something that is currently non-existent. By being ambitious and stretching out, it is possible that the firm leverages itself into the future. Hamel and Prahalad like to talk about strategic management as stretch and leverage. This requirement of stretch forms the basis of core competence as dynamic capability (see Figure 4.7).

The dynamic resource-based view is almost per definition a corporate strategy–level type of strategic thinking. It urges a firm to constantly explore for new business. This makes it unavoidable that a firm becomes a multi-business firm, juggling the exploitation within its existing activities with the exploration to develop new business. If a firm is able to combine exploration with exploitation, it is said to be 'ambidextrous' (O'Reilly III & Tushman, 2004). This is not an easy thing to do because the requirements of exploitation – doing the same thing over and over again – contradict exploration – actively looking out for things to change.

Nevertheless, the reason why a particular single business is better off as part of a larger entity is found in the core competence that allows for this exploration to take place and which is only available to an SBU because it is part of a larger whole. The environment is seen as a volatile and ever-changing place. Dynamic capability is expected to deal with this and fuels a deliberate strategy of exploration (March, 1991). The overall strategic intent should be one of stretch: of

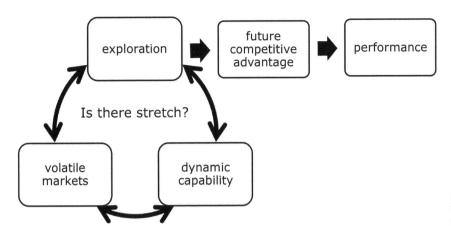

Figure 4.7
The dynamic resource-based view

reaching just beyond the horizon. Without stretch, so the argument goes, the firm never develops beyond what it is already doing, and eventually will wither away.

Additional features

A specific branch of the resource-based view has singled out knowledge as the key resource on which everything else hinges (Grant, 1996; Kogut & Zander, 1992). Their argument is based on the observation that the world economy essentially is a 'knowledge-based economy', and that economic performance is determined by what you know. There exist various types of knowledge, and a common distinction is the one between explicit knowledge and tacit knowledge (Polanyi, 1967). Explicit knowledge can be articulated and transferred. You find it written down, for instance, in procedures, manuals and in teaching materials like this book. Or it is materialized in equipment, machinery and IT that can be bought and installed. Obviously, explicit knowledge is transferable and can therefore not be a basis for competitive advantage. Tacit knowledge is what people know but that they are unable to express. Transferred to the realm of the resource-based view, it is this tacit knowledge that is bound to be unique to a firm, and the quest is on to manage and develop the inexpressible.

Ironically, what you know and how you understand things cannot only propel you forward but can also hold you back. The possibility of change combined with the temporality of a firm's resource-based competitive advantage gives rise to the concept of core rigidity (Leonard-Barton, 1992). Core rigidity refers to a past core capability that a firm is geared up to exploit but whose usefulness is surpassed by changing circumstances. It is obsolete knowledge but still used by the firm and its top management and employees to make sense of the world. A core capability has a tendency to be so ingrained in the functioning of a firm that it is very difficult to get rid of. What first made the firm successful now is a reason for failure. It adds another consideration for the explanation of performance. It needs to take core rigidity as a cause for failure into account (see Figure 4.8).

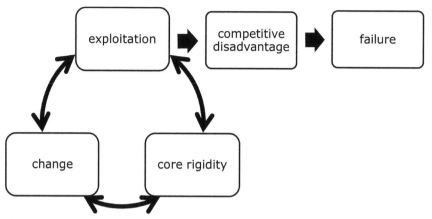

Figure 4.8 Core rigidity

Illustration 4.4 Core rigidity at NBL

NBL stands for North British Locomotive Company, a large Glasgow engineering firm with a proud history in producing railway steam engines (Fleming, McKinstry, & Wallace, 2000). The company was declared bankrupt in 1962. It could trace its history back 129 years, having produced no less than 28,000 locomotives and exporting them all over the world.

At the time, the firm and its management were fully aware of the development of new forms of traction with railway locomotives powered by diesel engines or electricity. It had reviewed its position and future in post-war Britain and concluded that there was still a market for steam locomotives for the time being, despite the inherent efficiencies that diesel and electricity hold over steam. Their analysis told them that the availability of oil is limited to a relatively small number of well-developed countries. They reckoned that diesel-powered locomotives would be a limited market in countries like the US, which happen to be rich in oil. The UK was an oil importing country but was furnished with coal. Electric traction requires an expensive additional infrastructure of electric power supply, either through overhead catenary or a third rail. The UK would not be able to afford these investments for some time. The distances in many of NBL's export markets were so large that electrification would not be a consideration there, either. On that basis, they had set themselves up to keep on selling and producing steam locomotives while exploring the possibilities of diesel technology. In fact, NBL did have a line in small diesel-mechanical shunting engines.

Diesel-mechanical technology was not suited for the high speeds and power requirements of mainline railway locomotives. To enhance their technological abilities, NBL entered licencing agreements with German diesel engine manufacturer MAN and with the German firm Voith for hydraulic transmission systems. The British government had nationalized the railways in the UK in 1948. By 1955, they were keen to modernize the railways and opted for dieselization. They made British Railways order small batches of diesel locomotives from various UK-based suppliers. This was much earlier than NBL management had expected. However, NBL secured orders for high-powered and medium-powered diesel-hydraulic locomotives, as well as medium-powered diesel-electric locomotives. This provided NBL with the opportunity to retool its production facilities for the new technologies. The diesel engines and the hydraulic equipment were going to be made by NBL by building licensed MAN and Voith designs. The electric equipment for the diesel-electrics was going to be brought in from the GEC.

On completion, the diesel-hydraulic locomotives suffered from very many teething problems. The diesel-electrics fared a bit better because of the GEC equipment. As it turned out, the NBL personnel who were perfectly capable of designing and building high-quality steam locomotives were having difficulty manufacturing diesel engines and hydraulic transmissions. The new technologies required much more precision and much tighter tolerances compared to steam. The teething problems turned out to be much more than that. British Railways stopped placing repeat orders, opting for designs from other locomotive builders instead. In the meantime, British colonies were gaining independence. These traditional markets for UK manufacturing firms took their business elsewhere. By 1962, NBL did not have any money left, was devoid of orders, and decided to enter into voluntary administration.

Doing resource-based view strategic management

As there is a static resource-based view and a dynamic resource-based view, there are two ways to go about here. The static resource-based view is more of an add-on to marketing-inspired strategic thinking or the industrial organization approach. It allows the strategist to assess the sustainability of a firm's competitive advantage and add that to the internal appraisal. The dynamic resource-based view departs from this and favours a way of doing strategic management that moves away from rational decision-making in favour of Schumpeterian entrepreneurship. Consequently, there are two sets of questions to answer. From a static resource-based view standpoint the two questions are:

1 Are there any issues that interfere with the firm exploiting its VRIN routines?
2 If there are, what can you do about them?

From a dynamic resource-based view standpoint, the two questions become:

1 Are there any issues that prevent the firm from stretching itself by exploring its future on the basis of its dynamic capabilities?
2 If there are, what can you do about them?

Answering Question 1: strategic analysis

To be able to find answers to these two sets of questions, the strategist should be familiar with the firm's resource base, whether there are any VRIN routines and how they are exploited, and whether the firm has dynamic capability and is stretching itself into the future. If this familiarity is not the case, the strategist needs to get up to speed first.

Getting up to speed

The static resource-based view provides a way to probe the sustainability of a firm's competitive advantage. Marketing-inspired strategic thinking conceptualizes the firm in terms of key or critical success factors. The industrial organization approach sees the firm as a collection of value activities that combine into a value chain. These success factors or value activities can be further examined to unearth the routines on which these are based. Competitive advantage based on certain success factors or particular value activities is sustainable when these are underpinned by core capabilities. Capabilities are core when they are valuable (remember these capabilities should be suitable for implementing a competitive strategy, like the ones mentioned in the marketing derived trade-off between value and price or the ecosystem cooperative roles and competitive generic strategies in the industrial organization approach). Furthermore, these capabilities should be rare, inimitable, and non-substitutable. In short, these should be VRIN.

To get on the tail of capabilities that are core, the strategist needs to identify the various routines that make up the firm (see Exhibit 4.1). These are the regular and predictable behavioural patterns by which the firm creates its goods and services. These routines can be broken down in terms of the basic resources and the firm members' individual abilities (see Figure 4.4). With regard to the people's individual abilities, skills refer to what an individual is able to do; motivation concerns whether an individual is willing to do it. On the side of the basic resources, physical resources concern the IT, plant, equipment, and materials available. Financial resources refer to the amount of money on hand. Knowledge resources concern information and shared understandings about how things can be done. Cultural resources refer to shared norms and values. Marketing resources refer to the various devices and artefacts by which a firm engages with customers. Organizational resources concern how a firm is organized to facilitate coordinated routinized activity. A common mistake to make here is to just provide an enumeration of basic resources – to generate a list that tells nothing more than that the firm has physical resources, financial resources, human resources, or knowledge resources – without providing any indication as to how these assemble into routines and whether these routines fulfil the VRIN criteria.

The extent to which a routine fulfils the VRIN criteria tends to be a matter of degree rather than an absolute yes or no. If a routine fails on one of the criteria, it is not a core capability. Also, it tends to be a combination of routines that make capability to become core capability. Obviously, when the core capabilities have been identified, there needs to be a check that these are being exploited.

Exhibit 4.1 Static resource-based view internal appraisal questions

- What routines are employed within the firm?
- What basic physical, financial, knowledge, cultural, marketing, and organizational resources are available for these routines?
- What abilities in terms of motivations and skills do employees and managers have to enact these routines?
- Do any or a combination of basic resources and people's abilities combine into core capabilities because they are valuable, rare, inimitable, and non-substitutable?
- Are the available VRIN routines exploited by the firm's competitive strategy?

For the purpose of analysis, there is no need to be concerned with factor markets. By addressing capabilities in this way, the strategist automatically implies the factor markets that are imagined existing. The question, obviously, is whether a particular factor market is perfect or imperfect. The answer is given as soon as a conclusion is drawn whether a capability fulfils the VRIN criteria or not. The static resource-based view does not contribute to the external appraisal.

The dynamic resource-based view leads to a completely different kind of analysis. It is not so much in aid of making rational decisions, as with marketing-inspired strategic thinking, the industrial organization approach, and the static resource-based view. Instead, it is an evaluation of a firm's ability to deal with changing circumstances by demonstrating Schumpeterian entrepreneurship.

Exhibit 4.2 Dynamic resource-based view starter questions

- Is there evidence of specific routines that indicate dynamic capability like product development, innovation, R&D, etc.?
- How successful has the firm been in generating new business as a consequence of these dynamic capability routines?
- Are there core competences?
- Are there core products?
- Is there a succession of businesses that have come out of these core competences and core products?
- Is there activity that is aimed at maintaining and developing core competences and core products?
- Is there evidence of core rigidity?

In line with the view that dynamic capability is found in specific routines that indicate a firm is actively engaging with the future (Eisenhardt & Martin, 2000), the strategist should try to identify these specific routines within the firm and assess their effectiveness (see Exhibit 4.2 and compare with Figure 4.4). Does the firm engage in new product development? Does it do R&D? Is it active in pursuing innovations, etc.? Whether a firm is engaged in acquisitions, strategic alliances, and joint ventures – in effect scouting the environment and taking an interest in interestingly new developments – is an activity that qualifies as a dynamic capability routine (Helfat et al., 2007). Also, the way in which the firm does its strategic management indicates whether there is dynamic capability. The argument can be made that if a firm develops strategy on the basis of a rigid strategic planning regime, it can be taken as an indicator of the absence of dynamic capability. Alternatively, if there is much questioning and discussion going on, as is advocated in this book, this can be taken as an indicator of the presence of dynamic capability.

However, anything that the firm has developed and achieved in the past does not necessarily mean that it will create something new in the future. There is only comfort in knowing that the firm is actually actively engaged with its future instead of doing nothing. Conversely, if the firm does feature specific routines that indicate dynamic capability, but these do not appear to lead the firm into new territory, the question should be asked whether there is some core rigidity present. Does the firm run around in circles and continuously end up doing the same thing?

If the view is taken that dynamic capability is a feature of the firm – like Hamel and Prahalad's (1994) core competence – the strategist should try to identify the firm's core competences and core products (see Exhibit 4.2 and compare with Figure 4.6). Additionally, the strategist should try to track the succession of businesses and products that have come out of these core competences and core products, as well as the activities that go into maintaining and developing the core competences and core products.

Strategy practice 4.1 A resource-based view SWOT analysis

The purpose of a SWOT analysis is to find out about threats and opportunities in the environment and about strengths and weaknesses with regard to the firm. But what makes an opportunity an opportunity, a threat a threat, a strength a strength, and a weakness a weakness? The resource-based view may be of help here.

The focus of the resource-based view is on the firm itself. With regard to a SWOT analysis, it is mostly applicable for evaluating whether there are any strengths and weaknesses. Strengths in static resource-based view terms refer to the core capabilities: the routines that are VRIN. Weakness is a firm that does not possess any core capabilities. From a dynamic resource-based point of view, strengths are expressed as featuring dynamic capability either in terms of specific routines by which the firm actively engages with the future, combined with a successful track record, or in terms of core competences and core products. An obvious weakness is the existence of core rigidity.

Strategy practice 4.2 Internationalization from a resource-based viewpoint

There is a top-down argument and a bottom-up argument here. Bottom-up, starting from the core capabilities of country subsidiaries of an MNC, Birkinshaw, Hood, and Jonsson (1998) distinguish between 'location-bound' capabilities and 'non-location-bound' capabilities. Location-bound capabilities only matter within a country and have no application elsewhere. Non-location-bound capabilities have applicability in more than one country. An MNC should seek out those capabilities and transfer and deploy them across its subsidiaries. Hamel and Prahalad's (1994) top-down core competence model implies that an MNC's core competence should be translated into core products and in turn into businesses and end products across various countries.

Continuous questioning and analysis

For strategic management as wayfinding, a comprehensive understanding of the firm's strategic position should be in place. On the basis of that, the static resource-based view adds an additional set of questions and considerations that should be taken into account (see Exhibit 4.3). Again, the continuous questioning should be focused on the question of fit. Adding the static resource-based view to the deliberations, this 'fit' question should consider the competitive strategy that the firm realizes and provided this strategy exploits the firm's core capabilities, whether there are any developments with regard to the VRIN criteria. Although there is sustainability with regard to the firm's current competitive advantage because of the VRIN qualities, the strategists should keep an eye out for anything that undermines the firm's core capabilities.

Combining the static and dynamic views, the strategy debate should also be about the tension between the continuity of exploitation and the change that exploration could create. This refers to ambidexterity (O'Reilly III & Tushman, 2004) and to simultaneously being a good competitor now while developing new competitive advantage for future success.

Exhibit 4.3 Static resource-based view continuous questioning

- Is something that is happening or that is about to happen going to lose a core capability its value?
- Is something that is happening or that is about to happen going to lose a core capability its rarity?
- Is something that is happening or that is about to happen going to lose a core capability its inimitability?
- Is something that is happening or that is about to happen going to lose a core capability its non-substitutability?
- Does any of this mean that the 'fit' is affected, as the chosen competitive strategy will not exploit core capabilities?

From a dynamic resource-based point of view, one thing to question is the firm's strategic management routine itself. As was argued earlier, having a lively continuous discussion can be seen as dynamic capability. Taking the criticism of the dynamic resource-based view towards marketing-inspired strategic thinking or the industrial organization approach to heart, conducting a strategic management that exclusively is focused on these two approaches, because of their static nature, indicates the possible presence of core rigidity. If a firm's strategic management demonstrates an over-reliance on marketing or industrial organization vocabulary and logic, it can indicate that the firm is too much engrossed in the present with an implicit expectation that what is happening now will continue very much unchanged into the future. The key subject for discussion here is about where to stretch into and whether the firm is actively engaged with a future that is different from how the firm competes today (see Exhibit 4.4).

Exhibit 4.4 Dynamic resource-based view continuous questioning

- How does the firm 'do' strategic management?
- Is the change that comes with preparing for and dealing with a new future at the expense of competing successfully in the here and now?
  - or –

- · Is competing successfully in the here and now at the expense of the change that comes with preparing for and dealing with a new future?
- · Is there 'stretch' towards an imagined future that builds on the firm's dynamic capabilities and core competences?

Strategy practice 4.3 A resource-based view strategy workshop

Top management teams periodically book themselves into a nice retreat over a weekend to discuss how they or the firm is doing. This is an ideal opportunity to do some questioning and analysis. Quite often, an external consultant is asked to design a programme for the workshop, to suggest topics for discussion, and to facilitate the workshop.

The static resource-based view can add to the workshop design that the consultant puts together. The consultant can have the management team discuss the core capabilities that the firm may have. It would be sensible to do this in addition to marketing's success factors or Porter's value chain. It provides an additional area for discussion by considering the sustainability of a firm's competitive advantage, because the success factors or the value adding activities in the value chain are supposed to be linked to core capabilities that are VRIN.

The dynamic resource-based view offers possibilities for discussing change and possible new futures. This is about questioning 'stretch'. They can discuss the presence and effectiveness of dynamic capability routines. If this is a multi-business firm, topics to talk about include the firm's core competences and core products, whether the firm has them, and how these are translated into current businesses and products. Moreover, the discussion should be about how to leverage the core competences and core products to create future new businesses and products.

A grimmer topic to debate during the strategy workshop is the possibility that the firm may suffer from core rigidity. Part of this can be members of a management team engaging in active self-reflection about how they do their strategic management and whether that closes down or facilitates change.

Answering Question 2: problem-solving and taking action

The co-existence of static and dynamic resource-based views means that the options of what to do can be arranged in an order of increasing ambition and difficulty. From a static resource-based point of view, if there is an issue, this will concern a firm not utilizing its core capabilities. To rectify this, the firm has to change its competitive strategy. In terms of the marketing-inspired trade-off between value and price, it has to move up or down so that it is based on the VRIN routines that make up the firm's core capabilities. In terms of the industrial organization competitive generic strategies and the cooperative roles in the ecosystem, it has to pick the right role and generic strategy. This is how the static resource-based view serves as an add-on to the aforementioned other two theoretical approaches.

If the issues that a firm is facing are a matter of the core capabilities being undermined, i.e., these are losing their VRIN qualities, or if the firm is suffering from core rigidity, then the remedy is to stretch into the future by developing new core capabilities. Now we are in the realm of the dynamic resource-based view. The process logic of the dynamic resource-based view sees the firm as trying to survive in a volatile environment. There are two ways of doing this, depending on whether you think that dynamic capability is found in specific routines by which new VRIN routines are developed, or whether you think dynamic capability is a firm attribute like core competence.

With regard to the latter, dealing with a volatile environment requires a firm to utilize its core competences to develop new core capabilities that can be exploited in new businesses (Hamel & Prahalad, 1994). As was explained earlier, businesses, like the leaves on a tree, come with the seasons, while a firm's core competences, like the roots and the trunk, make that the firm survives as it develops a continuous stream of new products and businesses.

The alternative of seeing dynamic capability as the firm having specific routines like product or business development, innovation, or R&D available, comes with an expectation that these routines provide a steady stream of new core capabilities that the firm can utilize. These in turn are activities that are associated with their own dedicated fields of study. Alternatively, the firm can team up with other firms in joint ventures and strategic alliances to develop new technology or business opportunities (Das & Teng, 2000), or it can acquire or merge with other firms to add to and refresh its capabilities (Schoenberg, 2003).

Illustration 4.5 The AT&T and Time Warner merger[*]

In October 2016, AT&T and Time Warner announced their intention to merge. AT&T's businesses are in the area of communication infrastructure. It is the second largest wireless carrier in the US, and after acquiring DirectTV, the company is the largest pay-TV distributor. Time Warner is a provider of content, as it owns HBO, CNN, and Warner Brothers. The new company is envisioned to be a combination of 'distribution' capabilities and 'content' capabilities. The combination is expected to be much more able to move along with change in the media industries.

* Angling for the future of TV, *The Economist*, 29 October 2016 (provided by Anup Karath Nair)

A larger and even more severe issue that a strategist can be confronted with is a firm lacking dynamic capability. In this case, the remedy would be to start developing or acquiring dynamic capability routines or core competence, if the firm can afford to do so. Change of this magnitude requires a complete metamorphosis. This is far from an easy matter.

Illustration 4.6 The transformation of Fujifilm

Fujifilm was in fierce competition with Kodak in what is referred to as chemical image processing; that is, the business of photo and film material. Fujifilm managed to surpass Kodak in sales in 2000. That was also the peak year for chemical image processing. From then on, this line of business went into a quick decline as a consequence of the emergence of digital image processing. Fujifilm realized it had to do something and embarked on a process of business development by translating its core competence in the chemistry of light into new businesses, while moving away from photo and film material. It developed new businesses in LCD screens, light protection coverings, photocopying and printing, and pharmaceuticals. It even became a player in digital photography (Komori, 2015). Kodak did not demonstrate it had such dynamic capability and ceased to be a major player in any business (Munir, 2005).

These are all ways a firm utilizes, maintains, and develops its resource base. From a dynamic capability perspective, the strategist should become more of a Schumpeterian entrepreneur than a rational decision-maker. Because renewal potentially disrupts the current state of affairs, entrepreneurship is a subversive activity (Hitt & Ireland, 2000). If not engaged in doing new and different things themselves, strategists should facilitate innovation and change within the firm. In its extreme form, this can mean a complete reversal of the strategic planning logic, with doing things first in a trial-and-error fashion, to then rationalize after the fact whether they have made any sense for future competitive advantage of the firm (Burgelman, 1983).

Strategy practice 4.4 Formulating a strategic business plan using the resource-based view

The static resource-based view allows for an extra qualification of the success factors of marketing-inspired strategic thinking or the value chain activities of the industrial organization approach. If the routines on which these are based happen to be VRIN, that part of the business plan that deals with the firm itself can be amended. The planned strategy has gained some more credence, as the competitive advantage on which it is based is now 'sustainable' competitive advantage because of identified core capabilities.

Putting together a business plan on the basis of the dynamic resource-based view is less straightforward. There are two levels of ambition here. First, the plan can entail aiming for the development of new core capabilities on the basis of the dynamic capability that the firm might have. To do this, it needs to be ascertained that the firm has dynamic capability. If this is the case, by definition, the firm knows how to go about it, defying the need to write a business plan about it. Second, if the firm lacks dynamic capability, it sounds obvious to then write a business plan about developing it. However, the question is whether dynamic capability is something that can be developed by writing and executing a business plan. What is impossible to do is the maths. You cannot make an estimate of expected turnover, costs, and profit margins for a business that still has to develop the dynamic capability to create new core capabilities that eventually can underpin competitive advantage, as both the required effort and the outcome are unknown.

Illustration 4.7 SKF from a resource-based point of view

Should SKF* compete on price and put in the lowest bid possible to retain a big US-based client, or should it step away and persist with its high-quality strategy?

What is important to consider here is which one of these two alternatives involves exploiting what are SKF's core capabilities. This refers to those routines that are valuable, rare, inimitable, and non-substitutable. The routines that need to be considered here are its manufacturing, sales, and servicing routines. SKF has a production process that generates high-quality reliable ball bearings for a wide range of applications. These are so reliable that they are commonly used in critical applications like jet engines and turbines, where a failure can lead to catastrophe. This has come about in the course of a firm history spanning more than 100 years. Within the SKF Service Division, this is combined with marketing and sales routines – backed up by a software tool – by which SKF sales representatives can demonstrate to a customer how much money they can save by using high-quality SKF ball bearings and have more reliable machinery that require less maintenance and last longer, even if the ball bearings are more expensive to buy. This supports SKF's competitive strategy of differentiation. Long-term reliable manufacturing at an overall lower cost level must represent value for an end user. Therefore, there is a sense that SKF has core capabilities as these routines are valuable as they underpin a competitive strategy, they are rare as SKF manufacturing and marketing is a unique combination, they are inimitable as it requires high investments to equal SKF's know-how, and they are non-substitutable as there are no immediate alternatives available to the sales software but even more so to SKF's ball bearing manufacturing process. Staying away from competition on price and continuing with the differentiation strategy exploits SKF's core capabilities. Giving in to the price competition and participating in the reverse auction does not.

* Value Selling at SKF Service, IMD-5–0751, 2009

Criticisms and unanswered questions

The static resource-based view comes from the same rational decision-making mould as marketing-inspired strategic thinking and the industrial organization approach. They all assume that there is a knowable business reality out there about which information can be gathered and processed to generate strategic decisions that are then implemented. They all assume top management to have the power and ability to initiate and realize a strategy at will. It also has the same issue of not being able to incorporate and explain fundamental change.

The dynamic resource-based view has been developed on the basis of the older approaches ignoring fundamental change. Instead, change is put at the heart of the argument. Dynamic capability is about dealing with change, with the implication that this fundamentally is what strategic management should be about. However, it is questionable whether the dynamic resource-based view has solved it. The ultimate answer is that a firm should have dynamic capability, yet there is some confusion as what this actually is, let alone how you acquire or develop it. There is also little guidance with regard to evaluating the scope or the direction of particular changes and initiatives a firm can get involved in. Thus far, there are suggestions that research into dynamic capability should draw on the fields of organizational change, change management, renewal, adaptation, growth, innovation, organizational learning, and knowledge management to give it more substance (Easterby-Smith, Lyles, & Peteraf, 2009). We are still awaiting results.

You can expect that the argument will be made that a firm has to exploit the current core capabilities, as well as explore for new core capabilities on the basis of dynamic capabilities. The concept of ambidexterity makes that point (O'Reilly III & Tushman, 2004). However, this is easier said than done. March (1991) argues that exploitation and exploration are mutually exclusive. Concentrating on what the firm currently is doing, and learning to become better at it, diminishes the capacity and inclination to experiment and try out truly new things. Besides, doing new things generates costs while the future return is uncertain because you cannot know what it will bring. The pressure to perform now adds to further postponements of investing in the future. The other way around, stepping away from becoming better at what the firm currently is doing, leaves room for competitors to catch up and overtake in the current marketplace. Yet, this is the consequence from devoting attention to new things.

Furthermore, dynamic capability as it stands now is just about the aptitude to acknowledge and deal with change, not about where change should lead or how to bring it about. It is a concept that appears to have the attributes of the ultimate panacea, or solution for everything (Helfat et al., 2007). The term is coined to capture the ultimate prize in strategic management: continued firm survival and performance in the face of continuous and possibly fundamental change. As yet, it does not deliver in bringing us a fail-safe method to deal effectively with all the threats to the future success of the firm. You can even wonder whether this is at all possible.

Terms like core capability, core competence, dynamic capability, and ambidexterity have been branded as tautological (Kraaijenbrink et al., 2010; Priem & Butler, 2001). The criticisms are that these terms are put forward as explanations of a particular phenomenon like the sustainability of competitive advantage, a competence that translates into new products and services, the ability to adapt to changing circumstances, or the ability to simultaneously exploit a core capability and explore for new core capabilities – yet, the effect is implied in the term and you end up with a conflation of what explains it with what is being explained. Williamson (1999) argues that core competence is just a rationalization after the fact. To him, you can only know whether a competence is 'core' if it has been successfully translated into successful business and products. You cannot know this in advance.

In sharp contrast to the approaches in the previous chapters, the dynamic resource-based view adds subjectivity to strategic management. Top managers can get it wrong. Their field of vision can be limited and distorted. That is the implication of core rigidity. Like everybody else in the firm, top management's interpretations are informed and mediated by the knowledge they already possess: the specific knowledge that is implied with particular core capabilities. This is what made the firm successful in the first place. When this knowledge becomes outdated and obsolete, there is a danger that top management becomes part of the problem. In principle, any firm's strategic management can become subject to core rigidity. What does it mean for strategic management that the assumption of objectivity with top managers as impartial and unbiased information processors is at best nothing but an unattainable ideal?

Furthermore, the notion of 'stretch' as the ultimate ambition for firms to propel themselves into the future introduces subjectivity into strategic management, as well. Stretch relies on strategic intent, which in turn is based on an imagined future. Nobody knows what the future will bring, and any expectation has to rely on imagination and creativity. Imagination is very subjective. Imagining a future business reality – by definition – is a creative exercise of the mind. A future business reality does not exist out there to be measured and assessed, because it has not happened yet.

Exhibit 4.5 Resource-based view reflective questions

- In the performance logic, how does the static resource-based view understand the environment, the strategy, and the firm?
- What in the static resource-based view is the key question that a strategist should always be worried about and serves as the 'starter' question for a strategic analysis?
- What is a core capability, and how does it explain sustainable competitive advantage?
- From a static resource-based point of view, what can a firm do if it has to deal with a strategic issue?
- In the static resource-based view process logic, how are the environmental survival process and the organizational strategy process understood, and how is a strategist expected to contribute?
- Why is the static resource-based view considered to be objectivistic?
- In the performance logic, how does the dynamic resource-based view understand the environment, strategy, and the firm?
- What in the dynamic resource-based view is the key question that a strategist should always be worried about and serves as the 'starter' question for a strategic analysis?
- What is core competence, and how does it indicate dynamic capability?
- How do dynamic capability routines allow a firm to deal with a volatile environment?
- What is the difference between dynamic capability as a firm attribute and dynamic capability as a specific routine?
- Why does core competence apply to corporate strategy?
- From a dynamic resource-based point of view, what can a firm do if it has to deal with a strategic issue?
- In the dynamic resource-based view process logic, how are the environmental survival process and the organizational strategy process understood, and how is a strategist expected to contribute?
- Why is the dynamic resource-based view considered to be subjectivistic?

Case 4.1

Macy's

Macy's traditional Thanksgiving Day Parade on 26 November 2020 for the first time in nearly 100 years was virtual, thanks to the Covid-19 pandemic.[1] Macy's Parade started in 1924 as a modest gathering of Macy's employees and has grown into a multi-million-dollar event where hundreds of volunteers and performers parade through New York City, passing Macy's flagship store on Herald Square, holding massive balloons and accompanied by numerous marching bands. In 2019, it attracted a crowd of 3.5 million and was watched on TV by 50 million viewers.

In September 2020, Macy's presented itself as having 607 Macy's department stores of which six are Macy's Backstage outlets selling returned and heavily discounted out-of-season items. The firm also owns and operates 56 Bloomingdale's and 171 Bluemercury stores.[2] Macy's and Bloomingdale's are traditional department stores, while Bluemercury is a cosmetics and beauty store.

Macy's CEO Jeff Genette, in announcing a major turnaround plan in 2016, described Macy's as having three types of stores.[3] There are the 11 'flagships': "some of the best retail properties in America and each of these . . . are the #1 retail destination in the regional market. They have the best that Macy's has to offer"; these are "really an all-senses engagement through fashion, service and experience". There are about 50 'magnet stores': "the best of fashion, food and entertainment", with this concept being rolled out to a further 100 stores, and there are the 'smaller neighbourhood stores' which "offer convenience, fulfilment of online orders and basic things like skincare replenishment or casual wear". About 100 stores will be closed that fit neither of these concepts. Macy's target market segment is described as middle-class women between 16 and 34 who want to buy quality products at a reasonable price, but who lead busy lifestyles.[4]

A shop assistant (or sales associate, as Macy's prefers them to be called) describes how she is pressured to entice customers to sign up for the store card – much to the annoyance of customers – and having to reach sales targets, with floor managers constantly monitoring whether she asks customers if they want to sign up.[5] People working at the cosmetic counters are under pressure from both store management and from the cosmetic firms whose wares they are representing. In September 2020, Macy's had a 1.5 stars (out of five) rating for customer service on Trustpilot, with 77% of reviewers rating Macy's as 'bad'.[6] Based on a survey it conducted, Maya Mikhailov, co-founder and chief marketing officer of GPShopper, claims that "a third of all Americans literally feel nothing when they go to a store and nearly a third feel anxiety. So nearly 66% of your customers either feel nothing or feel anxiety".[7]

After the 2018 Christmas period, Macy's had to report that it had experienced lacklustre sales. A Moody's Investor Services report was cited in stating that department stores have the "dubious distinction of being the weakest-performing sector in US retail the past three years".[8] Retail analyst Nick Egelanian observed that department stores over the last decade or so have lost various of their departments to specialist retailers. This applies to electronics, appliances, toys, auto services, home goods, furniture, mattresses, and cosmetics. Stores like Macy's fill their floor space with apparel and more apparel. He also describes Macy's as a "a tale of two retailers". In California and the Northeast, it is high-end with flagship stores in New York, Boston, and San Francisco. In the rest of the US, it is nothing special, although Macy's is still considered an 'anchor store' of many malls.

Macy's acquired Story in 2018. Story is a one-location concept store in downtown New York.[9] Story has adopted a theme-based formula that is unique to retailing. It changes its theme every three months, being redesigned with every change-over, so that customers have a new experience every time they visit. It is expected that this will also entice customers to want to visit again and again. The idea is that Story will become part of every Macy's department store. Story founder and CEO Rachel Shechtman is appointed as Macy's brand experience officer. Macy's is keeping the Story team separate as it rolls out the Story format across the many stores.[10] The idea is that Macy's existing merchandising and store teams will learn from the new way of doing things. Omnichannel retail expert Chris Walton visited the Story's addition to the Macy's flagship Herald Square store in New York and Story in the Macy's in the Ridgedale Mall in Minnesota in 2019. In Minnesota "the concept looks nothing like the glossy PR photos from Macy's flagship Herald Square store in New York City. What the concept lacks in creative naming it tries to make up for by utilizing plush AstroTurf in a manner not seen since the halcyon days of the Houston Astrodome in the 1970s".[11]

Macy's launched a click-and-collect service in 2013 with its own digital wallet as part of the Macy's app.[12] In March 2019, Macy's announced its 'in-store fragrance finder'.[13] This is an app for in-store customers that allows them to shop by scent family rather than by brand, which they tend to do. It is meant to replicate the online shopping experience. The fragrance finder was created by New York-based retail tech company Perch. In 2020, Rightpoint boasted that it had developed an app for Macy's that delivers "Macy's immersive retail experience . . . of their flagship store, Macy's Herald Square in New York City".[14]

In 2017, Macy's invested in 'SMART by GEP' cloud-based sourcing, procurement, and spend software, to better manage its procurement and sourcing process while simultaneously being able to do spend analysis.[15] Two years later, Macy's appointed as chief supply chain officer Dennis Mullahy, who is tasked with overseeing the whole product journey from global sourcing, inventory management, store and ecommerce distribution, indirect procurement, supply chain systems, sustainability, and supplier diversity.[16] He will report to Macy's president Hal Lawton.

Just before the Covid-19 pandemic hit in February 2020, Macy's CEO Jeff Genette announced that an additional 125 stores would be closed.[17] It also aims to move away from malls and to test several Macy's and one Bloomingdale's as stand-alone stores. He told analysts that "we continue to believe that the best malls in the country will thrive. However, we also know that Macy's and Bloomingdale's have high potential [off]-mall and in smaller formats". He also wants to grow the Macy's Backstage outlet business. In the same call to analysts, Genette revealed that there would be a narrower than expected loss in the second quarter, as a consequence of a boost in online sales.

In a reaction to the plunge of $2 billion in sales and a $142 loss during the third quarter, when the pandemic fully hit,[18] JP Morgan retail analyst Matthew Boss commented that despite growing online sales,

Macy's top-line profile remains constrained by declining brick-and-mortar sales across the bulk of its full-line stores, with increased promotions and growing digital sales pressuring gross margin. Larger picture and multi-year, discretionary dollars continue to shift toward convenience (Amazon) and value (off-price), with lower visibility in the U.S. wholesale environment.

To manage the decline that came with the pandemic, Macy's had considerably reduced inventory at the risk of letting shoppers down by not having merchandise in stock.

To get through the pandemic, Jeff Genette announced that "everything on the digital agenda has been accelerated" and that Macy's will become omnichannel.[19] For that reason, fulfilment will be centralized, moving away from parallel structures for the store and for online. This brings supply chain planning and merchandising together for both channels.

A firm selling courses on retail management describes retail best practices as providing shopfloor staff with sufficient incentives, training, and benefits, as limiting sales and promotions, and as treating sales associates as people with passion and capability, thereby creating a shopping experience that the firm claims cannot be achieved online.[20] Besides, retail businesses thrive by operating a well-organized supply chain that can deliver merchandise to customers when they want it. Nevertheless, there is a balance to strike between keeping inventory as not to disappoint customers and having money tied up in stock at the risk of it not being sold.[21]

Notes

1 www.msn.com/en-us/news/us/macy-e2-80-99s-thanksgiving-day-parade-to-go-virtual-this-year/ar-BB1923Jd [accessed 19 September 2020]

2 www.macysinc.com/about/store-count-and-square-footage [accessed 19 September 2020]

3 www.retaildive.com/news/macys-on-the-brink/546080/ [accessed 19 September 2020]

4 https://etaileast.wbresearch.com/blog/macy-future-of-retail [accessed 19 September 2020]

5 http://ihateworkinginretail.ooid.com/20-confessions-former-macys-sales-associate/ [accessed 19 September 2020]

6 www.trustpilot.com/review/www.macys.com [accessed 19 September 2020]

7 www.retaildive.com/news/is-macys-about-to-reinvent-the-department-store/525655/ [accessed 19 September 2020]

8 www.retaildive.com/news/macys-on-the-brink/546080/ [accessed 19 September 2020]

9 https://news.alphastreet.com/macys-buys-concept-store-to-spice-up-shopping-experience/ [accessed 19 September 2020]

10 https://digiday.com/retail/year-acquiring-story-macys-using-format-refresh-stores/ [accessed 19 September 2020]

11 www.forbes.com/sites/christopherwalton/2019/08/22/whats-wrong-at-macys-look-to-story-for-a-clue/#19d6d5aa6d89 [accesses 19 September 2020]

12 https://etaileast.wbresearch.com/blog/macy-future-of-retail [accessed 19 September 2020]

13 https://pathtopurchaseiq.com/macys-reinvents-customer-experience [accessed 19 September 2020]

14 www.rightpoint.com/case-studies/macys [accessed 19 September 2020]

15 https://chainstoreage.com/technology/new-platform-helps-macys-hit-spending-targets [accessed 19 September 2020]

16 www.macysinc.com/investors/news-events/press-releases/detail/1554/macys-names-dennis-mullahy-chief-supply-chain-officer [accessed 19 September 2020]

17 www.cnbc.com/2020/09/02/macys-plans-rollout-of-smaller-stores-away-from-malls.html [accessed 19 September 2020]

18 https://finance.yahoo.com/news/macys-will-probably-disappear-before-you-know-it-strategist-180442564.html [accessed 19 September 2020]

19 www.supplychaindive.com/news/macys-accelerate-e-commerce-fulfillment-omnichannel/584653/ [accessed 19 September 2020]

20 www.retaildoc.com/blog/12-best-practices-of-retailers-from-ivory-tower-to-front-line-employee-performance-management [accessed 19 September 2020]

21 www.strategicsourceror.com/2019/04/macys-creates-new-role-in-supply-chain.html [accessed 19 September 2020]

CHAPTER 5

Agency theory and shareholder value

The origins of agency theory as it underpins shareholder value and its application to strategic management are located with Ross (1973) and Jensen and Meckling (1976). Agency theory concentrates on what has been labelled as the agency problem that comes with the principal-agent relationship – a problem that can be solved with efficient contracts. For a business firm, this is further elaborated in terms of shareholder value (Rappaport, 1986). It means that a firm's strategic management is expected to make the interests of shareholders paramount.

The process logic of agency theory and shareholder value

Economists like efficiency. They use it as a driver and explanation for almost everything. The market mechanism is their favourite theoretical device that – in various forms and disguises – explains how scarce resources are allocated efficiently. This has led to what in economists' eyes is something of a conundrum. Why do organizations exist, as they are clearly not markets? It is a question first put forward by Ronald Coase (1937). One suggested answer is agency theory (Eisenhardt, 1989; Jensen & Meckling, 1976). Agency theory turns a firm into a kind of a market by stating that the firm is a nexus of contracts, with these contracts needing to be efficient for everybody involved. These contracts can be signed agreements in the legal sense, but often are just semi-formalized arrangements between what in agency theory is referred to as the principal and the agent.

Agency theory's agency problem

Economists assume that people are utility maximizers. People put effort in up to the point where the gains of this effort equal the costs that they have to endure. This is referred to as the 'law of diminishing returns'. It allows for a market to be elaborated as a conjuncture of supply and demand, and to postulate that in a perfect market, everything clears at an equilibrium price. Thus, people involved in a firm are assumed to do their job up to the point where their gains (financial or otherwise) equal their efforts (also financial or otherwise). Because of these gains, people want to become involved in the first place. Such a mutual expectation allows economists to theorize about a firm as a nexus of contracts, of people getting involved up to a point where the gains equal the costs. They also postulate that the supply of efforts that should be put into the firm and the demand of gains that people can get out of the firm clear at an equilibrium price.

Unfortunately, there is a problem, referred to as the agency problem (Jensen & Meckling, 1976; Ross, 1973). A firm is awash with principal-agent relationships. A principal wants something done and hires an agent to do it. An agent is a person who has been hired to do something on behalf of a principal. Examples are the employer-employee relationship, the manager-subordinate relationship, and the shareholder-manager relationship. Figure 5.1 illustrates this for a firm with dispersed ownership, where shareholders often are pension funds, banks, insurance companies, or other investment vehicles which keep money safe for their clients. In a way, these clients are very often ordinary people employed across the same firms whose shares are kept by these institutional investors. The same circular relationship exists with public organizations between politicians, civil servants, and the members of the general public who pay taxes and vote politicians in or out. Non-profit organizations like charities feature a similar circle among the board of trustees, managers, workers, volunteers, beneficiaries, and finally the members who vote in the board of trustees.

The problem here is that the principal cannot be sure whether the agent will do what the principle wants. Can a manager be trusted to always act in the interest of the shareholder? Will employees always put in their maximum effort? There

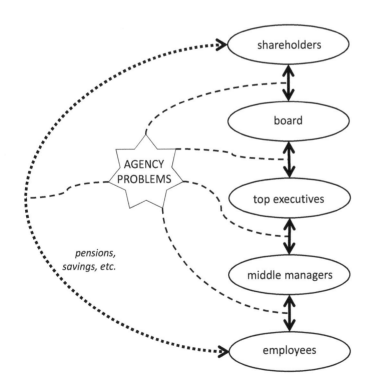

Figure 5.1
Corporate governance for a firm with dispersed ownership

are two reasons for this problem to exist (Eisenhardt, 1989). One reason is that the principal and the agent might want different and conflicting things from the relationship. Their utility functions might clash, posing a conflict of interests. This is often paired with information asymmetry in that the principal has difficulty knowing how much of the right effort an agent is putting in. The other reason concerns risk attitude. In pursuing their utility, agents might be comfortable with taking higher risks than principals, or the other way around. A contract that aligns the interests of the agent with the interests of the principal solves this problem. It is taken to be efficient if the costs and gains meet at an equilibrium where both principal and agent are happy.

Corporate governance and shareholder value

The relationship between shareholders, the board, and the firm's top team became the focus of agency theory research. How this relationship is organized is known as corporate governance. The argument starts with the expectation that the top team is hired to provide a return on the investment made by the shareholders by maximizing the firm's profits. This has been most famously expressed by economist Milton Friedman (1970, p. 6). He states that

> there is one and only one social responsibility of business – to use its resources and engage in activities designed to increase its profits so long as it stays within the rules of the game, which is to say, engages in open and free competition without deception or fraud.

Shareholder value is taken to indicate of a firm's profit potential (Rappaport, 1986).

The price at which a share is traded on a stock exchange is a consequence of two considerations. One is the expectation of the future profits that a firm will be generating. The other one is the amount of risk that a firm's future profits are exposed to. The combination of low risk and high profits is the stock market's favourite. The actual return on investment for a shareholder/investor is a combination of the firm's annual dividend and an increase in the share price as the firm's profit/risk profile improves.

Rappaport (1986) gives two additional reasons why shareholder value, to him, is so important. The first additional reason is the market for corporate control. If a firm is underperforming, and this is indicated by a low share price relative to comparable firms, the firm becomes a target for a hostile takeover. This is because it is obvious that shaking up such an underperforming firm to substantially improve its performance, and therefore its share price, will allow somebody to make money. Such a takeover involves turning the company around and sacking the top managers, who apparently were not doing their jobs. The second additional reason is that top managers compete for top jobs and they improve their bargaining power if they have a track record of creating high shareholder value.

To solve the agency problem for corporate governance, the contract between shareholders and managers should be put together in such a way that the interests are aligned. In this case, it will be a formal contract dealing with the terms of employment and remuneration of the top team. Most of the time, the solution is chosen to make top managers' earnings dependent on the share price. This, in turn, focuses the mind of top managers on shareholder value.

Illustration 5.1 The market for corporate control and Douwe Egberts

DE Master Blenders, the Dutch coffee, tea, and tobacco company commonly referred to as Douwe Egberts after its best known brand, was bought and taken off the AEX Amsterdam Stock Exchange by German firm JAB, an investment vehicle for Joh. A. Benckiser (JAB), in 2013.[*] Douwe Egberts had only been listed a year earlier, after it had de-merged from Sara Lee Corp. During these few months, the company was troubled by a fraud scandal in its Brazilian subsidiary and by severe differences of opinion within the executive team, leading to the resignation of the CEO. JAB had built up a minority shareholding before it offered to buy out everybody else. The share price had slumped and investors were very keen to take up JAB's offer. JAB's intention is to restore shareholder value for them by creating a multi-national coffee and tea firm around Douwe Egberts. JAB is doing so by taking charge of its management and combining it with future investments in this industry. In May 2020, the company was floated again on the Amsterdam AEX stock exchange as JDE Peet's NV.[**]

* NRC Handelsblad, 10 October 2012, www.nrc.nl/nieuws/2012/12/10/topman-douwe-egberts-stapt-op/; NRC Handelsblad, 28 March 2013, www.nrc.nl/nieuws/2013/03/28/grootaandeelhouder-komt-met-bod-op-douwe-egberts/#rel_expand=1; NRC Handelsblad, 16 August 2013, www.nrc.nl/handelsblad/van/2013/augustus/16/aandelen-douwe-egberts-massaal-aangemeld-1284527
** https://nos.nl/artikel/2335515-moederbedrijf-douwe-egberts-met-succes-naar-de-beurs-gebracht.html [accessed 25 November 2020]

The environmental survival process thus takes place in this market for corporate control (see Figure 5.2). The strategy process is primarily a matter of solving the agency problem, of putting contracts in place that align the interests of the shareholders as principals with the interest of the top team as agents. The strategist here is simply taken to be a utility maximizer, as economists assume all people are. This process logic has trickled down into the firm in that the various functions, management layers, and subsidiaries are expected to contribute to shareholder value, as well (Roth & O'Donnell, 1996), with the organization structure designed accordingly (Hrebiniak, 2006). For marketing, for instance, a relationship between customer satisfaction and shareholder value has been found (e.g. Anderson, Fornell, & Mazvancheryl, 2004; Gruca & Rego, 2005). For human resources management (HRM), research into the effect of various HRM policies that develop human capital and of employee payment schemes based on profit-sharing or stock ownership have been investigated, albeit being met with mixed results (e.g. Becker, Huselid, Pickus, & Spratt, 1997; Heinfeldt & Curcio, 1997).

Agency theory reasoning has also had an effect in public organizations and how government agencies are expected to realize performance. This movement is known as new public management. Among its attributes are the formulation of

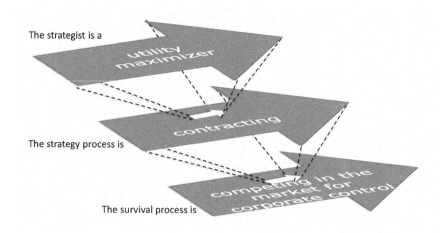

The strategist is a *utility maximizer*

The strategy process is *contracting*

Figure 5.2 The
process logic for
agency theory and
shareholder value

The survival process is *competing in the market for corporate control*

explicit standards and performance measures by which public organizations can be held to account, assuming that taxpayers are the principals who expect their interests to be fulfilled by government/agents, and the separation of policy makers (principals) and providers (agents), with provision of services being liable to outsourcing and privatization, governed by performance contracts (Hood, 1991).

Supply chains

The relationship between firms can also be elaborated in principal-agent terms, especially when it concerns a buyer-supplier link or an outsourcing relationship (Logan, 2000). It is the buyer who is the principal here. The buyer wants the supplier as agent to act in the buyer's interests. More specifically, a supplier would like the buyer to deliver what is specified at the right time and in the right place, yet a buyer might try to cut corners. Moreover, there is a common interest with regard to information sharing across the supply chain for everybody to plan the flow of services and goods better (Manatsa & McLaren, 2008). However, firms do not necessarily want to share, because this information can be commercially sensitive.

Applying agency theory, the solution is found in performance contracts that align interests between the various firms in the supply chain. Such a contract should stipulate what behaviours and what outcomes the supplier should deliver to the buyer, with the supplier paid and fined in accordance with how well it performs (Logan, 2000). Incentive schemes do not necessarily have to rely on punishment, but can also include rewards. These rewards can be monetary like cross-firm profit-sharing arrangements, but also non-monetary like preferred supplier status, exclusive access to products or to customers, or other exclusivity agreements (Manatsa & McLaren, 2008). Interestingly, this can work both ways in that the supplier and the buyer can secure the relationship for the long term by entering into these kinds of high commitment contracts (Hypko, Tilebein, & Gleich, 2010), which can include dedicated investments that make the two firms

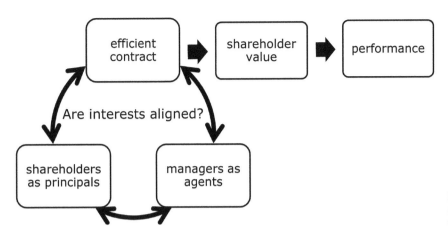

Figure 5.3
Agency theory and
shareholder value

mutually dependent (Hill & Jones, 1992). Good supply chain management is expected to make a contribution to the shareholder value of all firms involved (Christopher & Ryals, 1999).

The performance logic of agency theory and shareholder value

Firm performance here is primarily linked to shareholder value. The share price is a metric that expresses what a firm is worth in terms of its profit potential (Rappaport, 1986). Shareholder value has competitive advantage hidden in it, as profit potential is seen as a function of competitive advantage. This, in turn, is a consequence of the firm having solved the agency problems with efficient contracts so that the interests between principals and agents are aligned (see Figure 5.3).

Illustration 5.2 Shareholder value at Facebook

In November 2016, Facebook made a statement that revenue would "meaningfully" slow and that the firm was going to make "aggressive" investments*. This information was absorbed by the financial market and led to a reassessment of Facebook's profit potential. Facebook's share price dropped. As a consequence, Mark Zuckerberg, Facebook's founder and largest shareholder, found his fortune had shrunk by $2.5 billion.

* *The Independent*, 4 November 2016, www.independent.co.uk/news/business/news/mark-zuckerberg-facebook-shares-wealth-value-fortune-falls-drops-a7396876.html [accessed 4 November 2016]

Strategy, then, is a matter of putting efficient contracts in place. There is a choice between two types of contracts that each incentivize the agent differently (Eisenhardt, 1989): there is the behaviour-orientated contract, and there is the outcome-orientated contract. With a behaviour-orientated contract, the agent's effort is exactly specified and a pre-agreed reward is paid on display of this behaviour (e.g. a salary). With an outcome-orientated contract, the agent's reward is based on achieving a specified result (e.g. share price increase). With both contracts, there is the additional issue of information asymmetry in that the principal would have difficulty keeping track of the agent's efforts and results. To remedy this, every contract needs to have some form of monitoring system by which the principal can assess whether the specified behaviour is displayed, or whether the specified outcome is achieved. Such a monitoring system appears as a set of key performance indicators (KPIs).

Strategy practice 5.1 The balanced scorecard

Robert Kaplan and David Norton published a paper in *Harvard Business Review* in 1992 advocating an approach to KPIs that would go beyond financial parameters. In addition to financial measures, they argue that additional indicators need to be included that measure progress with regard to how customers see and appreciate the firm, whether there is any innovation and learning taking place, and where the firm is excelling. They labelled this the 'balanced scorecard'. A book published later presented the balanced scorecard as a key implementation tool (Kaplan & Norton, 1996).

Which type of contract aligns interests best – i.e. is the most efficient – depends on various aspects of the principal, the agent, and their relationship (Eisenhardt, 1989). If an effort is required that can be easily specified and measured, a behaviour-orientated contract works best. A monitoring system then can be based on measuring this required behaviour, with KPIs formulated accordingly. If the job is too complex and contingent, an outcome-orientated contract is called for, with KPIs formulated that are linked to outcomes rather than behaviour. If a principal wants to pass on risk to the agent, this also indicates an outcome-orientated contract rather than a behaviour-orientated contract. Duration of the contract is a consideration, as well. Short-term relationships are best established with a behaviour-orientated contract, and long-term commitments with an outcome-orientated contract.

The contract put in place between the top team of a firm and its shareholders tends to include an element of behaviour control with a relatively small base salary, and concentrates mostly on outcome by making the bulk of the top team's earnings dependent on the share price. Specifying top team behaviour is hardly possible. The board of directors and its supervision activities act as the monitoring system. Contracts for sales jobs or trading jobs also tend to be outcome-orientated with generous bonuses topping up low base-salaries if outcome KPIs are met. Middle-management and lower management jobs, as well as ordinary employees and workers, tend to be incentivized with salaries, wages, and career and employment prospects, and should then be monitored with behavioural KPIs.

Interestingly, with regard to top team behaviour, agency theorists and people who apply it expect a firm's strategic management to adhere to the strategic planning model and for the top team to use the language of finance and of the marketing-inspired and industrial organization approaches and the resource-based view (Rappaport, 1986; Zajac & Westphal, 2004). One could argue, as agency theorists tend to identify as organizational economists, that they are blind to strategy theory derived from the social sciences like the stakeholder approach or institutional theory. They expect that firm performance is driven by competitive advantage alone and ignore considerations of legitimacy or consider the firm to be legitimate if it is profitable.

Illustration 5.3 CEO remuneration at Microsoft

The Microsoft 2011 Proxy Statement* prepared for the annual meeting of shareholders contained an elaborate explanation of how much then-CEO Steve Ballmer was paid. For 2011, he received a $682,500 bonus on top of his $682,500 salary.

The non-executive members of the Microsoft Board of Directors, acting on recommendations of the Board's Compensation Committee, make the decisions on CEO pay at Microsoft. An independent compensation consultant advises the Compensation Committee. At the beginning of the fiscal year, the remuneration scheme is decided upon, as well as a set of specific targets with target incentive awards attached. At the end of the fiscal year, the CEO's performance is reviewed and decisions are made whether targets have been met, what award amount will be provided, and whether the basic salary will be adjusted.

Steve Ballmer was awarded a bonus because he presided over the partnerships with Facebook and Nokia, over improvements to Windows Azure and the Bing search engine, and over a number of successful product launches like the Kinect motion-sensing controller for the Xbox and cloud-based Office. The board did not award the full amount available because of lower sales than expected of the Windows Phone 7.

Steve Ballmer also holds 3.95% of Microsoft shares.

* Microsoft 2011 Proxy Statement, http://apps.shareholder.com/sec/viewerContent.aspx?companyid =MSFT&docid=8172917

Similar considerations about the type of contract depending on the specific circumstances apply to supply and outsourcing contracts between firms. The extent to which the exchange between firms can be specified and measured, the transfer of risk, and the duration of the relationship will indicate whether an outcome-orientated or a behaviour-orientated contract is called for.

Additional features

This is one of the areas where strategic management meets the law. In most countries, civil law defines all kinds of legal entities or juristic persons, which are not individuals. These can be companies, charities, government bodies, cooperatives, and partnerships, and are defined as endowed with statuary obligations and liabilities. This is done so that they can be parties in legally binding contracts with other legal entities and individual persons. The act of incorporation is a sort of contract by itself.

In almost all countries where a form of company law exists, the law defines only a small number of specific legal entities, all with somewhat different attributes. For instance, in the UK, the 2006 Companies Act defines the various legal forms a firm can take. The abbreviations of, for instance, 'Ltd' or 'Plc.' indicate what form for this legal entity has been chosen. 'Ltd' stands for 'limited' and means that the shares are not publicly traded. 'Plc.' stands for 'public limited company' and means that everybody can own a share in this company and you can find these companies listed on the London Stock Exchange. This distinction is made in many countries around the world and is often signalled with a particular abbreviation that is added to the company name.

When an organization is incorporated, it has to take on the form of one of these legal entities. The law prescribes specific corporate governance arrangements for each legal entity. For instance, the 'Plc.' in the UK should have a board of directors. The chief executive and the top executive team are responsible to the board. The board appoints and dismisses the top executives and sets their remuneration. The board of directors, in turn, is responsible to the shareholders. For this, the firm is obliged to organize an annual general meeting (AGM) where the firm is held to account. The firm is also obliged to publish an annual report on the accounts, which should be approved by an independent accountant.

Other legal entities come with different arrangements, yet they all organize the agent-principal relationship between various parties involved in the organization in specific and pre-set ways. There are also many variations between countries. For instance, in the UK, directors can either work for the company (executive directors) or not (non-executive directors). In The Netherlands, members of the Raad van Commissarissen, as it is called there, are required to be independent from the firm so all board members are non-executive.

Doing strategic management for shareholder value

To identify an issue here, the main concern is shareholder value and whether the firm is actually creating this. Whether shareholder value is created depends on the aligning of interests between the managers/employees/suppliers as agents and the shareholders as principals. If this is the case, the expectation is that shareholder value will be maximized. Therefore, the main focus is on whether the contracts that are in place allow for the incentivization and monitoring of the agents that is required. The two questions therefore are:

1 Are agents incentivized and monitored to create shareholder value on behalf of the shareholders as principals?
2 If this is not the case, what can you do about it?

Answering Question 1: strategic analysis

In order to continuously question the situation, the strategist should know about the incentivization and the monitoring that is taking place. Moreover, the strategist should know about the firm's shareholder value and whether it is on par with what can be expected. The strategist needs to get up to speed first if this is not the case.

Getting up to speed

The first item to consider is who the shareholders are and what they expect from the firm with regard to providing a return on investment. Are they in it for the long term, or the short term? Are they high-risk or low-risk investors? Did they invest in the firm for its steady annual dividend, or are they speculators banking on a steep increase of the share price? This all indicates what shareholder value they are looking for. Knowing what the profit/risk profile of the firm is would be helpful.

This should be paired with knowing what the share price is and how this compares with peers. Peers are firms which are in the same line of business and whose performance is therefore comparable to your firm. All firms in the same line of business face the same circumstances and are taken to be capable of a similar level of performance. If the share price is lower than your peers, you are undervalued and at risk of the market for corporate control doing its job of buying the firm, improving its strategic management, sacking the top team members, and restoring the share price to the level it should be at. Firms whose shares are freely tradable are exposed the most to the market for corporate control. If the share price is higher than your peers, you are overvalued. You then need to find out why investors are so keen on your firm and whether this is warranted.

An understanding of whether the share price is where it should be or not can be developed by doing a valuation of the firm. This is not the place to explain about how such a valuation should be done, as this is the realm of corporate finance. Nevertheless, Rappaport (2006) indicates that cash flow and long-term multi-year value should be favoured over short-term earnings that require finance and accounting wizardry that is often practised to make the firm look good for a quarterly report.

Whether the share price is on par with what it should be depends on how well the firm as a nexus of contracts has its incentivization and monitoring organized in the right way. This concerns all principal-agent relationships inside the firm, as well as with its buyers and suppliers. If there are any relationships where interests are not properly aligned, an issue has been identified. If shareholders are aware, this can have an effect on the share price and explain why a firm is undervalued.

It is also useful to understand which legal framework the firm is operating under and what implications this has for how corporate governance should be organized. A firm is always incorporated in a particular country, whose company law then applies. Many countries have additional codes of conduct that indicate what corporate governance practices are expected beyond the letter of the law. A publicly tradable firm is incorporated in the country where it is listed on the stock exchange. Some large multi-national companies are listed on more than one stock exchange, and as a consequence have to adhere to the requirements of more than one country. If something is amiss, this could have a negative effect on shareholder value.

The strategist should bear in mind that the value of a firm as an investment opportunity is relative to all other investments that can be made. Investors can put their money in government bonds, precious metals, art, property, commodities, classic cars, or in a savings account, to name but a few other options. These all have a profit/risk profile, and all are valued relative to each other, so share prices also go up or down as a reaction to a price movement in any of the other investment opportunities. It is not necessarily all down to the firm and its top team.

Exhibit 5.1 Agency theory and shareholder value starter questions

- Who are the shareholders, and what are their expectations?
- What is the current share price? Is the firm considered overvalued or undervalued when compared with its peers?

  - This tells you about the extent of shareholder value that is being created

- How is the top team incentivized and monitored?
- How are managers and employees incentivized and monitored?
- The firm as buyer: how are its suppliers incentivized and monitored?
- The firm as supplier: how is the firm incentivized and monitored?

  - This tells you whether the right contract is in place for each relationship

- How is the firm incorporated, in which country, and what are the legal requirements in terms of corporate governance?

  - This tells you about the legal requirements for how corporate governance should be arranged

---

Strategy practice 5.2 Maintaining investor relations

Many listed firms actively maintain investor relations. A firm's website contains elaborate pages where they show what the current share price is. There is large PR effort explaining what a wonderful investment opportunity the firm is. This is also the place where you can download annual reports and spreadsheets with quarterly results. The CEO and other top executives regularly appear in press conferences, hold presentations, and organize briefings. These are predominantly aimed at 'financial analysts'. These are people working for large institutional investors who hold most of the shares in publicly traded companies around the world. Their opinions on the soundness of a firm's strategy can make or break a firm's reputation in the financial markets. This reputation in turn not only affects the share price, but also the conditions by which these firms can access other sources of finance. CEOs and the top teams have to devote considerable time to satisfy the needs and concerns of these 'financial analysts'.

Continuous questioning and analyzing

For strategic management as wayfinding, the strategists should know about the incentive and monitoring schemes present in and around the firm, and what the shareholder value of the firm is. The strategist can expect things to happen that might make how the incentivization and monitoring is arranged obsolete.

Furthermore, for outcome-orientated contracts, the outcomes that have been specified might have become irrelevant. The same can happen with the specified behaviour in behaviour-orientated contracts. Also, the rewards for compliance with the contract might lose their utility. The effect of all of this is that interests become mis-aligned.

From a shareholder value point of view, a prime indictor that something is amiss is the share price going down, especially if the share price of peers does not show a similar drop. The main thing to do is to monitor the share price for upward or downward jolts, and discuss what may be the cause for this. Another indicator to keep an eye out for is when certain outcomes or behaviours associated with a particular contract are no longer realized. In effect, the contract appears to effectively be dissolved as the principal or the agent – or both – stops delivering on it. Investors not willing to invest and the associated collapse of the share price in a way is a special case of the contract between shareholders and the firm being ended.

The reason can be something exogenous to the firm that needs consideration and that maybe has to feed into the strategizing that is taking place in terms of any of the other theoretical approaches. If the jolt is traced back to the firm itself, and especially if it concerns a share price fall, the top team should seriously consider taking some kind of measure. If the drop in the share price is due to the shareholders losing confidence in the firm's top team, a replacement can be considered. Overall, whatever the firm does that negatively affects the share price: it basically means that the interest alignment between the firm and the shareholders is in disarray.

Exhibit 5.2 Agency theory and shareholder value continuous questioning

· Is the firm's share price going down relative to its peers?
· Are there contracts where the outcomes or the behaviours are not delivered anymore?
· Is there any change to what an agent or a principal want to get out of the relationship? Are interests changing?
· Is there still alignment of interests between shareholders and top management?

Strategy practice 5.3 A shareholder value strategy workshop

Top management teams periodically book themselves into a nice retreat over a weekend to discuss how they or the firm is doing. This is an ideal opportunity to do some deliberate strategy debate. Quite often, an external consultant is asked to design a programme for the workshop, to suggest topics for discussion, and to facilitate the workshop.

Shareholder value can be one of the topics to be discussed. This would require some preparation by getting the share price trends of the firm itself, as well as those of comparable firms. Such a discussion would be very useful if the firm is underperforming. It would prompt the top management team to 'face facts' and discuss where they apparently are going wrong.

Strategy practice 5.4 Internationalization from a shareholder value viewpoint

The tendency has been observed that capital markets become increasingly globalized (Stulz, 1999). However, there are countries with restrictions on foreign ownership of locally registered companies. Some countries also regulate capital flows. This is diminishing, however, and for a country to become a member of the World Trade Organization (WTO), these kinds of restrictions have to be eased. Unrestricted capital flows and allowing foreign ownership has at least two effects. On the one hand, the overall cost of capital tends to come down, meaning that firms find it easier to finance their strategies. On the other hand, the market for corporate control becomes a worldwide phenomenon, meaning that firms and their top management are monitored and scrutinized by a wider range of people, with the takeover threat coming from every corner of the world.

Answering Question 2: problem-solving and taking action

When action should be taken, there is a question of who the strategists are here. All previous theoretical approaches more or less assume that the strategists of the firm are its top managers. Here a distinction has to be made between the top team of executives who are in charge of managing the firm on a daily basis, and the directors and board members who have a supervisory role on behalf of the shareholders. If the shareholder value goes down, it can be blamed on the members of the firm's top team and their strategic management. They should feel compelled to rethink what they are doing. They should reconsider and redesign the various contracts – the incentivization and the monitoring arrangements – that exist with and around the firm and which have become a cause for concern, in order to make them fit the situation again.

There is one contract where the top team needs to be strategically managed by the board of directors. This concerns the firm's corporate governance and how it is arranged. From an agency theory point of view, and also from a legal perspective, the supervisory board members should step in when members of the top team are deemed to have failed in their task to create shareholder value. The supervisors/directors are in charge of the corporate governance of the firm, which extends to the hiring and firing of top executives and making decisions on their renumeration. One option they have is replacing the CEO or maybe the whole top team. They can also look at the remuneration arrangements to check whether the incentive schemes do align the interests of the top team members with the shareholders. If not, a redesign is called for. Such episodes indicate that there is 'trouble at the top'.

If the existing supervisory board does not deal with the problems in an adequate manner, chances are that the 'market for corporate control' steps in. Somebody will realize that an underperforming firm with a low share price can be bought relatively easily. When such a person becomes a majority shareholder, this person is in control and is able to appoint the members of the supervisory board, who in turn control the hiring and firing of the top team. This creates a powerful platform from which a turnaround effort can be launched. Alternatively, if this is a multi-business firm, the new owner can decide to split up the firm and sell the more viable parts, liquidate the less viable parts, and make a profit from that.

Strategy practice 5.5 Formulating a strategic business plan using shareholder value

The concept of shareholder value indicates what the business plan should achieve: a sound investment opportunity. To make this point, the numbers that need to be part of the plan should calculate the firm's earning potential in a way that indicates that shareholder value will increase when the business plan is implemented. In short, the business plan should incorporate a valuation of the firm.

Criticisms and unanswered questions

Agency theory and its association with shareholder value is probably the most contentious strategy theory of the six presented in this book. There is criticism with regard to it inspiring quantification and financialization, its narrow focus on shareholders, and its over-reliance on strategic planning. There are unanswered questions that concern its assumptions about a knowable future, its performativity, and its moral stance. Its position with regard to the objectivism-subjectivism debate is somewhat confused.

The contracts that need to be put in place require specification of behaviours or of outcomes, which then are translated into KPIs that need to be monitored. This poses a measurement problem in that there often is a discrepancy between what is taken as a KPI and the outcomes or behaviours that these KPIs are supposed to capture. In devising KPIs, quantification and visibility tends to be favoured over relevance, leading to a discrepancy between what is aimed for and what is achieved (Kerr, 1975). This is often paired with rewards being solely expressed in terms of money. Jensen and Meckling (1976) carefully argue that the utility that is driving principals and agents can be anything they value. Nevertheless, in the course of their paper and in practice, this utility tends to be solely expressed in financial terms, assuming that money can buy everything. However, much of what people want is not necessarily for sale.

Whether shareholders are the 'be all and end all' of firms is heavily debated, and the stakeholder approach in the next chapter disputes this. Critics reckon that firms have many more responsibilities than just making a profit, and have obligations to live up to these responsibilities – even at the expense of shareholders. This points at an underlying question of morality. Does a manager serve society best by just concentrating on making money for shareholders, or does the strategic manager have to face up to additional responsibilities that may not necessarily lead to increased shareholder value? Interestingly, agency theory does question the impartiality of managers. In fact, it is very much part of the theory that the interests of the top team do not align with the interests of the firm as a money-making entity. This is in sharp contrast with other strategy theories that assume top management to be unbiased in their information processing and decision-making. It adds another form of subjectivity to the equation by recognizing the inherent political nature of strategic management.

Illustration 5.4 Is shareholder value losing its shine?

The 'Business Roundtable', a US business group, issued a statement that redefined the purpose of business, now promoting "An Economy That Serves All Americans"*. This statement was signed by more than 180 US companies, including Amazon, American Airlines, and JP Morgan. In effect, these firms declare that firms' responsibilities go further than just making a profit for shareholders. Johnson & Johnson CEO Alex Gorsky was quoted saying that "This new statement better reflects the way corporations can and should operate today. It affirms the essential role corporations can play in improving our society when CEOs are truly committed to meeting the needs of all stakeholders".

* www.bbc.co.uk/news/business-49400885 [accessed 24 November 2020]

Rappaport's (1986) reliance on strategic planning and the strategy theories based on competitive advantage as an indicator of sound strategic management completely ignores Mintzberg's (1994a, 1994b) criticism, as well as the research into what top managers actually do to get things done (Watson, 1994), or how strategies are actually realized (Johnson, 1987; Pettigrew, 1985; Quinn, 1980; Sminia, 1994). Moreover, the belief that strategic planning is the benchmark for sound strategic management can be severely questioned when the considerations that come with the stakeholder approach – and especially with the recognition that strategic management is as much a process of negotiation as it is of rational decision-making – come into play, as will be explained in Chapter 6. Similarly, institutional theory adds another layer of criticism when the effects of organizational culture are added to the equation, anticipating what will be explained in Chapter 7: the expectation that sound strategic management equals strategic planning could be a myth that is perpetuated by people who adhere to agency theory and the financialization that it generates only because that is what they believe in, creating an effect of isomorphism.

The concept of shareholder value is a deliberate attempt to deal with the future. It relies on estimating earnings and what profits the firm will make in the period stretching away from the investment decision that potential shareholders make. Nevertheless, the future is unknown. Therefore, there is a question whether strategy theories have predictive power. Is it possible to prejudge what will happen and how much money a firm will make on the basis of applying a strategy theory – or a finance theory, for that matter?

Economic theories and agency theory in particular have been accused of performativity (Callon, 1998; MacKenzie, 2006; Veldman & Willmott, 2020). The notion of performativity expresses that theories do not capture and describe and explain what exists out there. Instead, the argument is that these theories create the world because people, by believing these theories are true, start behaving in accordance with them.

For that reason, respected management scholar Sumantra Ghoshal (2005) considers agency theory to be a bad theory because it leads to bad management practices. He particularly argues against agency theory's basic assumption that people are only motivated by self-interest. By claiming this as 'good' theory, managers are taught that to be selfish is a good thing, and in believing this, they behave selfishly and hence generate the empirical reality within which the theory apparently applies. Agency theory then has become performative. Ghoshal's assessment of agency theory as bad theory has found some empirical backing when it comes to performance appraisal (Evans & Tourish, 2016). Besides, Germany still holds on to an approach to corporate governance that is more in line with the stakeholder approach, which has proven to be a viable alternative (Bottenberg, Tuschke, & Flickinger, 2016).

With regard to the objectivism-subjectivism debate, the position of agency theory is somewhat confused. On the one hand, with its reliance on specifying efficient contracts, it takes an objectivist stance, but on the other hand, with recognizing that interests between shareholders and the top team can be different, some subjectivism has crept in.

Illustration 5.5 SKF from a shareholder value point of view

Should SKF* compete on price and put in the lowest bid possible to retain a big US-based client, or should it step away and persist with its high-quality strategy?

SKF is listed on the Stockholm stock exchange**. Swedish shareholders own 64% of the shares. Since the 2008 economic crisis, SKF shares had been on a downward trend, but they had started to recover. An announcement that SKF will lose a big account would not help with maintaining shareholder confidence. However, giving in affects the profit margin and the long-term earning ability of SKF.

* Value Selling at SKF Service, IMD-5–0751, 2009
** SKF 2009 Annual Report

Exhibit 5.3 Agency theory reflective questions

- In the performance logic, how does agency theory understand the environment, the strategy, and the firm?
- What with agency theory is the key question that a strategist should always be worried about and serves as the 'starter' question for a strategic analysis?
- What is the purpose of shareholder value?
- What is a principal, and what does a principal want?
- What is an agent, and what does an agent want?
- What is the agency problem, and why does it exist?

- How is the agency problem solved?
- How and why do agency theory and shareholder value apply to corporate governance?
- How and why do agency theory and shareholder value apply to supply/demand relationships between firms?
- What type of contracts can a strategist choose between, and what would indicate which type of contract would be preferable?
- According to agency theory, what should be part of every contract?
- In the process logic, how are the environmental survival process and the organizational strategy process understood, and how is a strategist expected to contribute?
- What moral questions does agency theory generate?
- Why is agency theory considered to be performative?
- What is agency theory's position with regard to the objectivism-subjectivism debate?

Case 5.1

Judges Scientific

In May 2016, during its annual general meeting, Judges Scientific warned that its order book was lower than expected.[1] The share price dropped 19% to 1,470.00p. Things had picked up again by September 2019, with Judges Scientific announcing increasing its interim dividend from 12p per share to 15p per share, after a successful first six months.[2] The share price then stood at 3,687.00p. Chairman Alex Hambro was quoted saying that the delivery of record revenue, adjusted profit before tax, earnings per share, cash generation, and dividends for the first half are testament to the group's pursuit of operational excellence. Orders to date are in line with our expectations, despite a subdued second quarter. The strong first half financial performance and healthy order book give the board confidence that full year adjusted profit before tax and earnings per share will exceed current consensus market expectations.

In February 2020, Judges Scientific expected some impact from the Covod-19 pandemic.[3] "With the current scale of the outbreak, and provided it does not last more than three months and remains largely contained within China, it is not expected that there will be a significant impact to the group 2020 trading".

Judges Scientific presents itself as "an AIM-quoted group specialising in the acquisition and development of a portfolio of scientific instrument businesses".[4] In May 2020, it did its 18th acquisition: Heath Scientific, a company specializing in calorimeters.[5] Among its larger subsidiaries are Scientifica, FTT, Sircal, PE Fiberoptics, and GDS.[6] Scientifica manufactures advanced imaging micro-positioning and photomanipulation systems for neuroscience research. FTT is a supplier of fire testing instrumentation. Sircal makes gas purifiers for spectrometers. PE Fiberoptics manufactures test equipment for measuring optical fibres and cables. GDS develops and makes equipment and software for testing soils and rocks.

AIM is the "London Stock Exchange's market for small and medium size growth companies".[7] Two weeks after reporting interim results on 22 September 2020, the 'Simply Wall St' website considered the Judges Scientific share price of £49.70 to be significantly above what it saw as a fair value of £24.99.[8] By the way, Chairman Alex Hambro declared with the interim report that "The outbreak of the coronavirus, with the consequential lockdowns in most of our markets, has had a material impact on the Group's trading performance, particularly on order intake which fundamentally drives all other Group key performance metrics".[9]

Alex Hambro wrote in the 2019 annual report, published in March 2020, that "delivering returns to our shareholders remains the core objective of the Group and as such the Board is pleased to be recommending a final dividend of 35p, making a total of 50p in respect of 2019, a 25% increase on the prior year (2018: 40p)". The strategy to do that is "to acquire small/medium-sized scientific instrument companies, paying a disciplined multiple of earnings and to finance any acquisition, ideally, through existing cash resources and/or bank borrowings".[10] This is referred to by the company as the 'buy and build model'. CEO David Cicurel added that in 2019, "the main drivers of growth within our businesses were the effect of the efforts deployed since 2018 to improve their operating performance and the continuation of very favourable exchange rates prevailing since the Brexit vote".[11] He continued by writing that market demand is being driven primarily by increased worldwide investment in higher education and a growing trend towards optimisation across science and industry; optimisation requires measurement. Despite these positive long-term trends, the markets across which Judges and its peers operate are characterised by a degree of shorter-term variability, influenced mostly by government spending, currency fluctuations and the business climate in major trading blocs, particularly the USA and China.[12]

He also referenced Covid-19 and the uncertainty this creates. And although orders are down, the order book is still 'robust'.

The 'buy and build model' is further specified as consisting of four components: (1) 'Leverage expertise and capital', (2) 'Accumulate sustainable established business', (3) 'Create an environment where businesses can thrive', and (4) 'Repay debt and reinvest profits in further acquisitions'.[13] With regard to (3), the aim is "to create additional opportunities through guidance, business support, expertise and capital, under an umbrella of robust financial controls".[14] To encourage employees to feel like they own the firm, a Judges Share Incentive Plan is in operation, which allows employees to buy shares using their pre-tax earnings. One-third of employees are shareholders.[15]

According to Malcom Wheatley, investment writer with Motley Fool UK, the risks associated with Judges Scientific are currency fluctuations, as it is selling worldwide, and the broader global economy.[16] Additionally, with the firm specializing in acquisitions, one might go wrong. However, he considers the biggest risk is its CEO David Cicurel, who celebrated his 70th birthday recently, retiring and stepping away from the business. Malcolm Wheatley sees him as pivotal for the company's continued success, especially with regard to securing favourable takeover deals.

Finance director Brad Ormsby explains that there are four KPIs at group level: earnings per share, operating margins, return on invested capital, and cashflow generation.[17] When asked, David Cicurel explained that for him, when it comes to the individual businesses, two KPIs are the most important: cash flow and order intake.[18] That is what gets reported every week. Additionally, COO Mark Lavelle has loads of KPIs. He calculates them every month and then talks them over with the businesses. David Cicurel also explains that subsidiary managers appreciate the freedom they gained after their companies were acquired by Judges Scientific. Mostly, these companies were founded and built up by an entrepreneur who – having achieved retirement age – wanted to get out. When these entrepreneurs were building their businesses, they tended to be more inclined to micro-manage and leave less room for others to take responsibilities.

Over 2019, CEO David Cicurel was paid £190k in salary, £48k as a bonus, and £5k in benefits. The other two executive directors, Brad Ormsby and Mark Lavelle, were paid £166k, £42k, and £2k; and £172k, £43k, and £18k, respectively.[19] All three received a 25% bonus on top of their salary because the earnings per share target was exceeded. Brad Ormsby also received an £8k pension contribution. Salaries for 2020 were decided by the board to be £200k for Cicurel, £180k for Ormsby, and £220k for Lavelle. All three executive directors will receive 1,000 share options; 84% of ordinary shares are not in public hands.[20] Table 5.1 provides an overview of the major shareholders. Notwithstanding the Judges Share Incentive Plan, subsidiary managers earnings are mostly determined by their salaries. David Cicurel explains that large bonuses do not work because you cannot get a mortgage with a bonus.[21] Besides, he said, people working for Judges' companies are engineers and scientists who are not predominantly motivated by money.

Table 5.1
Ordinary shares

David Cicurel (director: including SIPP and SIP, and 44,000 non-beneficial)	759,430	12.2%
Liontrust	561,414	9.0%
Odin Global	356,435	5.7%
JP Morgan Asset Management (UK)	352,234	5.7%
Guy Naggar	320,000	5.1%
Stephen Upton and Jacqueline Upton	188,100	3.0%
Hargreaves Lansdown	176,318	2.8%
Brown Shipley	167,882	2.7%
Banque de Luxembourg	141,803	2.3%
NFU Mutual	125,128	2.0%
Polleitt & Reichert Investment Management	122,270	2.0%
Berenberg Asset Management	110,085	1.8%
Directors (excluding those listed separately above)	196,789	3.2%

Source: www.judges.uk.com/financial-performance/disclosures.html [accessed 6 October 2020]

Notes

1 www.lse.co.uk/news/JDG/judges-scientific-shares-hit-as-pick-up-in-orders-fails-to-materialise-ep87qr4heweqzyh.html [accessed 14 September 2020]
2 www.lse.co.uk/news/JDG/judges-scientific-posts-record-interim-revenue-and-hikes-dividend-fa4fdvrry979akg.html [accessed 14 September 2020]
3 www.lse.co.uk/news/JDG/judges-scientific-says-coronavirus-won-t-have-significant-impact-on-trading-qqrfxeh8272db1e.html [accessed 14 September 2020]
4 Judges Scientific plc 2019 annual report
5 https://polaris.brighterir.com/public/judges_scientific/news/rns_widget/story/w91j61x [accessed 6 October 2020]
6 Judges Scientific plc 2019 annual report
7 www.londonstockexchange.com/raise-finance/equity/aim [accessed 6 October 2020]
8 https://simplywall.st/stocks/gb/capital-goods/aim-jdg/judges-scientific-shares?utm_medium=finance_user&utm_campaign=conclusion&utm_source=post&blueprint=1224886#information [accessed 6 October 2020]
9 https://polaris.brighterir.com/public/judges_scientific/news/rns_widget/story/w91j61x [accessed 6 October 2020]
10 Judges Scientific plc 2019 annual report, p. 6
11 Judges Scientific plc 2019 annual report, p. 7
12 Judges Scientific plc 2019 annual report, p. 8
13 Judges Scientific plc 2019 annual report
14 Judges Scientific plc 2019 annual report, p. 10
15 Judges Scientific plc 2019 annual report
16 www.fool.co.uk/special-free-report/one-top-small-cap-share-from-the-motley-fool-uk/?source=uhwsppcl10000001 [accessed 14 September 2020]
17 Judges Scientific plc 2019 annual report
18 Interview with David Cicurel, 6 October 2020
19 Judges Scientific plc 2019 annual report
20 www.judges.uk.com/financial-performance/disclosures.html [accessed 6 October 2020]
21 Interview with David Cicurel, 6 October 2020

CHAPTER 6

Stakeholders and organizational politics

The stakeholder approach originates with R. Edward Freeman (1984) and points at the wider purpose of the organization in the eyes of the various people who have some kind of stake in it. It builds on earlier work that recognizes the organization as a political arena (e.g. Cyert & March, 1963; Etzioni, 1964; Pfeffer, 1981), where conflicts of interests need to be resolved and coalitions emerge. This is also the place where corporate social responsibility comes to the fore. Overall, the focus is on people – either individuals or collectives – and whether their interests are met.

The process logic of stakeholders and organizational politics

The stakeholder approach is formulated to recognize the many different people and organizations that are dependent on or may be affected by the actions of a focal organization. A stakeholder is defined as "any group or individual who can affect or is affected by the achievement of an organization's purpose" (Freeman, 1984, p. 46). The basic idea is that because an organization depends on others for its livelihood, it has to take their interests into account to survive. In addition, and not unimportantly, it is often stated that every organization has a moral obligation to those who are affected by its activities. The stakeholder approach is therefore descriptive in the sense that it identifies the various types of distinguishable stakeholders, instrumental in the sense that it explains how stakeholders affect performance, and managerial in the sense that it aims to tell managers how to deal with stakeholders (Donaldson & Preston, 1995).

Distinguishing between the various types of stakeholders provides quite a list of individuals, groups, and organizations all having a stake of some sort or another in a focal organization. Such a list includes stakeholder categories like the owners/shareholders, the wider financial community, customers and customer advocate groups, employees and their trade unions, managers, trade associations, competitors, suppliers, various layers of government, and assorted activist and political groups (Freeman, 1984). Some argue that there is a corporate social responsibility to society as a whole (Wood, 1991). But it is through stakeholders that organizations are forced to face up to their accountability (Clarkson, 1995).

From a stakeholder's point of view, the notion of performance becomes a somewhat troubled concept. The economist Milton Friedman (1970) infamously suggested that the sole and only social responsibility of a business firm is to make a profit, but to do that within the confines of the law. This also underpins the concept of shareholder value (Rappaport, 1986). Their argument is that businesses should not engage themselves with any other causes, however noble these might be, because this means that managers are adding costs to the operations of the firm at the expense of the firm's profit margin. They effectively would spend money that is not theirs to spend but should be made available as dividends to the shareholders. If money needs to be spent on good causes, it should be left to the shareholders to decide what they want to spend their money on. If there are unwanted side effects associated with the operations of the firm affecting other stakeholders or society as a whole, government should legislate against these. Consequently, to create shareholder value, a firm has to deal with only those stakeholders who negatively affect the firm's profit margin and leave any other cause or stakeholder group alone, clearly stating that the shareholders should be the prime focus of management.

Illustration 6.1 Mutual dependence in the automotive supply chain

There are many firms involved in producing cars, effectively creating a network of interdependent relationships. Car manufacturers rely on suppliers not only to provide them with the various parts that assemble into a car, but also to develop new features and engineering solutions for the next generation of car models. US car manufacturers tended to be more aggressive and antagonistic, often asking one supplier to develop something for them as a one-off solution only to then change to another cheaper supplier when they had incorporated the new feature in one of their models (Sturgeon et al., 2008). The emphasis on costs forced suppliers to seek out savings at the expense of quality. They also felt little obligation to invest in a relationship that is always at risk of being terminated. This resulted in US carmakers producing cars with high failure rates as a consequence of using low-price/low-quality parts, and cars that were less innovative (Womack, Jones, & Roos, 1990). Consequently, US car plants had to put considerable effort into rectifying faults in new-built cars before these were shipped out, and their cars were still suffering from low reliability, eventually affecting sales. Japanese car makers tend to be more loyal and develop enduring relationships with a range of suppliers, allowing for continuous improvements shared across firms in the course of the lifetime of a model, but also from model to model. Consequently, cars coming out of a Japanese supply and manufacturing chains were almost faultless, having been built with higher quality parts, creating an image of reliability and quality. This not only was valued by customers; it also created a dynamic in the supply chain whereby firms were allowed to make a contribution and benefit from it, generating better cars and higher market share and profits.

This shareholder view is contested (Freeman, 1984; Freeman & Reed, 1983). From a stakeholder approach point of view, shareholders are but one category of stakeholders. A firm has a moral obligation to take everybody's interests into account. Performance, then, becomes a very multi-faceted phenomenon, with the firm being judged on its ability to meet the many different interests that the various stakeholders and stakeholder communities may have. Measuring performance in financial terms then becomes less relevant and other and possibly more qualitative indicators are called for, as well. This discussion whether to adopt a shareholder view or a stakeholder view is obviously not important to public or third-sector organizations without shareholders. Performance assessment of not-for-profit organizations has been a continuous source of debate.

Strategy practice 6.1 Corporate social responsibility

Many larger organizations take their corporate social responsibility seriously enough to devote part of their websites to it. There very often is a link to pages that come under the label of 'responsible business', of 'being a responsible company', or just 'CSR'. What you will find there is information on, for instance, how the firm is protecting the environment, what it does with regard to climate change, how well it is treating its employees, and how it ethically sources its supplies. It is interesting to note that the contradiction between going for shareholder value and being socially responsible is dealt with by having one area of the company website devoted to investor relations and another area to corporate social responsibility.

To indicate what kinds of demands and interests a stakeholder may have with an organization, and also to provide a more elaborate understanding of an organization's performance, we can look more closely at the requirement of legitimacy. "Legitimacy is a generalized perception or assumption that the actions of an entity are desirable, proper, or appropriate within some socially constructed system of norms, values, beliefs, and definitions" (Suchman, 1995, p. 574). A stakeholder's interests can be described in terms of the legitimacy they demand from a focal organization. Suchman suggests that this legitimacy can be pragmatic, moral, or cognitive, and is often a combination of these three.

Pragmatic legitimacy is derived from the idea of exchange. A stakeholder and a focal organization stand in some kind of mutually dependent relationship to each other. The level of legitimacy deriving from this relationship depends on the satisfaction that both parties get from the exchange that is taking place. Pragmatic legitimacy from the perspective of a stakeholder refers to the level of fulfilment the stakeholder receives from the focal organization.

Moral legitimacy concerns the norms and values to which a stakeholder subscribes. The activities of an organization are judged in accordance with what a stakeholder considers to be morally right or wrong. The interest of the stakeholder lies in upholding the formal and informal rules that the stakeholder sees as important. Moral legitimacy from the perspective of a stakeholder refers to the

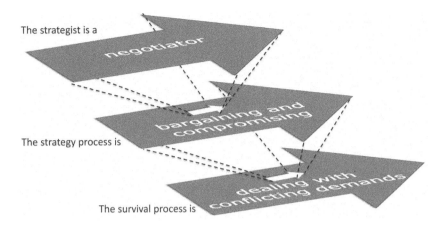

The strategist is a *negotiator*

The strategy process is *bargaining and compromising*

The survival process is *dealing with conflicting demands*

Figure 6.1
The process logic
for stakeholders
and organizational
politics

level of compliance the focal organization achieves regarding the stakeholder's norms and values.

The idea of cognitive legitimacy is based on the recognition that situations may be perceived differently. The activities of an organization are judged in accordance with how the stakeholder understands what is going on. It is in the interest of a stakeholder that an organization acts at least in accordance with a mutually shared definition of the situation or preferably that the organization adapts to how the stakeholder likes to see it. Cognitive legitimacy from the perspective of a stakeholder refers to the extent to which the definition of the situation is shared.

With multiple stakeholders, it is a normal state of affairs that an organization is confronted with different demands, as each stakeholder may have different ideas about what makes an organization pragmatically, morally, and cognitively legitimate. Stakeholders also hold power over the organization, and they may exercise this power, depending on how much of a stake they have in the organization (Frooman, 1999; Pfeffer & Salancik, 1978). It is not difficult to see that the different demands that may be levied on an organization lead to different and conflicting ideas about what is considered as good or bad organizational performance. On top of that, the organization itself may have ideas and interests of its own, which do not necessarily align with the interests of the stakeholders. From a stakeholder perspective, the environmental survival process, thus, is a process of dealing with conflicting demands (see Figure 6.1).

Illustration 6.2 Stakeholders around how drugs are priced

A drug called Orkambi, manufactured by Vertex Pharmaceuticals, costs $250,000 per year*. It is a drug that keeps sufferers of cystic fibrosis alive. Mylan is a generic drug company which raised the price of their EpiPen to $608; it was priced at about $100 in 2007. An EpiPen is an injection device that contains epinephrine, medicine that people need to use when they are struck by a deadly allergic reaction. People who are prone to such allergic reactions tend to keep one in their fridge to have it handy for when they need it.

Drug pricing is one of those issues where you find that stakeholders have conflicting interests. Commercial drug companies have to make money for their investors and shareholders, but they also argue that the R&D needed to develop new drugs is becoming more and more expensive. People with health issues have a desperate need for medication, especially if they are facing deadly deceases for which a cure is available. However, there is a limit to what they can afford. Of course, they can take out health insurance, but insurance companies have to strike a balance between what they charge, what cover they offer, and how much profit they have to make. Governments are often involved – directly or indirectly – either by providing healthcare themselves, regulating health insurance, or providing some form of healthcare regulation. In the US, for instance, many people have their healthcare needs covered by Medicare, which in 2016 spent $112 billion on drugs every year. However, according to current rules, Medicare is not allowed to negotiate with drug companies, while drug companies incentivize doctors to prescribe more expensive drugs. Private health insurers in the US do negotiate to keep their costs down, and in that way, pricing levels are established with which Medicare then has to comply. However, it is easier for private health insurers to restrict coverage or increase premiums than it is to take on the drug companies, leaving individual people who are desperate for life-saving drugs struggling to afford them.

In the US, in a way, there is a coalition among shareholders, drug companies, and insurance firms, which jointly keep drug prices high. In Europe, many governments have intervened on behalf of patients and formulated legislation that puts a cap on what a drug company can charge. Whatever compromise is reached, it is a compromise between who gets what, how the situation is defined, and what morally is acceptable.

* Drugs in America: Seizure-inducing, *The Economist*, 3 September 2016 (provided by Anup Karath Nair)

Stakeholders are not confined to just the environment, either. An organization consists of many groups and subgroups, which each have different ideas and interests. These can be collectives like departments, subsidiaries, or professionals, managers, workers, or any other category an individual may identify with, or these can be individual executives, managers, or staff members. Some of these subgroups or individuals can band together with external stakeholders and act as their representatives within the organization. Organizations are described as a 'negotiated order' (Fine, 1984), whose functioning depends on whether inherent contradictions and conflicts of interests can be overcome (Benson, 1977), and which essentially is run by a 'dominant coalition' of internal stakeholders who have found some common ground (Cyert & March, 1963). The interests of internal stakeholders are also described in terms of pragmatic, normative, and cognitive legitimacy.

With the recognition that stakeholders – external as well as internal – have different claims on the organization, and that these claims may be contradictory and result in conflicts of interest, it can be expected that the organization becomes an arena where the various stakeholders exercise power to have their interests come out on top. Managing an organization, then, essentially is a political process. This is the conclusion drawn by many strategy scholars who have studied how strategic decision-making actually takes place (e.g. Bower, 1970; Hickson, Butler, Cray, Mallory, & Wilson, 1986; Jarzabkowski & Balogun, 2009; Narayanan & Liam, 1982; Pettigrew, 1973).

Strategy practice 6.2 The strategy workshop and organizational politics

When a top management team retreats into a nice hotel in the country for a weekend to discuss the firm's strategy, its members might appear to debate the next strategic move or discuss an issue that has come up and what to do about it. From an organizational politics point of view, what actually is happening is that they are negotiating. They know that any decision that will be made will affect the area they are responsible for. They may get more resources out of it, or maybe they lose out. They may be arguing for their point of view (mediated by their mental map) and vigorously oppose another point of view (mediated by somebody else's metal map). Such debates can become quite heated and occasionally feature open conflict.

Quinn (1980) labelled this process of continuous negotiation as 'logical incrementalism'. He described strategic management as a process of aligning conflicting demands and viewpoints arising from the different subsystems of the organization. Any organization has limited means at its disposal. What is available is not sufficient to cater for all the ambitions that may exist. The various subsystems interact through negotiation, but Quinn believes that they still share an overarching purpose of sticking with the organization as a whole. Their subsequent compromises make that the organization develops in a step-by-step incremental fashion, as the limited means are successively committed to the different causes of each subgroup.

It follows that the strategist's role in all of this is taking part in these negotiations. This can be an arbitrator and *primus inter pares*, Latin for first among equals. Yet on many occasions, the strategist can be identified with a specific subgroup and has adopted its pragmatic, cognitive, and moral legitimacy, or strategists just act to foster their own individual interests.

Illustration 6.3 Decision-making at Toxichem

Toxichem is a pseudonym for a chemical company that had its strategic decision-making investigated (Wilson, 1982). The chemical manufacturing process requires Toxichem to produce its own steam. At some point, their existing low-pressure 80 psi boiler had to be replaced. Expectations were that higher pressures would be needed in the future, so Toxichem purchased a high-pressure 400 psi boiler. As it turned out, the higher pressures were not needed. However, the new boiler had to be fired up to 400 psi first before it could operate at the lower 80 psi level. This incurred an additional cost. On that basis, the works director had the idea that the spare capacity could be used by Toxichem to generate its own electricity. He calculated that this would save the company £39,000 per annum. However, an additional investment in a generator was needed – money that Toxichem did not have at the time.

A few years later, Toxichem had grown so much that it needed a second boiler. The works director saw a new opportunity for pushing the electricity idea again, but the high-pressure boiler that was needed to allow for electricity generation was too expensive. Toxichem could not afford that amount of capital outlay. The purchasing director was against the idea on these grounds altogether and preferred a low-pressure boiler. While the Toxichem board was considering the options, by pure coincidence, the National Coal Board let it be known that it had large stocks of low-quality coal available at a very low price. To take advantage of this and to be able to supply steam with this low-quality coal, a high-pressure boiler was needed, although it would not have to operate at this higher pressure. The numbers added up for Toxichem, and the purchasing director now agreed with the larger investment in a high-pressure boiler. The works director did not push the electricity idea any further, but was delighted that the option was still open with two high-pressure boilers available.

Growth continued for Toxichem, and a third boiler was needed to keep up with demand. The works director took this opportunity to again make the case for electricity generation. The purchasing director remained against the idea. Both produced reports with opposing arguments. The firm reached an impasse. Each report was based on assumptions and projections that could not be independently verified. Would the staff running the boilers be able to also run a generator? How reliable would the whole setup be? What would be the future costs of coal and electricity?

One of the key variables was the cost of standby arrangements. How much would the power company charge Toxichem if it needed to temporarily reconnect to the grid in case the generator broke down or when it was out for maintenance? The power company was not keen on firms generating their own electricity, and it refused to provide a quote. The works director then asked for quotes from two generator manufacturers and requested them to include standby charges in their tenders. For some reason, the power company did provide this information to the generator manufacturers. They were told that standby charges were £5 per kilovolt-ampere (kVA) per annum. This was too expensive, and the electricity generation idea was shelved again.

Some time later, the managing director of Toxichem announced his retirement and both the works director and the purchasing director were considered to be candidates to replace him. It was known within the company that their track records were measured in terms of their success in getting their ideas implemented. The electricity idea featured heavily in this assessment. This inspired the works director to revive the plan one more time. He asked around about the £5 per kVA standby charges and found out that this was ridiculously high, and some error must have been made. Investigating this further, he unearthed solid evidence that the actual charge would be about £1 per kVA. This made the whole proposition viable again. Months of discussion ensued within Toxichem, with everybody in the firm forced to take sides. It dominated board meetings and lunch breaks. The arguments became ever more personal, with the works director and the purchasing director challenging each other's competence to do their jobs. As no definitive case in favour or against could be supplied, it was put up for a vote. The majority was in favour of electricity generation. Engineers, who had more sympathy with the works director and his ideas as a fellow engineer than they had with the purchasing director, dominated the board. The works director was promoted to managing director a year later.

The performance logic of stakeholders and organizational politics

As previously explained, performance is a somewhat troubled concept within the confines of the stakeholder approach. Different stakeholders have different stakes in the organization, and therefore have different expectations and ideas about what performance means to them. It is the stakeholders' pragmatic, cognitive, and moral legitimacy which defines beneficial outcomes for them (see Figure 6.2). The contradictions and conflicts that arise as a consequence need to be dealt with. The ability of an organization to perform therefore depends on whether and how the organization achieves sufficient legitimacy among the many stakeholders to keep on functioning (see Figure 6.2).

Illustration 6.4 The legitimacy of coal

As a consequence of worries about climate change, the use of fossil fuels is becoming less acceptable*. US insurance companies Chubb and Axis Capital, and the Australian insurers QBE and Suncorp, are no longer providing insurance for new coal-fired power plants. They joined other – mostly European – insurance companies which pulled out earlier, with the expectation that others will follow. When insurance cannot be provided, new coal-fired power plants will not be able to be constructed and become operational. In effect, coal-fired power plants are in the process of losing their legitimacy, and as a consequence, they are threatened with extinction.

* www.theguardian.com/environment/2019/dec/02/coal-power-becoming-uninsurable-as-firms-refuse-cover?CMP=share_btn_link [accessed 24 November 2020]

The obvious solution for any organization to remain legitimate among all relevant stakeholders is to meet all their interests. This will be impossible. Realistically, an organization can at best prioritize and negotiate with stakeholders who are the most essential for an organization's survival. Mitchell, Agle, and

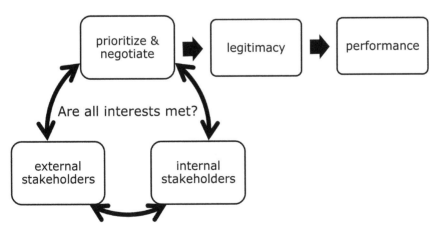

Figure 6.2
The stakeholder approach

Wood (1997) provide a framework by which stakeholders' relative importance can be assessed, based on the three variables of legitimacy, power, and urgency (see Table 6.1). In this way, eight different types of stakeholders, with each type being of more or less relative importance to the organization, can be distinguished.

The legitimacy variable refers to the extent to which the stakeholder's claim fits within what is considered legitimate in the then current situation (Wood, 1991). What is considered to be legitimate depends on how stakeholders are congregating in various coalitions and whether a dominant coalition has emerged. It is very rare that a single stakeholder can dictate what is legitimate and what is not. Stakeholders tend to band together, which allows them to further their individual causes as a member of a larger coalition of interests. It is in this context that a certain agreement on what is considered legitimate becomes established. Again, the distinction is made between pragmatic, cognitive, and moral legitimacy (Suchman, 1995). Whether a stakeholder should be taken care of depends on how the stakeholder's claim and the organization's claim compare to what is considered legitimate in the current context. The stakeholder who comes closest to what is expected more generally has the upper hand here.

Emerson's (1962, p. 32) classic definition – "the power of actor A over actor B is the amount of resistance on the part of B which can be potentially overcome by A" – indicates the usefulness of power in situations of conflict and contradiction. Mitchell et al. (1997) draw on Etzioni (1964) to distinguish between three bases for power. Coercive power is based on the use of force and threat. Utilitarian power is based on the provision of (material) resources that acts as an incentive. Normative power is based on the application of norms and regulations. Each stakeholder has a powerbase that extends across these three, and on which it can draw to pursue its interests. Again, coalitions are to be considered here, as individual stakeholders might find a common course and band together to increase their relative power. The balance of power between various stakeholder coalitions of which a stakeholder has become a member and the organization indicates the relative importance of a stakeholder with regard to this variable. If the stakeholder has a strong powerbase or has joined a powerful coalition of stakeholders and the organization has little to balance it out with, this stakeholder scores high in this realm.

Finally, urgency refers to the degree to which a stakeholder needs immediate attention. When a stakeholder's claim is associated with an acute problem that should be solved instantly, there is more urgency when compared with a claim associated with an issue that has lingered on in the background for some time and will linger on well into the future.

Depending on the scores on the three variables of legitimacy, power, and urgency, a stakeholder or a coalition of stakeholders ends up as either one of eight different types (see Table 6.1). Mitchell et al.'s (1997) framework also distinguishes between four layers of importance. The stakeholder type that is the most salient is the 'definitive stakeholder'. This is a stakeholder with the most legitimate claim, who is powerful and needs urgent attention. The next important stakeholders on the list are the dependent, dangerous, and dominant stakeholders, who score on two of the three variables. The least important ones are the discretionary, demanding, and dormant stakeholders, who only score on

Table 6.1
A stakeholder typology

Stakeholder type	Power	Legitimacy	Urgency
Definitive stakeholder	✓	✓	✓
Dominant stakeholder	✓	✓	
Dependent stakeholder		✓	✓
Dangerous stakeholder	✓		✓
Dormant stakeholder	✓		
Discretionary stakeholder		✓	
Demanding stakeholder			✓
Non-stakeholder			

Source: Derived from Mitchell et al. (1997)

one variable. The non-stakeholder, who neither has power nor legitimate claim, nor needs urgent attention, can be ignored. This, of course, refers to both internal and external stakeholders.

However, this is a typology, which means that no stakeholder will perfectly fit any of these categories. A typology is put forward – for the sake of argument – to pinpoint the distinguishing features of specific categories with no expectation that anybody or anything will completely match such an ideal type. Nevertheless, stakeholder salience has its use, because what can be expected is that stakeholders move up and down. Some become more salient as they are gaining legitimacy, power, or urgency; others see their salience diminished when they lose legitimacy, power, or urgency. It is this dynamic that should be at the heart of managing stakeholders strategically. Expect a constantly shifting landscape – like a kaleidoscope – that the organization continuously needs to deal with as things change.

Additional features

A tool to deal with stakeholders is the mission statement. Campbell (1987) tells us that an organization's mission statement has to indicate the relative attention that various stakeholders can expect to get. It should be a statement of purpose that reflects the reason why and for whom the organization exists. It should contain a vision of where the organization is destined for, as well as whom the organization is trying to serve. An explicit listing of organizational values should also be part of the mission statement. An organization's existence only makes sense if it is worthwhile in the eyes of its stakeholders.

On a different note, the notion of management cognition resonates with the basic idea that different stakeholders have different points of view and different ideas about cognitive legitimacy. The way in which the minds of strategists work has an effect on what they perceive and do not perceive, how they process information, and ultimately on the strategic decisions that they take (Schwenk,

1984). These effects are predominantly elaborated in terms of cognitive limitations. Herbert Simon (1957), for instance, built a theory of the organization on the basis that managers are limited with regard to their information processing abilities. He came up with the notions of 'bounded rationality' and 'satisficing' to denounce any expectation that managers will always come up with the optimal decision if all information is available. He argues that people can only consider so many alternatives, and can only deal with a limited amount of information. Because of that, their rationality is bounded, and they pick the first alternative that solves the problem, not necessarily the best.

Cognitive limitations can also have an effect in generating all kind of biases, which in turn affect the likelihood that one alternative is preferred over another one. For instance, Tversky and Kahneman (1974) did some famous experiments in which they demonstrated that choices people make are based on all kinds of decision heuristics or mental shortcuts.

Strategy practice 6.3 Mental mapping

Mental mapping is a practice whereby a group of people, like members of a management team, have a meeting to find out how they understand a situation. There are techniques available by which a collective cause-and-effect map can be generated, often with the use of a software package that allows individual participants to enter their views. During the mental mapping session, these individual views are collated and put together so that the group as a whole can discuss and settle on a shared view of the situation. This not only clarifies the mind of each individual participant, but also often results in a shared action plan of how to deal with a problematic situation. Ackerman and Eden (2011) provide one of the more sophisticated examples of this kind of practice, featuring the 'Decision Explorer' software package.

The basic idea that management thought is pre-structured is derived from cognitive psychology (Sims & Gioia, 1986). Things like 'schemas' (a mental structure which serves to organize knowledge), 'implicit theory' (a scheme of naive, personal collections of assumptions of how things are related and how the organization works), and 'scripts' (specific schemes about how events are supposed to organize into sequences) always are already in strategists' minds and inform how they make sense of the world.

Management cognition also feeds into cognitive legitimacy and is therefore closely intertwined with how stakeholders perceive their stake in the organization. Every individual stakeholder is seen as equipped with a 'mental map' that informs them how they understand the world around them. It also allows them to navigate their way in and around the organization. These maps are profoundly individual, although there are many instances where people's individual mental maps with regard to specific areas of understanding are largely similar, especially when these people have shared the same or similar experiences.

Doing strategic management as a political process

From a stakeholder approach point of view, strategic management is an opportunity for political behaviour – for instance, when doing an internal and an external appraisal, picking objectives, and formulating a strategic plan, everything is expected to be subjected to negotiation and bargaining. A strategic planning procedure, as Quinn (1980) observed, is a site were the various subsystems and internal stakeholders meet, arrange themselves in coalitions with common interests, and arrive at compromises. There are also many other occasions when people interact and effectively negotiation behaviour takes place. This is referred to as micro-politics. Doing strategic management here means taking part in these negotiations. By nature, this happens continuously and it therefore requires a continuous approach.

Strategy practice 6.4 Issue selling

To champion a cause or to get something on the agenda, middle management has to engage in 'issue selling' (Dutton, Ashford, O'Neill, & Lawrence, 2001). Issue selling is a deliberate attempt to draw attention to a situation by affecting people's understanding about it. From a cognitive and political point of view, nothing is a self-evident problem. It takes effort on the part of people who choose to champion a particular cause or issue to make people understand. Top management officials can expect to be approached constantly by people who perceive a particular problem and ask for guidance or support. They might even have a solution ready and only want the 'go ahead' and the resources to tackle it. In a way, there is constant competition for attention – and the best 'issue sellers' can expect to win out. It also leaves unaddressed the problems that are put forward by people who happen to be poor 'issue sellers'.

An organization also has to deal with the various outside stakeholders, coalitions, and their conflicting claims on the organization as a whole. However, a strict distinction between external and internal is not always straightforward. Some stakeholders can appear both as internal stakeholders and as external stakeholders, and therefore need to be taken into account as such. For instance, unions represent employees, while professional bodies represent professionals like accountants or medical doctors. In a similar vein, the marketing department represents customers, and the procurement department represents suppliers. All stakeholders can be expected to take every opportunity to put more pressure on the organization to have their interests met. Therefore, there is a constant dynamic of challenging, shifting, and jockeying for attention in and around the organization. This creates the continuously changing landscape – or kaleidoscope – of conflicting demands that needs constant attention.

As the organization has to keep the most important stakeholders happy to maintain sufficient legitimacy to continue to function and perform, it has to keep track of the changing landscape and consider everything that is occurring. As this takes place continuously, it therefore requires dealing with on a continuous basis. The most common way in which stakeholder claims and contradictions manifest themselves are open conflicts. For this reason, strategists need to keep their eye on all conflicts that are occurring. The two questions to answer here are:

1 Are there any conflicts of interest that manifest themselves, and by which stakeholders are becoming more or less salient?
2 If there are, what can you do about them?

Getting up to speed

Because the stakeholder approach requires continuous attention by definition, as the landscape is changing continuously, it becomes a bit of a nonsense to separate analysis from implementation, as is done with the previous approaches. Instead, managing stakeholders is a continuous and relentless process, with interventions needed all the time. To be able to track the dynamics among the various stakeholders, a strategist needs to know what conflicts are present in and around the organization, how stakeholders appear within these conflicts, what interests they have, and which coalitions they are members of. If you do not know about these factors, you do need to get up to speed.

The performance logic, and the Mitchell et al. (1997) stakeholder typology on which it is based, generates a set of basic questions by which you can get a sense of what is going on (see Exhibit 6.1). Answering these questions provides insight into what conflicts are present, who the stakeholders are, what conflicting claims they have, and which stakeholders are becoming more or less salient. What is important to learn, as well, is how the organization is actually dealing with these stakeholders and whether some currently are prioritized over others. Although the key question in the stakeholder approach is whether all interests are met, this will never be achieved. What the organization can aim for is to reprioritize stakeholders as they move up and down the Mitchell et al. (1997) stakeholder typology.

Assessing stakeholder claims is especially difficult with regard to understanding legitimacy differences. Pragmatic legitimacy may be the relatively easy one. For this, the strategist should find out what is exchanged between a stakeholder and the organization. Cognitive legitimacy may be more difficult. For this, the strategist should be able to understand the organization from the perspective of another stakeholder. The strategist should find out how somebody else defines the situation. This is extremely tricky, because cognitive psychology tells us that a strategist's own schemas, implicit theory, and scripts bind up any understanding of anybody else's perceptions. Finding out about a stakeholder's moral stance in comparison to one's own may be similarly difficult. Furthermore, this can be even more muddled when stakeholders have banded together in coalitions.

Exhibit 6.1 Macro-politics starter questions

- What conflicts of interest are manifesting themselves?
- Which stakeholders are appearing in this conflict?
- What coalitions have formed around this conflict?
- What pragmatic, cognitive, and moral claims on and expectations of the organization does a stakeholder have?
- What is the powerbase of a stakeholder, and how does this balance out against the power of the focal firm?
- How urgently should this stakeholder be dealt with?
- In what way is the organization dependent on each stakeholder?

  - These answers provide an overview of the conflicting demands, the relevant external stakeholders, stakeholder coalitions, and the interdependence between them and the focal organization

- Has the organization prioritized the (external) stakeholders in accordance with the relative importance of each one?

A strategist should also understand the various ways in which power is wielded, which powerbases are available, and whether various individual stakeholders and stakeholder coalitions bring them into play. Etzioni (1964) describes the use of brute force and the coercive power this generates. Utilitarian power comes with the provision and withholding of certain (material) resources in an exchange situation. He also writes about rules, norms, and values that allow people to sanction and to be sanctioned, effectively creating normative power. Each one of these powerbases is available in each relationship between a stakeholder and an organization. The organization and strategists also have power to wield but can also appear to be relatively powerless.

And finally, there is the specific matter at hand for which a claim is made. From the perspective of the organization, there is a need to appreciate its relative urgency, and whether it is an issue that should be settled now or can be left to simmer in the background.

This also works the other way around from the perspective of an individual stakeholder. Stakeholders can evaluate their relative position in terms of power, legitimacy, and urgency among all other stakeholders. A stakeholder will seek to strengthen its power, legitimacy, and urgency by joining a coalition with which it finds some common cause. However, joining a coalition already is making a compromise because you very rarely find that all members of a coalition want exactly the same things from the focal organization. The organization itself can seek to join a coalition with like-minded stakeholders, as well. Evaluating one's position provides the organization, as well as the stakeholders, insight into whether they bargain from a position of strength or a position of weakness. From the perspective of the organization, the strategist needs empathy to not only have an awareness of his own point of view, but also to be able to appreciate where other stakeholders and coalitions are coming from.

The macro-politics point of view assumes that a strategist can do this disinterested analysis on behalf of the organization. In effect, the interests of the organization are assumed to be the interests of the strategist.

Continuous questioning and analyzing

Strategic management from a stakeholder point of view turns almost always into micro-politics. It is individuals who have to do the negotiating, either safeguarding their own interests or representing a specific stakeholder or coalition of stakeholders. The assumption of the disinterested strategist comes under pressure in this micro-political realm. Is it realistic to assume that a strategist always acts in the interest of the organization as a whole? Or do strategists have their own interests that they will try to safeguard, even at the expense of the organization?

Exhibit 6.2 Macro-politics continuous questioning

- Is something that is happening or that is about to happen going to affect what is considered to be legitimate?
- Is something that is happening or that is about to happen going to affect the balance of power?
- Is something that is happening or that is about to happen going to make a stakeholder more or less urgent?
- Are stakeholders rearranging themselves in new coalitions, or is a stakeholder changing its allegiance?
- Is there a new stakeholder appearing on the scene, or has an existing stakeholder disappeared?
- From a disinterested position, does any of this mean that a stakeholder's salience is moving up or down, or are there new interests to be met by the organization, and does that mean that existing interests need to be reprioritized?

When we assume that the strategist as this disinterested party who acts on behalf of the organization, the continuous questioning is about the other stakeholders. To start, the strategists should know who these stakeholders are, what coalitions they are a member of, how the legitimacy of their claim is being considered within the context in which a conflict appears and how it differs from the organization's take on this, how urgent each claim is, and how dependent the organization is on various stakeholders. The analysis then should focus on any changes that might be occurring to consider whether stakeholders need to be reprioritized. Exhibit 6.2 lists a range of more specific questions that should be considered.

Strategy practice 6.5 Internationalization from a stakeholder viewpoint

If there is one thing that operating internationally adds, it is that the sheer number of stakeholders and coalitions multiplies. Every country an organization operates in comes with another set of stakeholders. You then have multiple governments, multiple workforces, multiple pressure groups, etc. It is also not uncommon that there are differences in interests within stakeholder categories. For instance, not every government wants the same thing, and local workforces, managers, or customers may have different expectations. Also, within the organization, there are bound to be differences of interest between internal stakeholder categories across countries. Yet there may also be commonality between stakeholders from various national backgrounds, with international coalitions emerging. These internal conflicts of interest are often bound up with the level of centralization and decentralization within the organization. A local organization within a country would very much like to be fairly independent of the headquarters (HQ), especially if the HQ is located in another country. This would help enormously with being locally responsive. However, to be able to act as a global organization, the HQ has to coordinate across countries, limiting the degree of freedom local organizations have.

Strategizing takes on a completely different dynamic if we take strategists to have their own individual interests that they want to take care of, or if strategists identify more with a specific subgroup like a department, a subsidiary, or an external stakeholder than with the organization as a whole. Whatever is being done, it becomes part of the overall struggle for power and for whose viewpoints and interests will dominate the organization. The strategist is still interested in the same questions, but interpreting the answers will be more geared towards whether anything that may be going on will affect the strategist's own interests rather than the organization as a whole. When there are any changes, they spark a flurry of renegotiation. New claims gain prominence, and some existing claims loose significance.

Exhibit 6.3 Micro-politics continuous questioning

· Who are the individuals who take part in the negotiations, and who do they represent?
· What expectations and interests do they have in the organization, and are these becoming more or less legitimate?
· What powerbase do they have, and is it increasing or decreasing?
· Is an individual's claim on the organization becoming more or less urgent?

  · Answering these questions will allow negotiators to evaluate their relative position vis-à-vis fellow negotiators

· How do individual negotiators understand their position, the organization as a whole, and the way it works as part of the larger environment?
· Is there any movement in how individual negotiators perceive the situation?

- Answering these questions allows a negotiator to gain insight into a fellow negotiator's mental map
- Whose interests and mental maps align with each other, and whose interests and mental maps contradict each other?
- Is there any movement with regard to how interests and mental maps align and contradict?
  - Answering these questions will allow a negotiator to gain insight in the coalitions that may gain or lose dominance

Strategy practice 6.6 SWOT analysis, management cognition, and organizational politics

The purpose of a SWOT analysis is to find about threats and opportunities in the environment and about strengths and weaknesses with regard to the firm. But what makes an opportunity an opportunity, a threat a threat, a strength a strength, and a weakness a weakness? When you factor in organizational politics and management cognition, the analysis takes on a different meaning.

Qualifying something about the organization as a strength or as a weakness may have more to do with the political 'pecking order' inside an organization than with an attempt to assess the organization's abilities. Any part of the organization openly exposed as 'weak' or championing another part as 'strong' has an effect on whether these parts are able to defend their interests. These interests do not necessarily have to be completely selfish. A label of 'weakness' can deter investing in that part of the organization, although it may desperately need it. The manager in charge of this weak part probably has little power in the management team as well, hampering his ability to secure resources. Similar affects are created with labelling something as opportunity or threat.

From a management cognition point of view, these labels are also indicative for the mental map of each individual manager. Opportunities have a positive ring, and threats are perceived as negative. When somebody labels issues positively or negatively, it reveals his or her way of thinking. Also imagine, for instance, a CEO qualifying something as an opportunity instead of a threat. By doing this, the boardroom discussion is primed with an initial understanding of where the CEO thinks the organization should go. Using the strength and weakness labels has similar effects.

Answering Question 2: solving problems and taking action

From a stakeholder approach point of view, the options are indicated by the three ingredients of strategy, organization, and environment in the performance logic. With regard to strategy, the option is to reprioritize and renegotiate in accordance with the changes in legitimacy, power, and urgency that have been observed.

With regard to either the internal stakeholders or the external stakeholders, there is the option to alter the level of mutual dependence. By reducing dependence, a stakeholder's claim's importance is diminished and the threat to the organization's legitimacy lessened.

When we look into how to do this, we enter the realm of micro-politics. Any activity a strategist undertakes here – either from a disinterested or self-interested point of view – boils down to engaging in negotiations. It is about reaching compromises, in which some stakeholders may lose out while others gain. It is also about which coalitions to join and which ones to oppose. While all these deals are struck, the stakeholder performance logic (see Figure 6.2) tells us that to stay viable, the organization should remain sufficiently legitimate among all the stakeholders on which it depends. This can drive the willingness of all the stakeholders with their conflicting claims to eventually compromise, and also to prioritize the interests of those stakeholders whose claims are the most urgent and legitimate, and who have the most power.

So, from a stakeholder point of view, a strategist should constantly be involved in building coalitions of consensus. If strategists are taken to be primarily concerned with their own interests, this coalition and consensus building is driven by the specific stake a strategist has in the organization. When we assume that the strategist's interests are similar to those of the organization as a whole, the strategist becomes the negotiator on behalf of the organization. On the basis of this assumption, a strategist can fulfil a role in the realm of macro-politics in representing and acting in the organization's interests, to maintain and develop the organization's legitimacy among the various stakeholders and their conflicting demands. This means giving in to those stakeholders or coalitions who are very powerful and have interests that are highly legitimate and urgent. It also means that the organization – and therefore, the strategist – has room to manoeuvre vis-à-vis stakeholders and coalitions who are less powerful and whose claims are less legitimate and urgent.

Strategy practice 6.7 Implementing a strategic plan as overcoming resistance?

Implementing a strategic plan is often associated with overcoming resistance (Ford, Ford, & D'Amelio, 2008). This resistance, in turn, is seen as being caused by stakeholders' self-interest. From a strategy implementer point of view, resistance is often branded as irrational and emotional. So, overcoming resistance then becomes a matter of 'stakeholder management'. The question can be asked whether 'stakeholder management' is a euphemism for forcing stakeholders to comply with what already has been decided. Or is it a serious attempt at dialogue and compromise, based on a willingness to realize a strategy that caters for a wide range of interests? A related question is whether stakeholders are to be considered after a strategic plan has been formulated and attention has turned to how to implement it. Or are stakeholders a permanent feature, or even participants, in a continuous strategy debate?

Criticism and generating further questions

The stakeholder approach turns strategic management into a political process. It also introduces subjectivity into the management process. The possibility of an objective benchmark to measure right or wrong against is lost, as everything is 'in the eye of the beholder'. This refers to an organization's performance, as well as the strategy by which this performance is achieved. What is legitimate is subject to constant renegotiation among the stakeholders. The organization's purpose is essentially what the dominant coalition makes of it. The question about the organization's purpose, therefore, is an almost permanent cause for debate – and the answer moves with the times.

The stakeholder approach brings a realization with it that top management officials are seen as another stakeholder, just as anybody else. They are seen as having their own interests, interpretations, and moral obligations. So, what role do they have in the strategic management of the firm? Are they the *primus inter pares* who serve as an arbitrator among the various stakeholders, or are they a separate stakeholder category with their own interests and a particular stake in the survival and success of the organization, or are they divided up amongst themselves because they identify individually with a specific part of the organization like a department or a subsidiary, or maybe even with an outside stakeholder, or are they just only acting to further their own individual interests? Thinking this through could lead to the conclusion that strategic management as an activity to make a firm or an organization perform and to maintain an organization's or firm's ability to perform nothing more than an *idée fixe*: an obsession in the minds of managers and some strategy scholars with little empirical grounding.

The stakeholder approach also brings into focus that the strategist's choices and activities have moral implications. First of all, the stakeholder approach is at odds with the concept of shareholder value. The stakeholder approach points out that any organization – and by implication, its managers – has a moral obligation to everybody who can be described as a stakeholder. Shareholder value implies – for business firms – that managers only have a moral obligation to shareholders. It is expected that there are situations when a decision in favour of a stakeholder will be at the expense of shareholders. Research by Hillman and Keim (2001) indicates that taking care of stakeholders can have a negative impact on profitability because it leads to additional costs that are not always recouped by increasing sales. This is where the strategist has to employ judgement and has to decide what to do about this moral dilemma. To make matters worse – and this concerns all organizations – these kinds of situations also occur when the strategist has to take sides between stakeholders with conflicting claims, especially when these refer to issues of moral legitimacy. It is at such moments that the strategist has to decide what corporate social responsibility really means to him or her personally. In the end, a strategist cannot hide or shirk away from this responsibility and accountability.

The stakeholder approach is predominantly subjectivistic. The notion of management cognition and mental maps points at an essential subjective point of departure, as what managers think is what managers see as their reality. All these multiple and essentially unique and personal realities are, then, all that there is.

Illustration 6.5 SKF from a stakeholder point of view

Should SKF* compete on price and put in the lowest bid possible to retain a big US-based client, or should it step away and persist with its high-quality strategy?

There are internal and external stakeholders who would be differently affected by what will be decided. SKF does not directly deal with the US-based client. A distributor acts as a go-between. The client which wants to hold the reverse auction is the distributer's main account. The distributor also sources from other ball bearing manufacturers and acts as the main channel by which the US-based client fulfils its ball bearing needs. That will remain after the auction. The auction is going to determine the price at which the client will procure its ball bearings. The distributer will get paid on the basis of a fixed cost-plus arrangement. The distributor is pressuring SKF to at least take part. The distributer wants to keep representing SKF – also with other clients – because, due to premium pricing, it is one of its more profitable product lines. SKF not taking part would jeopardize the relationship with this distributor, and could lose it all other clients the distributor deals with, as well.

This dilemma translates into conflicting positions within SKF, too. SKF's global manager for customer value is opposed to taking part. He was the architect behind the software tool with which sales representatives go around to demonstrate why SKG ball bearings are expensive but worth the money. He believes in SKF's value strategy, and believes that giving in would damage SKF's brand. Furthermore, it would inspire other clients and distributors to ask for similar deals. After some time, he reckons, this client would realize that just using price as the selection criterion would backfire and it would come back to SKF and its value proposition. The SKF account manager who deals with the distributer wants to take part because he is afraid that SKF would lose all business that is conducted through the distributor. The decision is escalated up to the SKF Service Division president. Because this is so tied in with SKF's strategy, he is charged with making the final decision. However, this problem only reached him five days before the auction will be held, so there is some urgency to this issue.

Pragmatically, this involves a considerable chunk of turnover. Morally, there is a question of loyalty. Is SKF going to stick with a distributor with which it has enjoyed a long-standing relationship? Cognitively, there is the question of how the reverse auction needs to be interpreted. Will this be the exception and all other SKF clients will stick with the value proposition, or will this become the rule and all other clients will start emphasizing price? All three players in this – SKF, the distributor, and the client – are mutually interdependent, and what happens will define who holds power over whom. As this is a dilemma, from a stakeholder point of view, there is no clear indication what the right decision is. The increased urgency does indicate that both the distributor and the client move up in terms of stakeholder salience. Maybe there is a possibility to engage in direct negotiation with the client to reach a compromise.

* Value Selling at SKF Service, IMD-5–0751, 2009

Exhibit 6.4 Stakeholder approach reflective questions

- In the performance logic, how does the stakeholder approach understand the environment, strategy, and the firm?
- What in the stakeholder approach is the key question that a strategist should always be worried about, and what will be the answer?
- What is legitimacy, and why is it important for organizations?
- Why do you need to keep an eye on conflicts of interest to understand how stakeholders appear in and around the organization?
- Why is the distinction between internal and external stakeholders, or every stakeholder categorization, actually not that relevant?
- Which three indicators can tell you about changes in stakeholder salience?
- Why would you want to keep an eye on changes in stakeholder salience?
- What effect can coalitions have on stakeholder salience?
- From a stakeholder approach point of view, what can a firm do if it has to deal with a strategic issue?
- In the process logic, how are the environmental survival process and the organizational strategy process understood, and how is a strategist expected to contribute?
- What is the effect of management cognition?
- Why is the stakeholder approach regarded as subjectivistic?

Case 6.1

Inditex

US author Dana Thomas released her book *Fashionopolis* in September 2019, in which she explains what she sees as a vicious circle of fast fashion, cutthroat competition, and bad labour practices.[1] In it, she references 24 April 2013, when the Rana Plaza factory complex in Dhaka, Bangladesh, collapsed, resulting in 1,027 deaths.[2] These were mostly women working in the many garment factories that were located in the building, and which were operating as subcontractors for many Western clothing brands. She also mentions the US sweatshops in Los Angeles employing immigrant workers who she sees as victims of wage theft, as well as workers in China and Vietnam.

H&M, as the largest user of the Bangladeshi garment industry, along with Inditex, C&A, and Primark, signed a building and fire safety agreement on instigation of a number of labour groups, which used the tragedy to pressure these firms into signing up just after the Rana Plaza disaster had happened. Helena Helmersson, H&M's head of sustainability, said that they are committed to a garment industry "in which no worker needs to fear fires, building collapses or other accidents that could be prevented with reasonable health and safety measures".[3] Scott Nova, executive director of the Worker Rights Consortium, explains that many clothing brands who use Bangladeshi suppliers claim that they are holding them to high standards, but that corruption and disregard for building safety make these claims suspect.

Zara, H&M, and Forever 21 are fast-growing fast fashion brands that dominate the Asian markets, with consumers in these economies perceiving these brands as premium as they are moving away from local brands like Padini in Malaysia or Penshoppe and Bench in the Philippines.[4] Forever 21 went bankrupt at the end of 2019, mostly as a consequence of lagging behind in online shopping.[5] Penshoppe appears to be holding out, but is under pressure from online shopping, as well.[6]

Fast fashion has been associated with high environmental costs.[7] It is alleged that offering new collections in fast succession at a low price leads to fast fashion companies cutting environmental corners.[8] Textile dyes cause water pollution. Man-made fibres like polyester shed micro-fibres that end up in the natural environment. Cotton production requires large quantities of pesticides. People buying new clothes in quick succession amplify these problems and also generate large quantities of textile waste. Zara and sister brands Pull & Bear and Bershka announced in 2017 that by 2025, they would only sell sustainable clothes. Pablo Isla, CEO of Inditex, which owns these brands, declared that: "Sustainability is a never-ending task in which everyone here at Inditex is involved and in which we are successfully engaging all of our suppliers".[9] Inditex presents itself as "one of the world's largest fashion retailers, with eight brands (Zara, Pull & Bear, Massimo Dutti, Bershka, Stradivarius, Oysho, Zara Home and Uterqüe) selling in 202 markets through its online platform or its over 7,000 stores in 96 markets".[10] On its webpage, Inditex explains its 'commitment to people' and 'commitment to the environment'.

Stanford Graduate School of Business Professor Hau L. Lee showcases Inditex as a successful company which managed to develop Zara into a successful brand by inventing new and superfast supply chain practices, relying on subcontractors – mostly working exclusively for Inditex – in its home country of Spain to manufacture the 'high fashion styles' while it relies on Asian subcontractors for the more 'basic styles'.[11] Zara has a design-to-retail cycle of about five weeks, but is being beaten by Missguided, which releases about 1,000 new products every month.[12]

Some claim that consumer attitudes are changing away from fast fashion. Taken to represent millennials in Malaysia and Singapore, Melissa Chi is quoted as saying that: "The whole mentality that we should buy more because it's cheap just didn't seem right anymore".[13] In the UAE, a debate was staged whether fast fashion brands should be boycotted.[14] However, MarketWatch found that consumers tend to forget about unethically made products, as they prioritize ease of purchase and price over sustainability.[15]

The Covid-19 pandemic appeared to slow down clothing retailing, with Inditex and H&M reporting lower sales in March 2020, when the first lockdowns were instigated; in the US, Zara and H&M app activity fell 14%, leading to speculation that the crisis might influence consumers to consider sustainability to be more important in their shopping choices.[16] Inditex and H&M have been telling shareholders that dividends will be cut. A number of fast fashion producers, suddenly being stuck with unsold inventory, stopped paying their suppliers, who in turn laid off workers. The US-based Center for Global Workers' Rights and the Worker Rights Consortium calculated that garment factories and suppliers had lost at least $16.2 billion in revenue as a consequence of clothing brands cancelling orders or refusing to pay for orders they had placed before the coronavirus outbreak, although H&M and Zara, after having been put under pressure, have reversed their decision.[17]

Fast fashion firm Boohoo was implicated with a flareup in Covid-19 infections in the city of Leicester, England, which instigated a local lockdown. The virus allegedly had been spreading in Leicester's many clothing workshops, where Boohoo is the dominant buyer after rival firms Asos and Missguided started avoiding the Leicester factories because of concerns about modern slavery, illegally low wages, value-added tax (VAT) fraud, and inadequate health and safety measures.[18] Business and Human Rights Centre labour rights researcher Thulsi Narayanasamy was quoted as saying: "I've been inside garment factories in Bangladesh, China and Sri Lanka, and I can honestly say that what I saw in the middle of the UK was worse than anything I've witnessed overseas".[19] As a consequence, the Boohoo share price collapsed by 23% to 279p.[20] A couple of days later, the share price was back at the old level after Boohoo had indicated to investors that it would clean up its supply chain.[21] A couple of months later, Boohoo reported increased sales and profits, but also announced it would set up its own Leicester factory.[22] Martin Buttle of activist group ShareAction wrote to 31 major Boohoo shareholders who together hold a 29% stake to urge them to hold Boohoo to account.[23]

Notes

1 www.nytimes.com/2019/09/03/books/review/how-fast-fashion-is-destroying-the-planet.html [accessed 29 September 2020]
2 www.bbc.co.uk/news/world-asia-22476774 [accessed 29 September 2020]
3 https://eu.usatoday.com/story/money/business/2013/05/13/hm-sign-bangladesh-labor-agreement/2154991/ [accessed 29 September 2020]
4 https://fashionunited.com/executive/management/what-would-become . . . ands-in-developing-asia-as-fast-fashion-takes-over/2017070516435 [accessed 29 September 2020]
5 www.vox.com/the-goods/2019/8/29/20838793/forever-21-consider-bankruptcy [accessed 8 October 2020]
6 www.euromonitor.com/apparel-and-footwear-in-malaysia/report [accessed 29 September 2020]
7 www.forbes.com/sites/theyec/2019/05/13/three-reasons-why-fast-fashion-is-becoming-a-problem-and-what-to-do-about-it/ [accessed 29 September 2020]
8 www.independent.co.uk/life-style/fashion/environment-costs-fast-fashion-pollution-waste-sustainability-a8139386.html [accessed 29 September 2020]
9 www.bbc.co.uk/news/newsbeat-49022453 [accessed 29 September 2020]
10 www.inditex.com/en/about-us/who-we-are [accessed 16 October 2020]
11 www.ft.com/content/3f581046-cd7c-11e9-b018-ca4456540ea6 [accessed 29 September 2020]
12 www.vox.com/the-goods/2020/2/3/21080364/fast-fashion-h-and-m-zara [accessed 29 September 2020]
13 www.scmp.com/lifestyle/fashion-beauty/article/2152687/why-fast-fashion-brands-hm-are-losing-millennial-customers [accessed 29 September 2020]
14 www.thenational.ae/lifestyle/fashion/the-great-debate-should-we-boycott-fast-fashion-brands-1.969305 [accessed 29 September 2020]

15 www.marketwatch.com/story/why-people-conveniently-forget-that-child-labor-made-their-jeans-2018-01-11-14884835 [accessed 8 October 2020]
16 www.forbes.com/sites/shelleykohan/2020/03/30/fast-fashion-leaders-hm-and-zara-weathering-the-pandemic/#21a2f04f17a2 [accessed 29 September 2020]
17 www.theguardian.com/global-development/2020/oct/08/worlds-garment-workers-face-ruin-as-fashion-brands-refuse-to-pay-16bn [accessed 8 October 2020]
18 www.theguardian.com/uk-news/2020/jul/04/boohoo-booms-leicester-garment-factories-linked-lockdown [accessed 9 October 2020]
19 www.theguardian.com/uk-news/2020/jul/04/boohoo-booms-leicester-garment-factories-linked-lockdown [accessed 9 October 2020]
20 www.theguardian.com/business/2020/jul/06/boohoo-leicester-factory-conditions-covid-19 [accessed 9 October 2020]
21 www.theguardian.com/fashion/2020/jul/09/boohoo-shares-bounce-back-after-pledge-to-improve-factory-conditions [accessed 9 October 2020]
22 www.theguardian.com/business/2020/sep/30/boohoo-reports-sales-surge-despite-leicester-supplier-scandal-covid [accessed 9 October 2020]
23 www.theguardian.com/business/2020/oct/08/boohoo-investors-called-upon-to-hold-firm-to-account-over-promises [accessed 9 October 2020]

CHAPTER 7

Institutional theory and organizational culture

Institutional theory has become prominent in management research (Powell & DiMaggio, 1991), developing its own take on strategic change (Hinings & Greenwood, 1988). It urges us to consider the regular interaction patterns on which an organization relies to function and exist. It also brings the underlying expectations and interpretations into focus of those who are involved in these interactions. It therefore points at social structure and organizational culture (Schein, 1992). On the whole, the focus is less on people and more on the interactions in which they are engaged, and on the social structure to which they are subjected. The basic premise in institutional theory is that people – either as individuals or collectives – are defined by what they do and how they do it.

The process logic of institutional theory

The concepts of institution and institutionalization are key terms in sociology (Berger & Luckmann, 1966). Some argue that this is what sociology is about: the explanation of social order and social organization. An institution is "more or less taken-for-granted repetitive social behaviour that is underpinned by normative systems and cognitive understandings that give meaning to social exchange and thus enable self-reproducing social order" (Greenwood, Oliver, Sahlin, & Suddaby, 2008, pp. 4–5). Organizations, which include business firms, operate in a society that consists of institutions. Organizations can be considered institutions themselves. But organizations also rely on this 'self-reproducing social order' to be able to function, exist, and perform. Such regularities in interactions make it so that organizations can be organized, that products can be sold, that public services can be delivered, that people can be employed, that investments can be made, and that money can change hands. For instance, money itself is such an institution. The money economy, prevalent and self-evident as it is now all over the world, is such a 'self-reproducing social order'.

Institutions develop over time. Some take centuries to come into being and seem to persist almost indefinitely; others come and go in a relatively short time span. Institutionalization is the process by which institutions emerge and change. Institutional theory is starting to get noticed by strategy scholars (Lawrence, 1999). This is happening for two reasons. One reason is that institutions impinge on the functioning and performance of any organization. Organizations thus should take notice of how they are affected to mitigate and manage their influence, or maybe make use of them to boost their performance. This is further elaborated under the header of 'isomorphism'. The other reason is that the idea has taken hold that organizations are actively involved in affecting the course of the institutionalization process and influence how institutions take shape to bolster their performance. This is elaborated under the header of 'institutional entrepreneurship'.

Isomorphism

The concept of isomorphism provides an answer to a question about a phenomenon that to Meyer and Rowan (1977) needs an explanation. Why do so many organizations claim that they have a formal organization structure and why do these organizations very rarely actually operate according to this formal structure? This goes back to the distinction between formal and informal organization. Anyone who goes into organizations to find out what is going on, astonishingly in a way, finds that what actually makes the organization work is not found in the formal structures and procedures. People improvise around these official arrangements, and very often have to, to get things done. Yet when asked to account for themselves, organizations maintain that everything progresses in an orderly fashion in accordance with pre-set and pre-designed standards and procedures. Meyer and Rowan (1977) suggest that formal organization is a myth. Organizations put up a front and conform to this image of formality and rationality because that is generally expected of them in society at large. People working in an organization know this. They often just 'act the part' to live up to this expectation but simultaneously deviate from it to actually get their job done.

Almost everybody who has any work experience has some familiarity with what appears to be this double standard. The difference between formal and informal organization is one of those truisms in organization and management theory. Meyer and Rowan's analysis points towards a more general effect. Organizations tend to conform to outside expectations, and they do so to appear legitimate. Suchman (1995, p. 574) defines legitimacy as "a generalized perception or assumption that the actions of an entity are desirable, proper, or appropriate within some socially constructed system of norms, values, beliefs, and definitions". Organizations need to be legitimate to maintain their reason for existence. Such 'socially constructed systems of norms, values, beliefs, and definitions', to which organizations have to conform, appear and are maintained in the form of specific institutions (Scott, 1995).

So, in institutional theory, legitimacy is connected with institutions. Regular interaction patterns have become institutions when they acquire a form of permanence independent of the interactions that constitute them (Berger & Luckmann, 1966). The norms, values, understandings, and resource exchanges, which are part of these regular interactions, become so taken for granted that they prescribe how the interactions have to take place. This effect that institutions take on an existence independent of the interactions that constitute them is referred to as a 'social structure'. This social structure contains common norms, values, and understandings. It stipulates how resources are supposed to be allocated. Individuals and organizations have to conform to the norms, values, and interpretations that the social structure dictates to remain legitimate. Overstepping the mark risks the peril of being sanctioned or losing the ability to function altogether.

Illustration 7.1 Volkswagen collides with the social structure*

In 2014, news broke that the California Air Resources Board had discovered that Volkswagen cars equipped with diesel engines were emitting up to 40 times the permissible amount of nitrogen oxides when driven on the road compared to when these cars were tested in a laboratory, when they appeared to comply with the regulations. Sometime later, a Volkswagen employee – going against instructions from Volkswagen management – revealed that these cars were equipped with engine management software that was able to recognize that the car was going through a test procedure and to then turn on emissions controls. These were turned off when the car was driven on the road. In developing diesel engines, Volkswagen engineers found it impossible to control emissions to comply with US requirements while simultaneously giving the car the performance US customers wanted. Volkswagen subsidiary Audi had developed this software, and Volkswagen managers decided to equip their cars with it.

More than two years later, Volkswagen pleaded guilty to criminal charges. The firm was ordered to pay a $4.3 billion fine, and six Volkswagen executives will be facing charges. When these announcements were made, Oliver Schmidt – head of compliance with Volkswagen's US division from 2012–2015 – had been arrested and was being kept in a Florida jail. Then-US Attorney General Loretta Lynch was quoted saying that "Volkswagen obfuscated, they denied, and they ultimately lied".

* BBC News, 12 January 2017, www.bbc.co.uk/news/business-38603723 [accessed 13 January 2017]

Institutions appear in all kind of shapes and sizes. Professions like accountancy or the medical profession are institutions, as are specific types of organizations like government, charities, hospitals, universities, and business firms – and within that, types of business firms, like for instance supermarkets or airlines. These are all institutions because they exist as regular interaction patterns prescribed by a social structure consisting of specific expectations and interpretations. Some of these expectations and interpretations, and sometimes institutions as a whole, are part of a formal system of rules and regulations. These can vary between the legal system of a country and the rules of play in the game of football. Others are more informal but can be just as compelling.

With regard to organizations, this tendency to conform to what the social structure prescribes leads to isomorphism – the phenomenon that organizations of a certain type tend to look alike. That is why a supermarket is recognized as a supermarket or a university as a university. That is why people can tell the difference between a rugby game and a football game. It also tells people how to act in the context of a supermarket or a university, or as a player on a rugby team or on a football team. Yet there is also the expectation that the supermarket or the university deals with them in a particular manner, just like a rugby player or a football player expects that their teammates, as well as the opponents, keep to the rules of the game. The realization to make here is that football and the social structure that defines it is only seen to exist if the game is being played. Likewise, a supermarket's social structural features only exist if people shop there.

There are three mechanisms of isomorphism (DiMaggio & Powell, 1983). Coercive isomorphism is the result of pressure put upon the organization to conform. This can be the consequence of a dependency that forces the organization to act in a particular way. It can also be 'peer' pressure, to be accepted as part of a community or group. Conformism here is forced upon the organization. Mimetic isomorphism is voluntary. An organization can decide to mimic another organization because it cannot think of anything else to do but follow a template or copy a good example. This is often prompted by uncertainty about the situation, and imitation then is the safe option. Normative isomorphism is a direct consequence of the limitations put upon organizations because they have to follow certain rules. For instance, legislation or professional norms and standards compel an organization to do things in a certain way.

All these regular institutionalized activities and the organizations and individuals associated with them, as well as the underlying social structure, are often collectively referred to as the organizational field. For DiMaggio and Powell (1983, p. 148), an organizational field consists of "those organizations that, in the aggregate, constitute a recognized area of institutional life: key suppliers, resource and product consumers, regulatory agencies, and other organizations that produce similar service or products". A field is seen as a collection of activities, conforming to a social structure and in which an organization takes part. The level of legitimacy an organization maintains determines this organization's membership, as well as its ability to function and perform within the organizational field, and this in turn is a function of the organizational field's social structure and the meaningful interactions in which the organization is able to engage as a consequence.

The organization itself is considered to be an institution, as well. The activities of people working on behalf of the organization are, to a large extent, taken-for-granted repetitive social behaviours. These regularities are reflected in particular normative systems and cognitive understandings. The normative systems and cognitive understandings part of an organization, in turn, is commonly referred to as the organizational culture (Fine, 1984). An organizational culture is

> a pattern of shared basic assumptions that the group learned as it solved its problems of external adaptation and internal integration, that has worked well enough to be considered valid, and therefore, to be taught to new members as the correct way to perceive, think, and feel in relation to those problems.
>
> (Schein, 1992, p. 12)

Organization culture, in effect, is the organization's social structure.

However, an organization can have different subcultures, associated with, for instance, different locations, departments, subsidiaries, or occupational groupings. Meyerson and Martin (1987) thus put forward three ways to appreciate organization culture. It can be integrative when everybody in the organization shares the same norms and values, and interprets situations in the same way. It can be divisive when the organization consists of various subcultures with different sets of norms, values, and interpretations, and an organization culture can be ambiguous when there are no clear expectations. What can be expected is that every organization has a little bit of all three. Some aspects of the organization culture are shared, others are contradictory, and a few more are not clear at all. It is also not uncommon that some subcultures within the organization share their outlook with outside institutions. For instance, medical doctors tend to identify with the rules of their profession more than the expectations of the hospital they work for. Yet what all organization cultures have in common is that they are created, maintained, and changed as a consequence of people's regular interaction patterns.

The integrative effect of organization culture is manifested in what Prahalad and Bettis (1986) have labelled as the 'dominant logic'. The dominant logic is top management's preferred way of interpreting an organization's situation. It is associated with the organization's 'paradigm': "a set of beliefs held relatively commonly throughout the organization" (Johnson, 1987, p. 216). It sits at the centre of a 'cultural web', with the paradigm reflected in the stories that people tell, in the symbols that signify what the organization is about, in the way the organization's structure and control systems work, in the rituals and routines that people engage in, and in who has power over what.

The paradigm's main effect appears when something happens, and a decision has to be made to deal with it (see Figure 7.1). This event will need to be interpreted to create a response. Johnson (1987) finds that there are three ways in which this happens: the problem is simply ignored and there is no reaction; or the problem makes perfect sense because it can be and is understood in terms of the paradigm, leading to the development of a solution; or the problem does not make sense because the paradigm does not provide a ready interpretation, and consequently, there is ambiguity. When this ambiguity happens, a struggle occurs about how the situation should be interpreted. This takes on the form of politics of meaning, with the most likely outcome that the paradigm prevails, and the initial ambiguity is accommodated within the belief system, with a solution developed accordingly.

There is one common denominator among these alternative ways to deal with a problem. The way people think and interpret a situation is governed by the paradigm, and this subsequently drives their actions. Simultaneously, the interaction patterns that are thus created nurture the paradigm. In this way, a self-preserving dynamic takes shape and the paradigm stays intact. Strategists, as well as the organization as a whole, maintain their organization culture and associated belief system, and continue to act in the same manner.

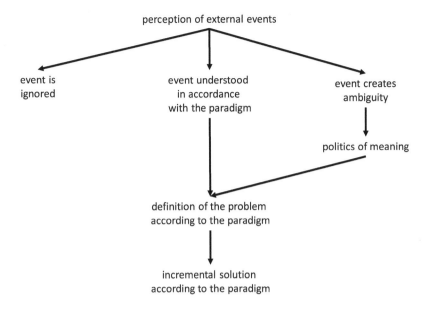

Derived from Johnson (1987)

Figure 7.1
Problem-solving and
the paradigm

To Johnson (1988), this provides another explanatory layer to Quinn's (1980) notion of 'logical incrementalism' (see Chapter 6). The negotiation process by which a firm develops in a step-by-step manner is seen as a manifestation of 'problem-solving-according-to-the-paradigm'. Within the paradigm, there is room for conflicting interests, and these are the problems that are being solved and negotiated about. There is also an overarching common understanding what the organization is about that puts the 'logical' in the 'incrementalism'. It keeps the organization together while the negotiations move it slowly forward.

The process logic for isomorphism sees the environmental survival process as taking place in the organizational field: this collection of regular interactions that in the aggregate constitutes a recognized area of institutional life (see Figure 7.2). To survive and be able to continue to interact, organizations have to yield to institutional pressure. They have to take part in the regular interaction patterns in the manner that the outside world expects of them. The result is isomorphism, with organizations appearing very much alike. The generalized perceptions and assumptions about the actions of the organization and their qualification as appropriate within some socially constructed system of norms, values, beliefs, and definitions at field level are expected to be reflected in the organization's paradigm. Consequently, the organizational strategy process takes on the form of 'problem-solving-

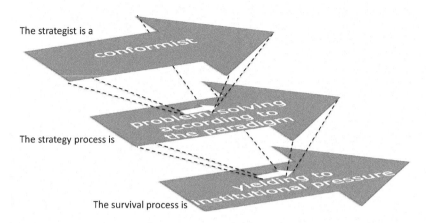

The strategist is a

The strategy process is

The survival process is

Figure 7.2
The process logic for
isomorphism

according-to-the-paradigm'. The strategist is a conformist: interpreting
situations in accordance with the paradigm and acting in compliance, maybe
without even realizing it.

Institutional entrepreneurship

Oliver (1991) suggests that organizations are able to take a more active
stance when it comes to dealing with institutional pressures. An organization
can opt for defiance. This is an act of resistance whereby the organization
openly demonstrates that it does not comply. One step further is the option of
manipulation. This means that the organization actively attempts to change the
demands that are made on it. It implies that the organization looks to achieve
deliberate institutional change. Such an active involvement in shaping the
institutional field is referred to as institutional entrepreneurship (DiMaggio, 1988).
The organization seeks to transform (part of) the organizational field and the
way interactions take place in order to suit its own needs. In effect, it attempts
to alter (part of) the organizational field's social structure. This is referred to as
fundamental change.

   In both instances, a reaction from the organizational field can be expected.
Either option results in a situation of controversy, with several parties joining in
to try to settle the dispute in a favourable manner. Because institutional fields tend
to feature contradictory and incompatible demands anyway, they often spawn
controversy and are seen as the reason why things change (Seo & Creed, 2002).
For instance, people who are engaged in investments and the financing of business
firms expect them to make as much profit as possible and therefore expect
management to keep the tax bill as low as possible within the confines of the law.

They like to see the firm engage in tax avoidance schemes and consider the use of offshore tax havens as quite legitimate. Others have condemned tax avoidance activities and expect firms to pay tax on their earnings in the country where these earnings are generated, even if this results in an overall higher tax bill.

Illustration 7.2 Airbnb defying the social structure

In 2007, Brian Chesky and Joe Gabbia rented out two airbeds in their San Francisco apartment for a couple of days because a large conference in the city meant that no hotel rooms were to be had*. This seeded the idea for a business whereby private people could rent out spare bedrooms for short-stay guests. They founded Airbed & Breakfast (subsequently shortened to Airbnb), and created a website where people could make the necessary arrangements. By 2016, the website listed two million properties in 191 countries. Bookings through the website were expected to add up to a total of $14.4 billion. The company at the time – if listed – was expected to be valued at $30 billion. That is more than the world's largest hotel chain, Marriott. Interestingly, Airbnb was valued at $100 million on its first day of trading when it appeared on the New York Stock Exchange in December 2020**.

The notion that private people go into private arrangements with total strangers to rent out rooms in their own private residences for short periods of time to make some money hardly existed in 2007. Normally, when you wanted to stay somewhere for a short period of time, you booked a room in a hotel. Airbnb has become an accepted alternative in a short space of time. However, not everybody sees this as a legitimate form of business for a number of reasons. It is now not uncommon that the spaces offered on Airbnb have been acquired especially for the very short-term letting market. The original concept was to make money out of a spare bedroom. More and more, houses and apartments are bought with every bedroom being offered for short-stay occupancy through websites such as Airbnb, and these types of lets tend to attract types of guests that create substantial levels of nuisance for neighbours and sometimes for whole neighbourhoods. Accommodations also tend to fall foul of the fire, safety, and hygiene regulations with which the local hotel industry has to comply. Moreover, owners are not paying tourists taxes or room occupancy taxes.

Various cities have had to come up with measures to accommodate the Airbnb phenomenon, often as a consequence of pressure by local hotels. New York banned rentals in residential blocks that last less than 30 days, as did Berlin (Germany). Barcelona (Spain) requires people to obtain a licence before they start renting out rooms. London (England) however, has started encouraging Airbnb-facilitated rentals as part of policy that favours the idea of the 'sharing economy'.

* The sharing economy: New York deflates Airbnb, *The Economist*, 29 October 2016 (provided by Anup Karath Nair)
** https://www.bbc.co.uk/news/business-55250359 [accessed 22 March 2021]

Table 7.1
Inherent contradictions

Agents	Contested legitimacy	Social structure
Individual interpretations	Cognitive legitimacy: to whom does it make sense?	Common definitions of the situation
Individual moral obligations	Normative legitimacy: whose rules?	Shared norms and values
Individual pragmatic considerations	Pragmatic legitimacy: what does it achieve for whom?	Distribution of material, financial, and organizational resources

Similarly, within organizations – and particularly in call centres – it is not uncommon that employees are told to provide excellent customer service and that the customer is always right. Simultaneously, employees are told to not incur additional costs and to stay within a limited set of instructions that they know will turn customers off. Individuals, organizations, and subcultures all can have different ideas about what is considered to be legitimate and be at odds with the overarching social structure (see Table 7.1). Most of the time, these contradictions are repaired or concealed (Lawrence & Suddaby, 2006), yet every latent contradiction can manifest itself in open controversy if somebody is inspired for some reason to take on the existing social order.

Many innovations and the rise and fall of markets and industries as a whole are found to be the consequence of institutional entrepreneurship (e.g. Garud, Jain, & Kumaraswamy, 2002; Hargadon & Douglas, 2001; Haveman & Rao, 1997; Leblebici, Salancik, Copay, & King, 1991; Lounsbury, 2001; Munir & Phillips, 2005; Sminia, 2003). Because institutional entrepreneurship takes on the existing social structure, a struggle between the existing order and the new initiative ensues. The course and outcome of such a struggle is impossible to predict, let alone control. Despite popular myth, these studies do not feature trailblazing organizations or heroic entrepreneurs who take charge and create a transformation from scratch. It appears to be safer to assume that such a process takes on the form of a concurrence of events coming together over time. The activities of the institutional entrepreneur and the innovating organization add events to the process, but they are not able to wield so much control that they can direct the process at will. Nor can those who are eager to preserve the situation as it is.

Pettigrew (1987, p. 659) provides a very apt description of how such a process takes shape inside an organization. He describes it as "politics as the management of meaning"; as a process in which "the content of strategic change is thus ultimately a product of a legitimation process shaped by political /cultural considerations, though often expressed in rational /analytical terms". The top management group of an organization meets, interacts, and discusses current issues all the time. The organizational paradigm (Johnson, 1987) and the dominant logic (Prahalad & Bettis, 1986) play their part. Many of the encounters effectively confirm existing beliefs about the state of affairs. Yet by careful staged but defiant behaviour, justified by different interpretations of the situation, maybe seizing the moment when difficult problems or full-blown crises manifest themselves,

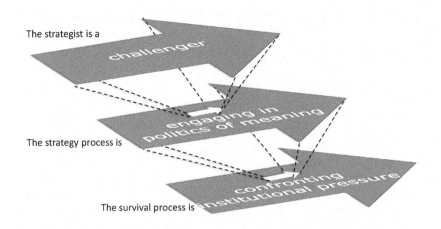

The strategist is a *challenger*

The strategy process is *engaging in politics of meaning*

The survival process is *confronting institutional pressure*

Figure 7.3
The process logic
for institutional
entrepreneurship

alternative interpretations can gain prominence. New ways of doing things are tried out and – if remotely possible – are described as successful to underline the necessity and validity of change.

The actual language that is used to justify the fundamental change features much of the vocabulary of marketing-inspired strategic thinking, the industrial organization approach, the resource-based view, and shareholder value. But there is another layer to what is discussed. The 'dominant logic' is challenged, debunked and eventually replaced with a new point of view. Burgelman (1983), Johnson (1987), Greenwood and Hinings (1988), Pettigrew (1985) and Sminia (2005) have provided these kinds of accounts of the strategy process. In effect, the strategy process is stratified (Sminia & de Rond, 2012). At the surface, managers discuss problems and solutions using the language and logics of the competitive advantage-based approaches. Simultaneously, they challenge or conform to the social structure and the organizational paradigm that sits underneath this surface layer, and which determines what is legitimate and what is not.

Illustration 7.3 Politics of meaning as a language game

Imagine that a scientific investigation has been commissioned to assess how dangerous the manufacture of the chemical compound metadioxine is. The resulting report will be used to decide whether a new chemical plant, where this compound will be processed, will get the go ahead. Now look at these two alternative conclusions:

"On the existing evidence, the committee can see no reason not to proceed".

"While the committee feels that there is no reason not to proceed on the existing evidence, it must be emphasized that metadioxine is a comparatively recent compound. It would be irresponsible to deny that after further research, its manufacture might be proved to be associated with health risks".

Both conclusions confirm that metadioxine is not found to be dangerous. However, the first conclusion means that those who have to decide whether the plant will be constructed can use the report to give it the 'go ahead'. The second conclusion allows the same people to say 'no'. Substantially, both conclusions are true. There meaning, however, indicates something completely opposite.

These lines are part of the British television comedy *Yes Minister*. This particular episode was first broadcast on 16 March 1981. Metadioxine is a fictional compound, and so is the chemical plant, as well as the problem. It was part of a plotline in which the Minister and his chief civil servant disagreed on whether the new plant should get ministerial approval. The Minister was against it. He persuaded the writer of the report to go with the second conclusion. This then allowed the Minister to disapprove the plans.

Of course, this is all fictional, but it does illustrate the effect the use of language has on decision-making. This is how 'management as the politics of meaning' plays out. It has been observed that many strategists play similar language games (Samra-Fredericks, 2003; Sminia, 2005).

Many studies into institutional entrepreneurship describe a very similar process, but now at the level of the organizational field (Garud et al., 2002; Hargadon & Douglas, 2001; Haveman & Rao, 1997; Leblebici et al., 1991; Lounsbury, 2001; Munir & Phillips, 2005; Sminia, 2003). Again, there is a dominant way of how things are done, underpinned by a social structure, and many organizations subscribe to this and are able to survive and be successful. Yet, on a regular basis, initiatives are taken that aim to upset the current state of affairs and to leverage in some kind of change – described by the initiators in terms of innovation and improvement. A struggle ensues between challengers and incumbents, and sometimes a new order will replace the old one. And again, this process features power, politics, ambiguity, contradiction, and controversy.

So, the environmental survival process for institutional entrepreneurship is very much a process of confronting the existing institutional order in an attempt to change an organizational field's social structure to benefit the challenger organization (see Figure 7.3). Within the organization, such a process takes on the form of politics of meaning. The strategist has an extremely difficult job of not only challenging the current state of affairs of how things are done and interpreted within the organization, but also to simultaneously preserve the organization as a purposeful actor; able to take part in the struggle that takes place at the level of the organizational field (Sminia & de Rond, 2012).

Illustration 7.4 Continuity and change in the US radio broadcasting industry

The Leblebici et al. (1991) investigation of the US radio broadcasting industry between 1920 and 1965 found that there were three distinct eras. Each of these eras lasted only for about 15 years; although each era, as the industry name implies, featured the broadcasting of radio programmes. The way in which this was done and how you made money was completely different between eras, with different activities and interaction patterns. Consequently, there were specific players that dominated each era, both in terms of the kind of businesses that were successful as well as with regard to the kind of jobs that people did working for these businesses. While there was a lot of continuity during each era, the industry was also in a continuous state of transition towards the next era.

Radio equipment manufacturers dominated the first era (1920–1934). Equipment manufacturers only made radio parts and held patents on specific components. At first, if you wanted a radio receiver or transmitter, you had to get parts from different manufacturers and put them together yourself. These manufacturers initially were competing on the basis of rival technologies, but also accusing each other of patent breaches. Creating a patent pool among these radio manufacturers solved this. Also, the Radio Corporation of America (RCA) was established by the main manufactures to build and sell complete radio sets using parts supplied by its constituents. To entice people to buy radio sets, these manufacturers and also some large retailers started to provide radio broadcasts. This gave people something to listen to. However, at some point, the market for radio sets became saturated. The manufacturers became less keen to provide radio broadcasts for free as programming's effectiveness for selling radio sets waned.

The impetus for solving this problem came from the periphery of society. A number of "sellers of questionable commodities" (Leblebici et al., 1991, p. 345) like hair loss remedies and fortune telling, and who were shunned by regular advertising media, had started to use radio broadcasts to advertise their wares. This seed of an idea developed into a mainstream business when it was picked up that advertisers could cover the costs of producing radio shows and even allow for a profit for a radio broadcasting station. This model became the basis of the second era (1935–1950), dominated by radio networks like NBC, CBS, and ABC. It allowed the also emerging fast moving consumer products firms to develop their brands on a nationwide scale. Branding products on that scale was a new phenomenon at the time, as well. These firms would sponsor shows, and in return, the broadcast would be named after them (the 'Palmolive Hour', the 'Lucky Strike Hour'). One problem was that radio transmitters only have limited reach. To get nationwide coverage, local radio stations were linked up and became part of these radio networks. Consequently, the networks became the key players in the industry. Alongside this, an advertising industry emerged which specialized in producing the sponsored radio shows that were being broadcast by the radio networks.

The competition for listening figures, and therefore value for advertisers, made the radio shows ever more extravagant and increasingly expensive to make. This was another reason for radio stations to band together. It also left out stations that missed out on becoming a network member. They could not afford the costs of the mostly live shows and had only limited – local – reach. The alternative they found was to use recorded music, i.e. playing records and to broadcast commercials in between. This cheap alternative brought down their cost base and also made it affordable for local businesses to advertise their wares to local customers. Radio shows became known for their type of music, attracting specific groups of listeners, which represented particular market segments. This allowed advertisers – both national and local – to target their commercial messages to their respective customers. This also saw the emergence of the disc jockey: somebody who developed a radio personality on the basis of his music choice and who also operated the record player and mixing desk himself. This was in sharp contrast with the division of labour between radio technicians and mostly anonymous radio announcers with the radio networks. With local radio stations now outcompeting the networks, the third era (1951–1965) of the independent radio stations had come into being. It also spawned another industry – and even, to some extent, another category of people. The music industry and the radio broadcasting industry had become entwined in producing and selling pop music to teenagers.

The performance logic of institutional theory

Looking at it from the perspective of isomorphism and the passive stance with regard to the institutional pressures an organization has to deal with, institutional theory covers the three ingredients of strategic management – strategy, environment, and organization – in a very specific manner (see Figure 7.4). The environment is an organizational field of regular and institutionalized interaction patterns underpinned by a social structure. The organization itself exists by way of the continuity in interaction patterns among the organization members as well as the interactions it has with the many participants in the organizational field, all in accordance with the field's social structure. Isomorphism implies that the organization conforms to the institutional pressures put upon it and that it maintains its legitimacy in this way.

There are, in fact three, different ways or strategies that an organization can conform to institutional pressures. There is a choice between acquiescence, compromise, and avoidance (Oliver, 1991). The option of acquiescence means that the organization fully accedes to the social structure. It subscribes to the 'normative systems and cognitive understandings' as well as the associated 'taken-for-granted repetitive social behaviours', which are prescribed by the social structure, by acting accordingly. The option of compromise comes into play when fully acceding to the institutional pressures results in an unworkable situation or when there are reasons to object to the standards put upon the organization. As was said earlier, institutional pressures often contradict each other. By compromising, the organization tries to find a mutually acceptable middle ground. The option of avoidance means that the organization conceals its non-conformity by only appearing to adhere to the standards. This is sometimes an unavoidable situation when a middle ground between contradicting expectations cannot be found, yet it can mean that the organization enters the realm of illegality (e.g. Sminia, 2011).

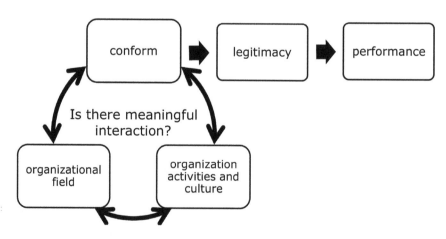

Figure 7.4
Institutional theory:
isomorphism

The overall requirement for the organization to remain viable is expressed by the question about meaningful interaction (see Figure 7.4). Interactions are meaningful when they comply with the social structure. The institutional demands from the organizational field, the organization's activities and associated culture, and the ways in which the organization conforms – all three have to combine so that the organization's activities as a part of the many interaction processes that the organization relies on to continue to exist, and are meaningful for all interaction partners. This refers to participants inside as well as outside the organization. As soon as this breaks down, the organization is in danger of becoming irrelevant. When the interactions the organization is involved in lose their meaning, they stop happening – and as a consequence, the viability of the organization is at stake.

The same requirement of meaningful interaction applies to the realm of institutional entrepreneurship, as well. The difference is that because of the change initiative that is at the heart of this, the meaning of a range of interactions has become ambiguous. Some pragmatic claims, definitions of the situation, or norms and values underpinning meaningful interactions are disputed. As a consequence, existing interaction patterns are put into disarray and have to institutionalize again. In effect, part of the social structure is suspended and has lost its power to make participants conform. With institutional entrepreneurship triggering controversy, the organization brings this on itself as a consequence of a strategy of transformation and of willingly challenging the status quo (see Figure 7.5). This is the effect of Oliver's (1991) more active strategies of defiance or of manipulation, as described earlier.

As was said, research evidence suggests that it is more or less impossible for an initiator to control the full process of institutional change and to direct it towards the most favourable outcome. Nevertheless, an organization that has initiated

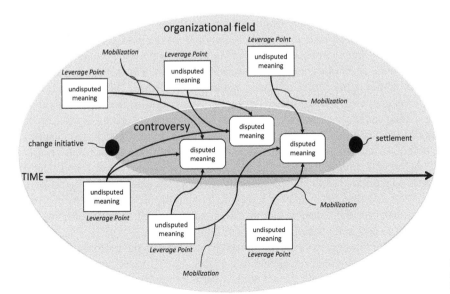

Figure 7.5
A controversy and
leverage points

change should at least try to affect the course the process takes. Sminia's (2003) analysis of how such an initiative failed horribly provides a few pointers as to what an organization can do.

The first thing to realize is that most of the time, a change initiative only affects part of the social structure that characterizes the organizational field. Neither all interaction patterns, nor the complete social structure, get in disarray – only the part that is directly affected by the change initiative. When a change initiative triggers a controversy, only specific interaction patterns and associated normative systems, cognitive understandings, and resource allocations are in disarray (see Figure 7.5). The meanings of the interactions affected directly by the controversy have become ambiguous and need to be resettled. There is effectively a dispute about what the interactions that are disputed achieve for whom, about how the situation is defined and what norms and values apply. Also, the resource exchange tends to be interrupted. In short, these interaction patterns have to regain meaning again.

The controversy is over when a settlement has been reached. A controversy thus only covers a limited part of the field's social structure referring to a specific subset of interactions. The process from start to resolution takes shape as a sequence of events over time, from initially being triggered by a change initiative to eventually being settled.

To affect the direction the controversy process will take and to shape the eventual settlement, the organization can mobilize leverage points. Mobilizations of leverage points are specific events that aim to move the process forward towards a specific settlement. A leverage point is a particular norm or value, a definition of the situation, a pragmatic claim, and quite often a combination of these three, which are not disputed, that have retained their meaning and that vindicate particular interactions. Leverage points are available in that part of the organizational field's social structure that is not disputed. These norms, values, interpretations, and exchanges are still legitimate. These leverage points are fixed points of reference indicating the normative, cognitive, or pragmatic legitimacy by which the situation gets settled again (Suchman, 1995).

In effect, leverage points exist because only part of the field's social structure is disputed. Many interactions are still meaningful and supported by common norms, values, beliefs, definitions, and pragmatic considerations. These meanings can be drawn on to direct the course of events and settle the dispute. Whether and how these leverage points are mobilized during the controversy process determines the eventual settlement that will be reached. The extent to which an organization is capable to come together and muster the skill to act in a unified way – despite the politics of meaning that take place inside the organization – determines how well the organization is able to affect the course of the change process and steer it towards a favourable settlement. Especially as various organizations who all have interest to settle the controversy in a way favourable for them, with some of them wanting to restore the situation to how it was, will all mobilize leverage points in opposition to and in favour of the change initiative.

This take on the process of institutional change informs the performance logic of institutional entrepreneurship (see Figure 7.6). The environment, or more specifically the organizational field, consists of leverage points that can be

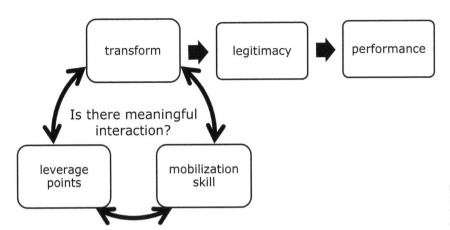

Figure 7.6
Institutional
theory: institutional
entrepreneurship

mobilized to direct the course of the controversy process towards a particular settlement. The organization should have mobilization skill to be able to identify and utilize these leverage points. It should be able to act in a coordinated and concerted manner to time and mobilize the available leverage points as the process progresses. This, then, supports the organization's transformation strategy to generate new legitimacy. The question of meaningful interaction is still relevant, as this is the eventual benchmark by which a settlement of a controversy is evaluated.

Illustration 7.5 Controversies with Sport7

In 1996, the Dutch football association (KNVB) sold the broadcasting rights for domestic league matches and matches involving the Dutch national team to a consortium of investors – of which it also was a founding member – for 900 million guilders. This consortium wanted to use these rights as a basis for establishing a dedicated sports TV channel under the name of Sport7. This move created three controversies (Sminia, 2003).

One of the controversies was triggered primarily between Sport7 and the Dutch public broadcaster NOS, which had broadcasted football matches previously, but it was not confined to these two. Football represents high viewing figures, so there was much at stake. The NOS was outraged, as it felt cheated by the KNVB with which they had been negotiating – while simultaneously and secretly, the KNVB was a member of a consortium that was trying to outbid the NOS. The Dutch viewing public was unhappy, as well. Sport7 was to become a cable station and wanted to charge a monthly fee of two guilders per cable connection. Before that, The Netherlands got their football for free on the public free-to-air NOS channels. Dutch football fans felt that football had been stolen from them. There were also principles of journalistic freedom at stake, with Sport7 wanting to ban filming at matches to safeguard exclusivity. TV journalists maintained that football is of national interest, which allows them to film matches and broadcast video as a news item.

A second controversy was triggered within the KNVB about the proceeds of the broadcasting rights contract. The KNVB wanted to distribute the money among the various professional and amateur leagues to boost football at every level. The top clubs in the Dutch premier league reckoned that it would get much more money by selling the broadcasting rights of matches itself, especially because that would mean it did not have to share with the lower-league clubs.

A third controversy concerned the cable companies. Charging households for individual channels turned their business model upside down. Before the Sport7 deal, cable companies made their money by charging commercial TV channels a transmission fee instead of charging viewers a connection fee. However, one of the larger cable companies was a member of the Sport7 consortium and was keen to transform the cable companies' business model.

All three controversies played out simultaneously. All parties involved drew on a range of leverage points to settle them in the way they wanted. The NOS went to court to challenge the deal, drawing on legislation that was not disputed. They also appealed to the government, which became involved to safeguard the principle of journalistic freedom. The top clubs drew on the KNVB bylaws to argue that the football association did not have the right to sell broadcasting rights on their behalf. The cable companies split in favour of or opposition to changing their business model. Sport7 contested the various legal challenges and tried to win over the Dutch viewers and the cable companies by promising that football coverage on TV would be raised to unprecedented levels of quantity and quality, mobilizing the existing and undisputed wants and needs regarding quantity and quality among the Dutch viewing public. Sport7 also approached other minor sports and offered increased coverage to them.

When Sport7 started with its first broadcasts, it had (temporarily) withdrawn the cable companies' requirement to charge 2 guilders to boost initial viewing figures. With the cable companies wavering, only a minority of viewers were able to watch Sport7. The first broadcasts were also mired by technical glitches, putting the promise of quality under pressure. Many viewers boycotted Sport7 and refused to watch. This affected the keenness of advertisers, another important source of income. The legal challenges led to compromises that meant that Sport7 did not have total exclusivity in covering football on TV. Four months after the first Sport7 broadcast, the consortium pulled the plug, as the numbers did not add up anymore.

Additional features

The notion of organizational culture is closely related to the concepts of vision and visionary leadership. A vision is "a mental image of a desirable future state" (Bennis & Nanus, 1985, p. 86). The visionary leader is the person who articulates this 'desirable future state' and who is expected to inspire others to follow the leader. In essence, a vision is a definition of a future situation to which the organization is supposed to aspire. It may well include statements of desirable norms and values the organization seeks to emulate and resource gains it might accumulate. Montgomery (2008) argues that strategists should formulate a vision for the organization. The claim is that this vision and the charisma of the leader are powerful enough to initiate and effectuate the strategic change an organization might need. In effect, transformational leadership aims to generate the fundamental change that within organizations often is referred to as cultural change. For realizing such change, the research on strategic change introduced earlier would suggest that charisma at least needs to be matched with the skill to play politics of meaning (Pettigrew, 1985).

Apart from organizational culture and belief systems propelling an organization into the future, it is also observed that they can hold organizations back. This is referred to in terms of 'strategic myopia' (Lorsch, 1986). It leads to what Johnson (1987) labelled as 'strategic drift' (see Figure 7.7). Taking the problem-solving according to the paradigm again – i.e. the strategy process as part of the process logic of isomorphism – over the long term, there have been numerous occasions when the paradigm was challenged by an initial ambiguous problem situation. Yet, most solutions will have reconfirmed the existing paradigm. In due course and in small steps, the organization's interpretations move further and further away from plausible alternative ways of looking at what is going on. Environmental change happens at a faster pace than the incremental changes the organization makes by implementing the solutions it comes up with. Eventually, the gap between the environment and the organization becomes too large and the organization finds itself out of touch. Normally when this has been going on for a while, there will at some point be one issue too many, with an initial minor problem escalating into an existential crisis. The organization then needs a major turnaround to remain viable. Such a turnaround takes on the form of a substantial cultural upheaval or paradigm change (Baden-Fuller & Stopford, 1994; Grinyer, Mayes, & McKiernan,

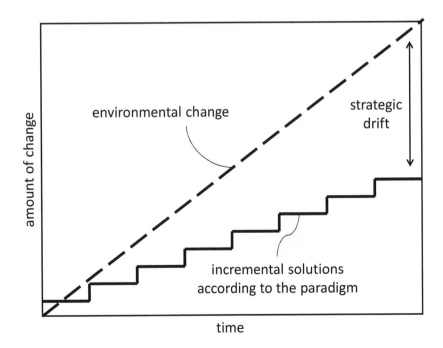

Figure 7.7
Strategic drift

1988; Hinings & Greenwood, 1988; Pettigrew, 1985). Such fundamental change is considered to be 'real' strategic change.

Analogous effects are observed at the level of the environment. A group of similar firms tend to adopt a common outlook on how to conduct their business. This then becomes prescriptive in order to be considered part of this business community. Spender (1989) labels this as the 'industry recipe', while Porac, Thomas, and Baden-Fuller (1989) write about 'cognitive communities' that see themselves as an industry even long after this industry definition has ceased to be a relevant demarcation. Top managers identifying with a cognitive community share an industry recipe that tells them how they should operate. As a consequence, they all operate in the same way, creating the effect of being this industry. Eventually, a whole group of firms can find that they have become obsolete by collectively becoming the victim of strategic drift.

Illustration 7.6 Strategic drift at Marks & Spencer

Marks & Spencer is a well-known chain of department stores that developed out of a trading stand on Leeds market in the 1880s. It had gained an image as one of the most successful British retailing firms ever, but entered into difficulty around 2000–2002 (Mellahi, Jackson, & Sparks, 2002). A century of success was born out of being unorthodox. It had a strict 'buy British' policy, sourcing stock from within the UK. It only carried the one St Michael brand. It did not do marketing or advertising, relying on the trust that people had with the company. It did not accept credit cards, but had a very successful store card, which at some point was the third most used card in the UK after Visa and Mastercard. The department stores were firmly rooted in British town and city centres. On that basis, Marks & Spencer enjoyed solid continuous growth up to 1998, when it plateaued, and slowly declined from 2002 onwards. Profits had plunged from 1998 onwards, as well.

The late 1990s were difficult times for British retailing, and Marks & Spencer responded by focusing on cost control. Simultaneously, a number of specialized competitors like Gap, Zara, Mango, Hennes & Mauritz (all clothing retailers), Lush (soaps and cosmetics), and La Senza (lingerie) appeared, offering value at a price that rivalled or improved upon the Marks & Spencer offerings. There was also the rise of out-of-town shopping malls, benefitting from more efficient logistical arrangements and pulling away trade from town and city centres.

The refusal to take credit cards was reversed in 1999, after repeated pleas from customers and shareholders, although it took nine months to adapt the payment systems. The 'Buy British' policy was abandoned reluctantly. Freeing trade with China and the rising production capacity in Southeast Asia meant that competitors were able to offer higher value for lower prices. However, it turned out to be a public relations disaster, with the national press and the trade unions deriding Marks & Spencer's decision to abandon Britain. Advances in IT also meant that efficient supply chains became widely available to everybody, and Marks & Spencer's advantage in this area eroded away.

Marks & Spencer's long history and the success it had enjoyed had given the company a sense of invincibility. The Marks & Spencer reputation was cherished, and change was interpreted as risky because it could tarnish the brand. Marks & Spencer management was very centralized, with the top management team far removed from the day-to-day realities in the stores. The focus of everybody in the firm was more on satisfying management than on satisfying customers. Middle and lower management numbers – a source of direct experience with customers – had been reduced as part of the cost-cutting measures. Also, the successes of the past had promoted certain individuals into powerful positions who had a vested interest in how things always had been done. Careers were made through a string of internal promotions. By rarely appointing anybody from the outside in middle and senior management positions, new ideas and points of view were kept at bay. By 2002, the once proud company had developed a reputation as a straggler of the High Street, of being out of touch, and offering merchandise that had lost its appeal with the British buying public.

Strategy practice 7.1 SWOT analysis and strategic drift

The purpose of a SWOT analysis is to find out about threats and opportunities in the environment, and about strengths and weaknesses with regard to the firm. But what makes an opportunity an opportunity, a threat a threat, a strength a strength, and a weakness a weakness? What does a SWOT analysis tell you about an organization in a situation of strategic drift?

When the top management team conducts a SWOT analysis, it will reflect the paradigm that characterizes the organization. It does not reveal strengths, weaknesses, opportunities, and threats as such. It reveals how the top team members see their own organization and what it has and has not picked up with regard to environmental change. You could even argue that the analysis does not provide any information about the organization or the environment at all. It is very informative about the people who have conducted the analyses, though. It provides an insight into their perspective on the world around them.

Doing strategic management in an institutionalized world

Although there is less conviction that strategists are capable of safeguarding the future of an organization, the requirement of meaningful interaction in which the organization should be involved within the context of the organizational field provides a possibility to do strategic management. From and institutional theory point of view, strategy is essentially stratified (Sminia & de Rond, 2012). There is a surface layer of purposefully interacting in accordance with the social structure and the paradigm, remaining legitimate and realizing performance. Simultaneously and often unwittingly, these purposeful interactions create an effect of continuity and isomorphism, and of keeping the social structure as it is. This second effect refers to the deeper layer that is inherent in regular interactions. That is the effect of conserving the social order by conforming to and confirmation of the existing social structure. This deeper layer is also the level of fundamental or institutional change, brought about by institutional entrepreneurship. In the case of institutional entrepreneurship, strategy aims to transform the state of play by attempting to alter the social structure. Nevertheless, this stratified understanding of strategy generates only one set of questions. The two questions are:

1 Are there any initiatives which may create controversy and upset the current institutionalized social structure?
2 If there are, what can you do about them?

Answering Question 1: strategic analysis

Strategic analysis from an institutional theory point of view needs to be continuous as a consequence of how the strategy process and the realization of performance are understood to be taking place. People and organizations interact continuously, and through these interactions, they conserve or alter the patterns by which institutions exist. Institutionalization is therefore taking place all the time. The organization is functioning both as and within a continuing process of ongoing interactions, which tend to conform to the social structure of the organizational field, as well as that of the organization itself. However, there is a perpetual possibility for this social order to be challenged, with fundamental change always on the horizon. Strategic analysis, therefore, is something that should take place continuously and instantly, to scout for initiatives that might spawn alternative interactions and meanings, and which eventually change (part of) the existing social structure, or the organization itself might contemplate an institutional entrepreneurship initiative by trying to initiate and realize fundamental change.

Getting up to speed

A strategist should know about the institutionalized interaction patterns and associated social structure. Strategists are supposed to know about the regular interactions inside and outside the organization on which the organization's survival and success depends. If you do not know what the current institutionalized interaction patterns are, how these are steeped in the existing social structure, and how well the organization conforms to them, you need to find out about them. You need to get up to speed first.

To check on conformity, the analysis should focus on whether the organization is sufficiently engaged in meaningful interactions. This requires using the isomorphism performance logic (see Figure 7.4). This logic generates specific questions about the social structure the organization relies on (see Exhibit 7.1). At the level of the organizational field, these concern the way in which the organization relies on norms, values, interpretations, and exchange expectations to provide its goods and services, as well as the interactions in which these goods and services are used. Within the organization, this concerns the interactions by which the goods and services are produced and how separate but interdependent activities are coordinated. All these interactions come with expectations in terms of a social structure of normative systems and cognitive understandings in which these interactions are couched. There is a good chance that some of these expectations contradict each other, and this is what the strategist should know about, as well (Besharov & Smith, 2014). The strategist should also know whether and how these contradictions are being accommodated through acquiescence, compromise, or avoidance (Oliver, 1991), yet the overall effect should maintain the meaningfulness of all the interactions.

Exhibit 7.1 Institutional theory starter questions

- What norms, values, interpretations, and exchange expectations (or social structure) within the organizational field does the organization rely on?

    - This refers to interactions in which the organization's goods and services are used, as well as interactions by which the organization provides its goods and services to those who use them

- On what norms, values, interpretations, and exchange expectations (or social structure) within the organization does the organization rely to produce goods and services?

    - This refers to the actual activities by which the products and services are produced, as well as how separate interdependent activities are coordinated

- Is the organization subjected to possibly contradicting demands and expectations when relying on these norms, values, interpretations, and exchange expectations, either internally (subcultures) or externally? Do these demands manifest themselves through coercion, mimicry, or normative pressure?
- How does the organization deal with the (contradicting) demands: by acquiescence, compromise, or avoidance?

    - These questions allow the strategist to gauge whether the organization is engaged in meaningful interaction that conforms to the prevailing social structure

---

Continuous questioning and analysis

As soon as the strategist is comfortable with knowing what the normal state of affairs is, a situation of continuous questioning needs to arise. The questioning and analysis should focus on at least three different possible developments. First, there is always a possibility of the organization being confronted by a change initiative or trigger event generating a controversy and possible fundamental change of the social structure on which the organization relies. Therefore, whether, when, and why such a trigger could occur is something to keep an eye on. Second, the organization, and its management in particular, should always wonder whether it is becoming subjected to strategic drift. If this starts to creep in, the organization will have difficulty keeping an eye on changes if and when they occur. Third, the organization itself should contemplate whether, when, and why it could and should want to initiate fundamental change and to trigger a controversy.

   With regard to keeping an eye on possible fundamental change, there are bound to be problems because of the inherent contradictions among and sometimes within institutions. Expectations in one institutional sphere can be at odds with expectations in another institutional sphere (Besharov & Smith, 2014). Because an organization has to deal with institutional contradictions within the organizational field, there are always latent issues that can manifest themselves as controversies that need to be settled again. There are also issues for people inside organizations as a consequence of the presence of subcultures, which can flare up because they have to deal with contradicting demands that are made on them. It is up to the strategists to keep track of these tensions, the way they are dealt with, and whether specific contradictions become more or less profound, and whether these inspire people or organizations to come out as an institutional entrepreneur. There is a set of more specific questions that fuels the debate here (see Exhibit 7.2).

To check on the occurrence of strategic drift (Johnson, 1987), the way in which the organization deals with problematic situations that appear on its path should be scrutinized continuously. The strategist – in a way – should be able to step away from the dominant logic (Prahalad & Bettis, 1986) to get a sense for the content of the organizational paradigm. Furthermore, the strategist should investigate how problems are dealt with to find out whether the implemented solutions predominantly confirm the existing organizational paradigm or whether there is significant variability in how problems are understood and dealt with.

Exhibit 7.2 Isomorphism continuous questioning

- What contradictions exist among the various institutional demands within the organizational field in which the organization functions, as well as within the organization itself?
- Which of these contradictions is prone to turning into controversy, and which of these contradictions is becoming less troublesome?

  - These questions allow the strategist to evaluate whether there are concerns with regard to maintaining 'meaningful interaction' and whether the stance toward certain contradictions should be changed

- What is the dominant logic among top management, and how does the organization understand itself – i.e. what is in the organizational paradigm?
- To what extent does the organization solve its problems in accordance with the organizational paradigm?

  - These questions allow the strategist to gauge whether there is any strategic drift

---

There is a different dynamic when it comes to institutional entrepreneurship. Instead of confirming to institutional demands, an organization has initiated, or is maybe contemplating initiating, institutional change within the organizational field, or an initiative by somebody else has stirred up a controversy. Any of these requires the organization to re-establish interaction patterns anew, to recast (part of) the social structure, and to be actively involved in a process of settling controversy (Lawrence, Leca, & Suddaby, 2009). Here, the strategist should focus on whether the controversy that is created as a consequence of a change initiative can be settled in a favourable manner for the organization (see Exhibit 7.3).

Exhibit 7.3 Institutional entrepreneurship continuous questioning

- Which regular interaction patterns, and what part of the social structure within the organizational field, are subjected to controversy? This includes interactions in which the organization's goods and services are used, as well as interactions by which the organization provides its goods and services.
- Who in the organizational field has reason to put up resistance to the change initiative?
- What leverage points in the organizational field are available to mobilize in favour of (by the change initiator) or in opposition to (by opponents) the change initiative?

  - These questions allow the strategist to gauge the chances of a favourable settlement of a controversy

- Which regular interaction patterns, and what part of the organizational culture within the organization, are subject to controversy? This includes the actual activities by which the products and services are produced as well as how separate interdependent activities are coordinated.
- Who in the organization may have reason to put up resistance to the change initiative that triggered the controversy?
- What leverage points in the organization are available to mobilize in favour of the change initiative?

  - These questions allow the strategist to gauge whether the organization can act as a purposeful actor and strive for a favourable settlement of a controversy; these questions are also indicative of and allow a strategist to play politics of meaning

---

At the level of the organizational field, the main focus should be on the leverage points that can be mobilized in favour of or in opposition to the change initiative. The strategist should find out which interaction patterns, as well as what part of the associated social structure, will become involved in the controversy and what will not. This is indicated by the ambiguity that is appearing with particular interaction patterns. Everything that remains outside of the controversy potentially provides leverage points, as this remains undisputed. Depending on what the leverage points are, these can be mobilized in favour of or in opposition to the change initiative. It is also good to know who in the organizational field would be engaged in this mobilization against the initiative and whether there might be any allies who would welcome the change initiative.

A similar evaluation should take place with regard to the inner workings of the organization itself. The purpose of this is to see whether the organization can act as a purposeful actor in the course of settling the controversy in a favourable manner, or whether the organization will become paralyzed as a consequence of internal turmoil. By doing all of this, strategists find out what they are up against and whether there is a fair chance of seeing the initiative through. In effect, the strategist has to engage in politics of meaning (Pettigrew, 1985).

Additionally, these considerations also allow the strategist to find out whether there may be any chance initiatives immanent that threaten the future existence of the organization, and whether the organization will be able to resist them or find a way to benefit from them.

Strategy practice 7.2 A strategy workshop doing scenario planning

Strategic management from an institutional theory point of view recognizes that people can have very different interpretations of the same situation. It also recognizes that there is no way to distinguish right from wrong. The consequence of accepting that people effectively have different interpretations is that a strategist has to reconcile different points of view. A strategist also has to recognize that nobody has a monopoly on the truth, just because a strategist is in charge. This becomes even more of an issue when you consider that strategy has its eye on the future, and any strategic analysis is an interpretation of a possible future state.

Scenario planning as developed by van der Heijden (1996) is a method to have 'conversations' about the future that aim to bring out a range of different interpretations. Scenarios are developed as a kind of 'practise of the mind'. By questioning the 'taken for granted', alternative interpretations are generated. The purpose is not to decide which is the most likely scenario and, as it were, predict the future. It is about developing sensitivity among the participants with regard to the various ways in which the future might be interpreted so as to help their understanding and to become more sophisticated strategists while the organization moves along with the times.

Strategy practice 7.3 Internationalization and country culture

Contradictions can originate from disparities between country cultures (Trompenaars & Hampden-Turner, 2004). What is considered to be pragmatically, morally, and cognitively legitimate in one country will be different in another country. Organizational field social structures can therefore vary across the world. There also is an effect of country culture on organizational culture and subcultures.

This can be especially troublesome for corporate social responsibility. It needs to be decided which set of norms and values is going to serve as a point of reference. For a firm operating in many different countries, will the mission statement be based on a universal declaration of norms and values, or will it be tailored to specific countries? If there is a universal declaration, will it be aligned with the home country culture, the country culture that is the strictest, or the country culture that is the most lenient?

Answering Question 2: problem-solving and taking action

Analogue to the strategic analysis being a continuous activity, taking action is continuous, as well. On the one hand, there is the organizational field, the regular interaction patterns, and the field's social structure. At the level of the organization, there are also regular interaction patterns, with the social structure referred to as the organization's culture. On the other hand, there are contradictions between various institutionalized arrangements and subcultures, continuously threatening to manifest themselves by triggering controversies. Taking action is about dealing with contradicting expectations and with the controversies that will arise.

Overall, these actions can be informed by either one of two strategic stances. One is to conform to the existing institutionalized interaction patterns and to accommodate the contradictions that come with them. The organization and its management then resist attempts at institutional change. They deal with contradictions through acquiescence, compromise, and avoidance (Oliver, 1991). This maintains isomorphism. The other one is to actively try to create institutional change and to go for institutional entrepreneurship. Contradictions then are actively engaged with through defiance and manipulation (Oliver, 1991) (also see under the institutional theory process logic earlier). To conform or to transform are the two basic choices of what a strategist can do.

With regard to how to do this, taking action here effectively means a choice between intervening and not intervening in the course of the organization's strategy process with the intention to also change the course of the organizational survival process. Institutionalization takes place continuously, both within the organization and in the organizational field. It is an unremitting process of continuity and change. If the strategist is happy with the course of events as a consequence of the interaction patterns by which the organization functions and exists, and if the strategist finds that the contradictions do not create any serious problems, then the recommendation is to not to intervene. The strategist basically lets the process run its course.

If the contradictions threaten to run out of hand and the survival and success of the organization is in jeopardy, the strategist should intervene in the organization's strategy process. Through that, the strategist also intervenes in the way the organization functions within the organizational field level survival process. The occurrence of strategic drift is an obvious indication of the need for an intervention. The strategy process takes on the form of politics of meaning with the strategists engaged in challenging existing interaction patterns. An intervention in the organizational field means that a controversy is triggered. Subsequently, leverage points need to be mobilized to direct the outcome towards a favourable settlement.

Strategy practice 7.4 Strategic planning as a culture intervention

Strategic planning is commonly understood as a procedure by which information is processed to formulate a strategic plan. Going through a process of strategic planning is also found to have an effect on the organizational culture (Jarzabkowski & Balogun, 2009). A multi-national company consisting of a diverse array of business units went through a strategic planning exercise. As a consequence, the business units became more unified as a common approach to how they did their strategic management developed. The centre also learned about local concerns and anxieties and how it could serve the business units better. Initial antagonism and misunderstandings made way for a common approach, eventually leading to a more unified and integrated multi-business firm.

Illustration 7.7 SKF from an institutional theory viewpoint

Should SKF* compete on price and put in the lowest bid possible to retain a big US-based client, or should it step away and persist with their high-quality strategy?

Clearly, the US-based client is engaging in some institutional entrepreneurship. The prevalent interaction patterns by which ball bearings are traded in the US involved distributors who negotiate with clients about what quality of ball bearings they want and what the best offer would be. Part of this is the common expectation that every new contract needs to come with a 5% reduction in price. By initiating a reverse auction, this specific interaction pattern is now suspended, and the question is whether this new way of going about the business with an even stronger emphasis on price will become institutionalized.

Underneath this, within many industrial firms in the US, there is another change process going on. The procurement function is gaining more prominence and has been at the heart of many cost-saving drives. By centralizing practices, reducing the number of suppliers, and negotiating harder, big savings are made. Company buyers are put on performance contracts to get the cheapest deals possible. Reverse auctions fit this pattern. The US-based client is under pressure to reduce costs as a consequence of the economic downturn. The question is whether centralized procurement and the emphasis on price will deliver the right quality of supplies, or whether it will be a matter of 'penny-wise and pound-foolish'.

On the basis of these considerations, it is in SKF's interest to resist the change in procurement practices and try to have it reverted back to how it used to be done. SKF should engage in isomorphism, stick with its strategy and use the evidence produced by its marketing and sales activities with quality and durability as leverage points to convince the client of the merits of long-term cost savings sticking by how ball bearings were procured. The importance of quality and durability does not appear to be disputed.

* Value Selling at SKF Service, IMD-5–0751, 2009.

Generating further questions

Institutional theory turns strategic management into a process whereby action and interpretation go hand in hand. The social structure that underpins the regular interaction patterns, and which is also maintained by them, creates a stratified business reality (Sminia, 2005; Sminia & de Rond, 2012). The surface layer refers to purposeful and meaningful interactions that conform to the social structure. The deeper layer concerns these same interactions but refers to the effect that these interactions confirm the social structure and also to the institutional entrepreneurship that changes the social structure, making way for new interaction patterns.

An organization relies on the social structure to be able to function and exist (de Rond & Thietart, 2007). This applies to both the organization culture and the organizational field's social structure. A sufficient degree of shared pragmatic, moral, and cognitive legitimacy is required for meaningful interaction. Without meaningful interaction, the organization ceases to exist. However, at the level of the individual, and also with regard to subcultures, alternative understandings of what is considered to be legitimate exist. Consequently, there are numerous tiers of meaning and many local truths, which account for a myriad of multiple business realities. Given such an essentially subjective world, what basis remains for a strategist to direct an organization into the future? Which business reality forms the foundation for a feasible future?

Alongside these questions, there is also the recognition that contradictions are commonplace and that people across the organization and the organizational field have different interests that are linked to different points of view (Besharov & Smith, 2014; Meyerson & Martin, 1987; Seo & Creed, 2002). It is up to the strategists to manage the organization through the differences and ambiguities, and through the controversies that will result from this and which will appear in regular succession. Change and confusion, indeed, then are the only things strategists can be certain about.

But who are these strategists? If it is just top management, there is a problem. On the one side, top management is expected to provide the visions and interpretations by which the organization moves forward. On the other hand, top management is a liability as they are subjected to the organization's paradigm along with all the other organization members. To acknowledge the relevance of organizational culture implies that the ideal of impartial, unbiased information processing, with top managers arriving at clear objectives and strategies, is nothing but an *idée fixe*: an obsession that lacks solid ground. Top management can get it horribly wrong without realizing it. That is what the concept of strategic drift implies (Johnson, 1988).

Fundamental change – change that involves the organizational field's social structure and the organizational culture – spans both the organization itself and the environment. Many case studies found that the seed corn of change, as well as the persistence of seeing it through, originated from the periphery of the organization (e.g. Burgelman, 1983; Regnér, 2003) and of the environment (e.g. Leblebici et al., 1991). It is found to be far more the consequence of emergent strategy than the result of deliberate strategy.

Processes of fundamental change are found to be longwinded, conflict-ridden, and complicated, both within the realm of the organization itself (e.g. Johnson, 1987; Pettigrew, 1985) and within the realm of the organizational field (Garud et al., 2002 e.g.; Hargadon & Douglas, 2001; Haveman & Rao, 1997; Lounsbury, 2001; Munir & Phillips, 2005; Sminia, 2003). Yet, it appears that no organization can avoid having to deal with or maybe initiating fundamental institutional change. If this process is so perilous, it poses the question whether we expect too much of top management and its ability to lead an organization to success and survival.

Nevertheless, institutional entrepreneurship is an attempt to take the initiative. The strategists – whoever they are – take the destiny of an organization in their own hands. Their vision of the future can be sketched out. Such an initiative means that the strategist makes the organization go against the grain. The organization violates the existing normative systems and understandings. Therefore, there is a question of morality here. On what basis does the strategist think that certain rules – probably mostly informal, but they can be formal – can be set aside?

Summing it up, institutional theory is predominantly subjectivistic in the objectivism vs. subjectivism debate. Nevertheless, there is an objectivist notion in the idea of an institutionalized social structure to which organizations and people submit. This dual position is referred to as the paradox of embedded agency (Lok & Willmott, 2019). This institutionalized social structure can be taken as an objective business reality out there about which information can be gathered while it simultaneously is created, maintained, and changed as a consequence of interactions based on interpretations and localized cultures, and therefore is utterly subjective.

Exhibit 7.4 Institutional theory reflective questions

- What is an institution?
- How does institutionalization happen?
- What is isomorphism, and why is it relevant?
- In the performance logic, how does isomorphism understand the environment, the strategy, and the firm?
- In the isomorphism process logic, how are the environmental survival process and the organizational strategy process understood, and how is a strategist expected to contribute?
- What is institutional entrepreneurship, and why is it relevant?
- In the performance logic, how does institutional entrepreneurship understand the environment, the strategy, and the firm?
- In the institutional entrepreneurship process logic, how are the environmental survival process and the organizational strategy process understood, and how is a strategist expected to contribute?
- In institutional theory, what is the key question that a strategist should always be worried about and serves as the 'starter' question for a strategic analysis?
- What is a controversy, and why is it relevant?
- From an institutional theory point of view, what can a firm do if it has to deal with a strategic issue?
- What is organizational culture, and why is it relevant?
- What is strategic drift, and why is it a problem?
- How do you play politics of meaning?
- What does it mean that strategy is stratified?
- In what way can institutional theory be regarded as objectivistic or subjectivistic?

Case 7.1

Waymo

Waymo was spun out of Google in 2016.[1] The company came forth from Google's 2009 initiative to develop a self-driving car. It claims self-driving cars are safer and improve mobility and quality of life. Over the years, it has been kitting out cars with lidar, radar, and vision systems, and has been testing technology and developing software. Lidar refers to light detection and ranging. In 2015, Waymo introduced the Firefly, a fully autonomous bubble car without a steering wheel; it was retired in 2017. As it has been active in self-driving technology for the longest, Waymo claims its cars have driven the most miles and therefore its software is the most advanced.

The latest development is Waymo One, a self-driving ride-hailing service in Phoenix, Arizona.[2] This service comes with a phone app by which you can summon a car that will take you anywhere in the Phoenix East area. Waymo Via refers to its developmental programme for self-driving trucks. Waymo has started to offer its self-developed lidar equipment to other users. The company acquired $2.25 billion of outside financing in March 2020, leading to speculation that Waymo's parent company Alphabet (Google) was losing interest.[3] Until then, Google had been the only financier of Waymo. Alphabet CFO Ruth Porat has been scaling down on a number of Google's 'moon shot' projects.

A 2019 American Automobile Association (AAA) survey found that 71% of Americans do not want to ride in a self-driving car, up 8 percentage points from the previous year; with that 2018 survey having been held just after the first deadly accident involving a self-driving car.[4] An Uber self-driving taxi killed a woman who crossed the road with her bicycle; the driver of the Uber who was supposed to intervene if the car was making a mistake was charged with negligent homicide.[5] A 2020 survey by PAVE (Partners for Automated Vehicle Education) found that 48% of the 1,200 adults that were asked would "never get in a taxi or ride-share vehicle that was being driven autonomously".[6] PAVE is "a coalition of industry, non-profits and academics with one goal: to inform the public about automated vehicles and their potential so everyone can fully participate in shaping the future of transportation".[7] The AAA, Audi, Cruise, Daimler, Ford, GM, Intel, Liberty Mutual, Lyft, Munich Re, Nvidia, Toyota, Waymo, and Zoox are among its members. The Society for Automotive Engineers recently has defined six levels of car automation. Level 0 is no automation at all. Levels 1–4 distinguish between increasing degrees of self-driving, but the driver is still required to be in control. Level 5 automation has eliminated the need for a driver.

John Rosevaer from the investment website 'The Motley Fool' reckons that self-driving technology has become investible, singling out firms which are active in either developing sensors like lidar, self-driving algorithms, or dedicated chipsets.[8] KPMG developed an 'Automotive Vehicle Readiness Index', using indicators like 'Policy and Legislation', 'Technology/Innovation', 'Infrastructure', and 'Consumer Acceptance'.[9] In the 2018 Top 20, The Netherlands came out on top, Singapore was second, the US third, the UK fifth, the UAE eighth, China sixteenth, and India twentieth. Companies involved in driverless technology are Google through Waymo, GM through Cruise, Intel through Mobileye, lidar company Luminar, Baidu from China, lidar company Velodyne, and Nvidia. Nvidia – in cooperation with German certification company TÜV SÜD – is developing a test protocol for autonomous vehicles: in effect, a driving licence for self-driving cars.[10] Sony started to test self-driving cars in 2020 as a means to develop its sensing and safety technologies.[11] Sony is the leading firm in image sensors for mobile phones.

Cruise revealed its self-driving Origin electric car designed for shared ownership in January 2020. Cruise presents itself as "a self-driving service designed for the cities we love".[12] The Cruise Origin is a vehicle without a steering wheel, rear view mirrors, or pedals, and the seats are facing each other. General Motors acquired a 75% stake in Cruise in 2016, while Honda was set to invest $2.6 billion.[13] While demonstrating the Origin to a journalist, co-founder Kyle Vogt claimed:

> By the time this vehicle goes into production, we think the core software that drives our AVs will be at a superhuman level of performance and safer than the average human driver. And we'll be providing hard empirical evidence to back up that claim before we put people in a car without someone in it.[14]

International treaties like the Vienna Convention on Road Traffic and the Geneva Convention on Road Traffic need to be changed to accommodate cars that do not have drivers. Both require that a driver must be in full control of a car at all times. Similar reformulations need to take place with regard to national traffic legislation. The US National Highway Transportation Safety Administration (NHTSA) declared Waymo's autonomous vehicle control algorithm a 'driver' in February 2016.[15] In 2020, 29 of the 50 US states had enacted legislation that covers autonomous vehicles.[16]

The Advocates for Highway and Auto Safety is a lobby group that opposes the US Self Drive Act, arguing that "deeply flawed legislation fails to ensure driverless cars will deliver on lofty promises of safety, accessibility, sustainability and equity".[17] Florida hopes that its legislation will entice autonomous car manufacturers to choose the state for developing and then manufacturing self-driving technology, yet it imposes a requirement of $1 million insurance coverage per incident on ride-sharing companies like Uber, Lyft, and Waymo.[18] The Insurance Institute for Highway Safety (IIHS) – a research institute financed by the US insurance industry – claimed that self-driving cars would only prevent a third of US vehicle accidents.[19] PAVE quickly countered this claim by saying that the research by IIHS underestimated the capabilities of driverless cars, while the auto industry body Alliance for Automotive Innovation issued the statement saying that reducing accidents by a third would be a major improvement.[20] According to Accenture, the US insurance industry would lose an estimated $25 billion in revenue – 12.5% of the total market.[21] Daimler and reinsurance firm Swiss Re have teamed up to start calculating the risks associated with automated vehicles.[22]

Audi abandoned its plan to offer Level 3 autonomous driving for its 2020 A8 model, which would have made it the first car offered for sale that would feature this ability, because they found their approach to be too costly and too unwieldy.[23] Most of the costs were in the chips and having them operate together. They combined a Nvidia Tegra K1 for traffic signal recognition, pedestrian detection, collision warning, light detection, and lane recognition with an Intel/Mobileye EyeQ3 for image processing, and Altera Cyclone and Infineon Aurix Tricore processors to tie it all together. Tesla has opted to develop its own dedicated chipsets.

Rodney Brooks, an Australian roboticist, explains that the Artificial Intelligence (AI) on which the software relies has a fundamental limitation in that it only learns from data that has already been gathered.[24] The AI that results from this cannot deal with new situations, a 'skill' that sets humans apart from robots. The driverless car is also at the centre of a moral dilemma[25]: in case of an imminent accident, should a car be programmed to save its passengers or save the people it is going to crash into? The US government intends to only lightly regulate AI and its applications, while the approach taken by the EU is to put a stringent set of rules in place, with both arguing that their approach will foster innovation.[26]

Amazon acquired Zoox in 2020 after it had already bought self-driving start-up Aurora Innovation and electric truck manufacturer Rivian.[27] Commentors speculated that Amazon's interests in autonomous vehicles lies with its attempts to develop its own logistics network, although Zoox is mainly involved in developing a robo-taxi to compete with ride-share and food delivery companies Uber and Lyft.[28] Self-driving trucks would present tremendous cost savings, being able to run 24 hours a day, only having to stop for fuelling and loading/unloading, and eliminating the human operator; it would also cut insurance costs, as there would be fewer accidents, but would make thousands of truck drivers redundant.[29]

Notes

1 https://waymo.com [accessed 15 October 2020]
2 https://waymo.com [accessed 15 October 2020]
3 www.forbes.com/sites/samabuelsamid/2020/03/06/waymos-30b . . . the-new-reality-of-automated-driving-is-sinking-in/#a8452fb6f355 [accessed 10 August 2020]
4 www.bloomberg.com/news/articles/2019-03-14/americans-still-fear-self-driving-cars [accessed 13 October 2020]
5 www.forbes.com/sites/bradtempleton/2020/09/16/uber-robocar-safety-driver-changed-with-negligent-homicide/#5ea7fcef1466 [accessed 13 October 2020]
6 https://drivetribe.com/p/it-turns-out-we-still-dont-trust-HlQUs8 . . . ZTpKWw?iid=Ms-k7Hv5SB-h1e4EAvoy_Q&utm_source=organic_apple_news [accessed 10 August 2020]
7 https://pavecampaign.org [accessed 15 October 2020]
8 https://nz.finance.yahoo.com/news/invest-self-driving-car-stocks-203800818.html [accessed 13 October 2020]
9 www.designnews.com/electronics-test/are-we-ready-autonomous-vehicles [accessed 13 October 2020]
10 www.alphr.com/cars/1010023/nvidia-driving-licence-driverless-cars [accessed 13 October 2020]
11 www.reuters.com/article/us-sony-autonomous-idUSKBN1Z60MF [accessed 13 October 2020]
12 www.getcruise.com [accessed 14 October 2020]
13 www.theverge.com/2020/1/21/21075977/cruise-driverless-car-gm-no-steering-wheel-pedals-ev-exclusive-first-look [accessed 14 October 2020]
14 www.theverge.com/2020/1/21/21075977/cruise-driverless-car-gm-no-steering-wheel-pedals-ev-exclusive-first-look [accessed 14 October 2020]
15 www.kitguru.net/channel/generaltech/jon-martindale/u-s-road-agency-declares-googles-autonomous-ai-a-driver/ [accessed 31 December 2016]

16 www.ncsl.org/research/transportation/autonomous-vehicles-self-driving-vehicles-enacted-legislation.aspx [accessed 13 October 2020]

17 https://saferoads.org/2020/09/23/self-drive-act/ [accessed 13 October 2020]

18 www.auto123.com/en/news/florida-self-driving-cars-loi-lyft-uber-waymo/66009/ [accessed 13 October 2020]

19 www.iihs.org/news/detail/self-driving-vehicles-could-struggle-to-eliminate-most-crashes [accessed 15 October 2020]

20 www.reuters.com/article/us-autos-selfdriving/self-driving . . . prevent-many-more-crashes-than-insurance-study-says-idUSKBN23C2T7 [accessed 10 August 2020]

21 www.freightwaves.com/news/with-driverless-trucks-trucking-would-not-be-the-same [accessed 13 October 2020]

22 https://uk.reuters.com/article/us-daimler-swissre/daimler-swiss-re-launch-mobility-insurance-venture-idUKKBN26X0VV [accessed 13 October 2020]

23 https://electrek.co/2020/05/04/audi-gives-up-plan-for-hands-off-autonomy-for-next-a8/ [accessed 10 August 2020]

24 www.economist.com/technology-quarterly/2020/06/11/driverless-cars-show-the-limits-of-todays-ai [accessed 15 October 2020]

25 www.media.mit.edu/projects/moral-machine/overview/ [accessed 16 October 2020]

26 www.politico.com/news/2020/01/08/self-driving-cars-regulation-096267 [accessed 13 October 2020]

27 www.forbes.com/sites/sabbirrangwala/2020/08/01/amazons-zoox-acquisition-is-lidar-next/#96438177eda8 [accessed 15 October 2020]

28 www.forbes.com/sites/peterlyon/2020/05/30/amazon-could-co . . . ers-as-it-makes-its-move-in-the-self-driving-space/#35a278455f1e [accessed 10 August 2020]

29 www.freightwaves.com/news/with-driverless-trucks-trucking-would-not-be-the-same [accessed 13 October 2020]

CHAPTER 8

Similarities, differences, and underlying assumptions

The six strategy theories in this book represent distinct ways to do strategic management. Nonetheless, it will probably not have gone unnoticed that there are many similarities and parallel arguments among these six theoretical approaches. There are also profound and fundamental differences.

To take the similarities and parallel arguments first, marketing-inspired strategic thinking, the industrial organization approach, and the static resource-based view all assume the strategist to be an unbiased information processor who is engaged in rational decision-making. These strategy theories have primarily been developed to assist the strategist with formulating a strategy and with making strategic decisions. These theories see strategy as a plan (Mintzberg, 1987), and in doing so, these three approaches presume the existence of a business reality out there, about which information can be gathered. This information can then be used to fill out these theoretical frameworks with concrete information about the situation at hand to then draw conclusions. The strategy process is seen as an ordered and organized process – referred to as strategic planning – that is largely the preserve of top management.

Some concepts and variables are common across these three strategy theories, as well. Obviously, all three take the environment to be competitive and centre on competitive advantage as the explanation of firm performance. All three are biased toward for-profit business firms and elaborate performance mostly in financial terms. Both marketing-inspired strategic thinking and the industrial organization approach use the concept of customer value, and both have put forward strategies of differentiation and focus. It is therefore possible to take, for instance, Porter's (1985) value chain and to use it to find out about a firm's key success factors. The other way around can work, as well. For instance, a marketing-inspired notion like the experience curve is useful for underpinning a firm's suitability for Porter's (1980) cost leadership. There are more possibilities for exchanging concepts between these two approaches.

The static resource-based view complements the industrial organization approach, as well as marketing-inspired strategic thinking (Barney, 1991). It provides a means to address the sustainability of a firm's competitive advantage. If the firm's core capabilities underpin the value activities that add the value by which a firm differentiates or focuses itself in an industry, as these capabilities are valuable, rare, inimitable, and non-substitutable, then the firm is on more solid ground. The same holds true for core capabilities backing up the critical or key success factors for a positioning strategy in a product market. It means that the firm has a 'sustainable' competitive advantage.

Agency theory and shareholder value build on marketing-inspired strategic thinking, the industrial organization approach, and the static resource-based view. The demand for shareholder value incorporates an expectation that managers – as agents for the shareholders – are incentivized through remuneration packages to be these rational decision-makers and to execute an ordered and organized strategic planning process to realize financial performance on behalf of the shareholders (Rappaport, 1986).

Yet, there are also profound differences. One important contrast between marketing and industrial organization is the difference between competing for market share and competing to appropriate value. From a marketing point of view, being a low-price/no-frills competitor in a product market, then, is a feasible strategy. Yet Porter (1980) vehemently warns against competing on price because it ends up in a situation of cutthroat competition. It makes everybody in the ecosystem (apart from the customers) worse off. Additionally, to Porter (1980, 1985), the only feasible strategies are his generic strategies. There is no middle way, as you will get stuck in the middle. In marketing-inspired strategic thinking, this is not necessarily the case. Any strategy based on balancing out price with perceived customer value is feasible, as long as there is a market (segment) for it.

Another contrast between marketing and industrial organization refers back to where and for what firms compete. From a marketing point of view, competition takes place in a product market. It takes place among competitors, and they compete for market share. From a modern industrial organization point of view, competition takes place within an ecosystem. A focal firm not only competes with rival competitors but also with complementors, suppliers, buyers, substitutes, and potential entrants in a value system. The competition is not about market share, but about who ends up with most of the money that a product or service sells for: i.e. value appropriation. Furthermore, in an ecosystem, the same firms with which you compete to appropriate value also can be the firms with which you have to cooperate to realize the product/service bundle that represents the sophisticated solution that end users value. Hence, the survival process is one of coopetition (Brandenburger & Nalebuff, 1996). Although both approaches draw on an understanding of strategy as position here (Mintzberg, 1987), the positioning takes place in different conceptualizations of the environment: i.e., product markets or ecosystems.

Although the dynamic resource-based view and the static resource-based view share the same roots in that the reasoning starts with the firm's resource base, they end up at diametrically opposed conclusions. This is not just about the tension inherent in the ambidexterity of pursuing a strategy of exploiting the current core capabilities while simultaneously exploring for future core capabilities (O'Reilly III & Tushman, 2004). More fundamentally, this is a tension between a mode of strategic thinking, which presumes continuity and predictability, on the one hand, and change and uncertainty, on the other hand.

The static resource-based view, alongside marketing-inspired strategic thinking and the industrial organization approach, are essentially static in the sense that they provide snapshots of situations (Pettigrew, Thomas, & Whittington, 2002; Porter, 1991; Whipp, 1996). They do not handle fundamental change. Fundamental change – among other things – refers to the emergence and disappearance of complete ecosystems or product markets. These approaches can cope with changes that follow a regular pattern like a life cycle, but they do not offer the strategist much understanding as to how fundamental change happens, and, as a consequence, how this should be managed.

The dynamic resource-based view takes change as its point of departure. It urges the strategist to follow suit. It offers concepts like dynamic capabilities and core competence. The recommendation is that strategists should strive for these kinds of capabilities. These concepts resonate perhaps best with an understanding of strategy as a perspective (Mintzberg, 1987), urging strategists to have the vision and creativity to stretch towards an imagined future and to translate core competences into new businesses.

Unfortunately, as it stands now, the dynamic resource-based view also does not incorporate an account of how fundamental change happens, leaving the strategist empty-handed as to how to manage change (Arend & Bromiley, 2009; Helfat & Peteraf, 2009; Kraaijenbrink et al., 2010). Nor does the dynamic resource-based view provide much indication on how to develop dynamic capability or core competence. Interestingly, the resource-based view puts in an argument for cooperation and strategic alliances in order for a firm to work on its resource base, denoting here as well that strategy is not exclusively about competition (Das & Teng, 2000).

Another sharp contrast can be found between shareholder value and the stakeholder approach (Freeman & Reed, 1983). Agency theory and shareholder value urge the strategist to manage the firm for the purpose of providing shareholders with maximum return on investment. Firm performance is ultimately understood in those terms. The stakeholder approach sees the shareholder as only one among many different stakeholders, who all expect different performances from the firm. This is more about arriving at a suitable compromise to remain legitimate. With this – and this is an important realization to make – comes a recognition that financial performance is not the only measure by which the success of an organization can be assessed. Different stakeholders have different stakes in an organization, and each stakeholder will see performance in terms of how well the organization is catering to their specific interests.

There are conceptual parallels between the stakeholder approach and institutional theory. They both centre on legitimacy. They both recognize issues of perception, interpretation, conflict, contradiction, and politics. They both are more focused on what is eventually realized than on what should be intended. Both approaches fit with an understanding of strategy as a realized pattern in an organization's activities (Mintzberg, 1987).

The stakeholder approach concentrates on the people or actors – either as individuals or collectives – who have a stake in a focal organization (Freeman, 1984). The emphasis is put on the conflicts of interest between people and on the politics which ensues. This is amplified by differences in perceptions as a consequence of (management) cognition and the way in which mental maps affect how people perceive the world around them differently (Schwenk, 1984). Striving for sufficient consensus among a dominant coalition about the overall purpose of the organization while recognizing that this requires constant renegotiation, then, is what it is all about. Continuously reaching new compromises is the strategy pattern that is realized over time, while smart political manoeuvring fits the ploy definition of strategy (Mintzberg, 1987).

Institutional theory concentrates on the activities by which an organization exists (Greenwood et al., 2008). Institutionalization takes place as a mutual reinforcing dynamic. People interact in a particular way, and these interactions in turn confirm that this is the proper way in which these interactions should take place, compelling them to keep on interacting in the way that they do and making them the actors that they are. In this way, a social structure – which takes on an existence of its own and compels people to keep on interacting in the way that they do – is generated and maintained. This effect is another way in which strategy as pattern appears (Mintzberg, 1987), but now tied into the social structure. Within the organization, the social structure is normally referred to as the organizational culture (Schein, 1985). In the environment, the organizational field has a social structure, as well. Albeit, there are contradictions within and among these institutionalized arrangements, fuelling controversy and possible fundamental change.

Within institutional theory, institutional entrepreneurship has been put forward as an attempt to understand how the process of fundamental change is brought about (DiMaggio, 1988). In that sense, it is a step ahead of the dynamic resource-based view. Institutional entrepreneurship and fundamental change is found to be a struggle (Seo & Creed, 2002), requiring strategists to engage in the politics of meaning (Pettigrew, 1985). Albeit, the outcome is unclear while the process of changing is mired with ambiguity. Yet, a pattern will be realized, with various participants embarking on ploys by mobilizing leverage points to attempt to move the process towards the outcomes they would like to achieve (Mintzberg, 1987).

In contrast to the theoretical approaches that are centred on competitive advantage, for which predominant counsel is about being different to out-compete competitors, institutional theory's concept of isomorphism urges the strategist to not strain too much from what is expected, in order to maintain legitimacy. By being very similar to your competitors, your business is recognized as cognitively, morally, and pragmatically legitimate.

Isomorphism, as well as the stakeholder approach, envisions organizations as progressing in a more logical, incremental fashion (Johnson, 1987; Quinn, 1980). Their starting point is continuity. Within the stakeholder approach, who the stakeholders are and what interests they have is not subject to that much change. What does change is their relative salience as they juggle for attention and form coalitions, with the organization urged to adapt by reprioritization and renegotiation. In a similar vein, isomorphism is about continuity and about conforming to a template that perpetuates the existing state of affairs.

Both in the stakeholder approach and in institutional theory, the strategy process and the role of the strategist are less clear-cut. What is clear and contrary to marketing-inspired strategic thinking, the industrial organization approach, and the static resource-based view is that this idea of the strategist/top manager as an unbiased and impartial information processor and rational decision-maker is dispensed with.

In the stakeholder approach, the strategist becomes a political animal engaged in negotiations, even when engaged in strategic planning. Strategists can just as well work on behalf of their own interests as on behalf of the interests of the organization as a whole. In institutional theory, strategists become managers of meaning and maybe visionaries, engaged in interpretation and sense-giving (Gioia & Chittipeddi, 1991). The concepts of strategic intent and stretch and leverage in the dynamic resource-based view (Hamel & Prahalad, 1994) have a certain resemblance to institutional entrepreneurship (DiMaggio, 1988). Moreover, the concept of core rigidity (Leonard-Barton, 1992) puts a strategist's subjectivity forward as a problem and is comparable to institutional theory's strategic drift (Johnson, 1987). In a way, agency theory also recognizes the political and subjective nature of management by introducing the agency problem into the shareholder-manager relationship (Jensen & Meckling, 1976).

The contrast between strategists as unbiased rational decision-makers, on the one hand, and political animals and managers of meaning or visionary leaders, on the other hand, strikes at the heart of what strategic management is about. Is strategic management – and the strategy scholarship that supports it – about top managers making the right decisions? Or is strategic management – and the scholarship that supports it – about understanding the limitations of dealing with a process by which an organization propels itself into the future, over which strategists/top managers have limited control? This contrast is demonstrated in a small debate (Mintzberg, Waters, Pettigrew, & Butler, 1990). Mintzberg, Waters, and Pettigrew argue that to represent strategic management as a process of decision-making is wrong, and that the full strategy process by which strategies are realized and by which organizations perform should be imagined as a semi-autonomous process of continuity and change. Butler argues against this, and maintains that you cannot rule out the possibility that a strategy is realized as a consequence of decisions that are made by strategists.

Different basic assumptions underpinning each strategy theory

The various overviews and reviews of the strategy field recognize the existence of contrasting ways of defining the field (e.g. Chaffee, 1985; Eisenhardt & Zbaracki, 1992; Elbanna, 2006; Haselhoff, 1977; Huff & Reger, 1987; Hutzschenreuter & Kleindienst, 2006; Johnson, 1987; Mintzberg, Ahlstrand, & Lampel, 1998; Pettigrew et al., 2002; Sminia, 2009; Whipp, 1996; Whittington, 1993). Mintzberg et al. (1998, p. 2–3) compared strategy scholars to the blind men in the poem by John Godfrey Saxe (1816–1887) about the blind men and the elephant. They all approach the elephant in their own way. The one who touches the skin describes the elephant as 'like a wall'. The one who feels the tusk describes the elephant as 'like a spear'. The blind man who feels the trunk describes the animal as 'like a snake'. The elephant's knee, its ear, and its tail lead to descriptions of 'like a tree', 'like a fan', and 'like a rope', respectively. The poem concludes that each man is partly in the right, but they are also all in the wrong.

This comparison begs the question: if they had the faculty of sight, would they not have seen the elephant for what it is? Can we achieve this with strategic management? If we do the research, will we eventually be able to generate the all-encompassing strategy theory that reveals everything and contains the guaranteed formula by which we can achieve enduring success? Or are we condemned to only be able to feel our way around as these blind men?

The blindness with regard to strategic management and strategy scholarship is due to very fundamental problems to which solutions do not readily exist. Scholarship – and, by implication, management – are bound by having to make basic assumptions. One assumption that was discussed with each strategy theory concerns the nature of reality. Is there an independently existing business reality out there about which information can be gathered, or are there as many realities as there are people thinking about it? Doing empirical research cannot solve this problem. Doing research requires you to settle on a certain research methodology. By choosing a particular methodology, you are making assumptions about the nature of reality.

The same issue exists for strategy theory. It was mentioned earlier in the book that the representation of the strategist as an unbiased rational decision-maker assumes the existence of an objectively business reality out there. The opposite assumption, as befits the strategist as negotiator or manager of meaning – that any description of what is taken to be the business reality is but a mere perception or interpretation, and that there is no way of knowing how accurate this representation is, or if a business reality out there actually exists – makes strategists as subjective in their judgements and decisions as anybody else. Going one way or the other on this is making an assumption about the nature of reality, about the nature of knowledge and information, and about the nature of strategic management (Smircich & Stubbart, 1985). Going one way or the other takes up a position in the philosophical debate between objectivism and subjectivism.

The common textbook approach to strategic management is biased towards the objectivist position in the debate. It puts the emphasis on combining marketing-inspired strategic thinking, the industrial organization approach, the resource-based view, and sometimes agency theory. It envisions strategic management as rational decision-making and as formulation followed by implementation (e.g. Johnson, Whittington, & Scholes, 2011; Thompson, Strickland III, & Gamble, 2013). It requires the strategists to do a full strategic analysis, utilizing and combining the performance logics of aforementioned theoretical approaches – maybe add a stakeholder analysis in, as well, to list the various parties that need to be taken into account – to formulate an intended strategy in the form of a plan; all in the belief there is an independently existing business reality out there, which this strategic plan is going to deal with for the next five years or so.

In the classic textbook approach, notions of organizational politics and organizational culture only come into play during the implementation phase, when it is recognized that a newly formulated strategy may require organizational change. Making this change happen then has to involve elements of negotiation to accommodate the various different interests that may exist, although there is a bias in the implementation literature that the organization and the people within it should submit themselves to top management and their strategic plan. In the same vein, implementation has to involve elements of organization culture simply because people are expected to change their understanding of their activities to fit the bigger plan. As a consequence, the common textbook approach tends to separate out thinkers from do-ers (Lenz & Lyles, 1985). It is therefore not really surprising that the major complaint of people subjected to such a strategy implementation process is the lack of clear communication (Hrebiniak, 2006), with the do-ers expecting to get clear instructions from the thinkers, which apparently the thinkers fail to provide.

However, when the subjectivism that is implied by politics and organizational culture is taken as the starting point for understanding the strategy process, it should not come as a surprise that communication is an issue. From a subjectivist point of view, the notion of 'clear instructions' becomes questionable. People will have different interests, cognitions, and understandings, and live and work in their own individual realities. Whatever the message was that an instruction was meant to convey from the perspective of the top of the organization, it will be interpreted and given meaning to locally, framed by the local subculture (Balogun & Johnson, 2005) or in accordance with somebody's unique and personal mental map (Schwenk, 1984). Most likely, the instruction will be made sense of differently, or does not make sense at all, because that is what will happen from a subjective point of view. And when it does not make sense locally, the cry will go out that there is a lack of clear communication. But can you expect communication to be clear when people in various parts of the organization have different interests, are parts of different subcultures, or are taken to each have their own individual interpretations?

Can we ever see the whole elephant? The answer is no – the reason being that, because of underlying basic assumptions that each strategy theory draws on differently, these can never be put into one overarching framework. Devising such a framework would require that basic assumptions with regard to, for instance, objectivism vs. subjectivism have to be made, which then disqualifies any theoretical approach for becoming part of the framework that does not make the same assumptions. Nonetheless, you can ask yourself what basic assumptions – wittingly or unwittingly – you have been making all the time.

Strategic management as wayfinding

This book puts forward that strategic management essentially is a process of wayfinding. It is a real-time continuous process during which strategists have to keep on asking themselves questions about the organization they are responsible for and to find solutions to whatever problem arises. Depending on the theoretical approach, these are questions about 'fit', 'stretch', 'interests', and 'meaningful interaction'. There never is a definitive answer, yet problems appear endlessly and the wayfinding moves on all the time. One reason for this is strategy scholarship and the different theoretical approaches it has yielded, as has just been explained. The other reason is the only certainty that exists, and that is that things will change; hence, the importance of recognizing that strategic management has to be a continuous and real-time activity.

If anything, this means that any way forward with regard to strategic management and strategy scholarship at best can only be pragmatic. This is the pragmatism of trying to make the best of the situation despite all the limitations. A way to get to grips with this is to distinguish between two types of change: change as variability and fundamental change.

Variability is change that can be captured and understood as variation of quantity or degree, but within, for instance, a product market, an ecosystem, a market for corporate control, or a set of persisting conflicts, or within an organizational field within the confines of an existing social structure. Wayfinding would then be a matter of navigation, of plotting your journey to arrive at an existing destination. You would be able to find your way by mapping out the situation as you find it to then deal with the variability and contingency as it appears. For this, you can use marketing-inspired strategic thinking, the industrial organization approach, the static resource-based view, the stakeholder approach, and isomorphism in institutional theory.

And there is fundamental change. This is the change that sees product markets and ecosystems appear and disappear. It sees conflicts of interest emerge and dissolve. It is about changes of the social structure and the ambiguity and controversy that appears. Wayfinding, then, becomes a matter of pioneering, of being on a journey without having a clear destination. The reason for being on the journey is to just continue travelling. This is where you can use the dynamic resource-based view and institutional entrepreneurship.

Figure 8.1 contrasts navigation with pioneering. Navigation makes a distinction between thinkers at the top of an organization and do-ers lower down in the hierarchy, with thinking happening before action is taken. Pioneering recognizes the value of dialogue and interaction between all members of the organization, with experimentation taking place by embarking on a course of action to then learn from what has been happening. Navigation anticipates possible problems before these arise to be ready with solutions. Pioneering means travelling into the unknown. Problems therefore cannot be anticipated and therefore have to be dealt with if and when these arise. Navigation plots the journey as a linear progression from A to B, which can be managed by checking whether you have reached predefined performance indicators. With pioneering, you do not know where you will end up, so it is impossible to pre-define any points that you have to pass through in advance. Instead, you can keep track of what you have learned along the way and see that as progress. With navigation, management is about enticing and forcing workers to keep going in the direction that has been set out. This is done by giving out instructions and by incentivizing people to act in a predefined way. With pioneering, management happens by people observing each other and reading the situation to get a sense of the direction that the journey is taking.

NAVIGATING	PIONEERING
• Top down	• Interaction
• Thinking before acting	• Acting is thinking
• Solving problems before they arise	• Solving problems when they arise
• Expectation of linear progression over time	• Expectation of a meandering experience in time
• Tracking progress with Key Performance Indicators	• Tracking movement through enhanced understanding
• Implementation through instruction and incentivisation	• Formulation is implementation is formulation

Figure 8.1
Wayfinding

Illustration 8.1 Debating SKF

Should SKF compete on price and put in the lowest bid possible to retain a big US-based client, or should it step away and persist with its high-quality strategy?

This issue has now been analyzed on the basis of all six theoretical approaches. Utilizing marketing-inspired strategic thinking, if there is a change in customer wants and needs, SKF should adapt. The industrial organization approach arrives at a similar conclusion. The buyer force appears to be on the increase and SKF's value proposition appears to not be powerful enough to withstand it. The resource-based view arrives at the opposite conclusion by arguing that SKF should continue to exploit its core capabilities. Giving in would mean that SKF would not be utilizing its competitive advantage. Shareholder value is fragile. From a stakeholder perspective, there is no clear conclusion. Institutional theory indicates SKF should resist the possible change in the organizational field. Where does this leave SKF? How do you weigh it all up?

There is no formula that combines and calculates what the preferred option should be. This is where the ultimate strategy debate comes in. What is the relative merit of each approach in this particular situation?

I know what I would go for. Just now, I would not give in. SKF has built this strong position as a quality supplier of ball bearings, and I would not be willing to give this up that easily. I also prefer to go with the theoretical approach that deals with change the best. There still is a chance that the US-based client sees sense and eventually comes back to preferring quality to price. SKF should go on the offensive and make the client see sense. But that is my judgement call.

This book starts with the statement that strategic management is about making a firm or an organization perform, and about maintaining the organization's or the firm's ability to perform (Sminia & de Rond, 2012). It explains how strategy theory is to be used to evaluate whether the firm or organization will be performing, whether the firm or organization will maintain the ability to perform, and what a strategist can do about it. It does so by introducing process logics and performance logics for six different theoretical approaches. Every one of the strategy theories has its role within this as fuel for the continuous questioning and problem-solving by which strategic managers find their way. Each approach at best contains a, albeit, partial truth. The utilization of a range of strategy theories enhances the quality of wayfinding. Strategy can be taken as a plan, position, ploy, pattern, perspective (Mintzberg, 1987), or even panacea; nonetheless, ultimately it is understood as a relentless and never-ending process. Helping to improve the quality of the questioning and problem-solving is the ultimate purpose of this book.

Case 8.1

De La Rue

In its 2014 annual report, De La Rue reported on the October 2013 opening of its technology centre.[1] The centre was meant to grow the company's patent portfolio in micro-optic technology and especially on security features for use in polymer. In the same annual report, chairman Philip Rogerson announced a 51% growth in underlying profit before tax from £51.3 million to £77.3 million. The use of polymer for banknotes started in Australia in 1996 to make forging more difficult, after the country was hit by a huge counterfeiting scandal.[2] Polymer banknotes also tend to last longer than paper notes.[3]

In February 2018, De La Rue announced selling its paper business to the Epris Fund II hedge fund for £61 million.[4] The two paper mills will continue as Portals De La Rue. De La Rue will retain 10% of the shares. Portals De La Rue will also be De La Rue's preferred supplier, with De La Rue committing to a pre-agreed volume of paper at a pre-agreed price. The rationale for this deal, as De La Rue explains, is to reduce De La Rue's exposure to the paper market while still securing its paper supplies as "the world's leading integrated banknote provider". Half of the paper mill's production was for internal use, while the other half was delivered to external customers. The proceeds of the sale are to be used for developing innovative technology for "the currency, identity and brand protection markets".

Her Majesty's Government announced on 18 April 2018 that the contract for supplying the new blue British passport was awarded to Gemalto. De La Rue had been making the red EU model British passport since 2009.

The 11.5-year contract has been awarded to Gemalto after a rigorous, fair, and open competition. With a contract value of approximately £260 million this will deliver significant savings compared to the £400 million contract awarded in 2009 and provide value for money to the taxpayer.[5]

The expectation is that this will add approximately 70 jobs to the UK workforce.

HM Passport Office would like to take the opportunity to thank all the bidders for their efforts throughout the procurement process, in particular to De La Rue with whom we look forward to continuing to work closely and successfully with for the remainder of the current contract.

Gemalto is headquartered in The Netherlands and has subsequently been acquired by Thales.[6] The new British blue passports are to be produced in Poland.[7]

While announcing the 2019/2020 half-year results, new CEO Clive Vacher announced a profit warning, with De La Rue suspending payment of future dividends. The main reasons given for this were boardroom mutations – with the chairman, the CEO, a senior independent director, and most of the executive team leaving the company – and overcapacity and pressure on price in the currency business. A turnaround plan has been put together. It had already been decided to create two separate divisions: Authentication and Currency. "Authentication is focused on providing physical and digital solutions to authenticate products through the supply chain and to provide tracking of excisable goods to support compliance with government regulations".[8] With Currency, De La Rue aims "to maintain a leading market position in banknote print and security features, and to focus our innovation in developing technology and products customers want to buy".[9] With Currency, it expects to be able to grow its polymer substrate business. Additionally, it intends to cut costs, manage cash better, and provide better management. De La Rue also recently sold its Identity Solutions business for £42 million.[10] This part of the business was responsible for passports and other security documents.

Unite the Union national officer Luisa Bull commented:

> The potentially precarious future of De La Rue, a major UK manufacturing
> company, should be ringing alarm bells across government. Unite will be doing all
> it can in supporting our members at this very difficult time and will continue to
> campaign strongly to keep vital printing work in the UK.[11]

De La Rue is close to breaching its banking covenants.[12] Its net debt should not exceed three times its earnings before interest and taxation. If the company is unable to turn itself around, the lenders can force the company into administration, and have it subsequently declared bankrupt. Demand for banknotes is expected to fall, as the world becomes more and more cashless. Of 2018/2019 De La Rue turnover, 77% came from its currency business. Nevertheless, 84% of transactions are still in cash. Despite the Bank of England's prediction that 91% of transactions will be cashless by 2028, banknote production is still rising.

De La Rue has been in trouble before.[13] In 2011, profits had significantly declined. Then newly appointed CEO Tim Cobbald devised a strategic plan with the intention to cut costs and invest in technology. Chairman Nicholas Brookes at the time blamed De La Rue's problems on issues with paper production, low demand for banknotes, senior management turnover, and a takeover approach. Confident the plan would be successful, De La Rue spent its entire profits on dividend payments the next two consecutive years. However, profitability did not rebound and the company's net debts increased from £31.2 million in 2011 to £111 million in 2015.

Cobbald was replaced by Martin Sutherland, who formulated another strategic plan aiming for "improved profitability, more effective use of capital and reduce the Group's reliance on a small number of material contracts while reducing some of the volatility of the business".[14] De La Rue developed new products like polymer banknotes and biometric passports. The costs that came with these innovations prevented De La Rue from reducing its debts. Sutherland was replaced by Clive Vacher in 2019. De La Rue is not considered to be a sound investment because debt is insufficiently covered by operating cash flow, there is a relatively high proportion of non-cash earnings, and shareholders have seen their investment substantially diluted.[15]

In February 2020, De La Rue reported progress on its now third turnaround plan.[16] The company is reporting a rising demand for banknotes, with a number of new contracts being signed. The cost reductions that are aimed for have been set at £35 million, with £10 million already realized. This would allow De La Rue to tender for currency contracts that it previously would not consider. On top of that, De La Rue sees an increasing interest in its De La Rue Safeguard® polymer technology. Growth in the Authentication division is expected to come from tobacco tax stamp schemes, as countries have to comply with the World Health Organisation Framework on Tobacco Control. De La Rue also aims to "improve efficiencies in terms of its manufacturing footprint, asset utilization and customer programme execution".[17]

On presenting the 2019/2020 annual report, De La Rue announced its intention to close its Gateshead, England plant and also a proposal to raise £100 million in capital to fund the turnaround.[18] Gateshead was one of De La Rue's banknote printing facilities and was also producing the red British passport. As that contract was running out, the company aimed to increase its efficiency by concentrating banknote printing in its other four sites, with the Gateshead machinery being redistributed. This meant that approximately 250 jobs were at risk.[19] Local MP Liz Twist was furious that De La Rue had once again let their brilliant workforce in Gateshead down. Since the loss of the British passport contract two years ago, senior management at De La Rue have promised their workforce in Gateshead more and more work, but in reality, they have handed down more and more job cuts. These are good, skilled jobs, so this is another huge blow for our region, which already suffers the highest unemployment across the country. I have demanded a meeting with the Chief Executive and Chairman of De La Rue, and I will be speaking with Government Ministers and Gateshead Council, to try and prevent further local job losses. I will continue to work with Unite the Union to support their members as the consultation period begins.[20]

Notes

1 De La Rue 2013/14 annual report.
2 https://theconversation.com/proceeds-of-crime-how-polymer-banknotes-were-invented-34642 [accessed 21 October 2020]
3 www.rbnz.govt.nz/notes-and-coins/notes/banknotes-in-circulation/about-polymer [accessed 21 October 2020]
4 www.delarue.com/media-center/de-la-rue-secures-strategic-relationship-for-its-paper-business [accessed 15 September 2020]
5 www.gov.uk/government/news/gemalto-awarded-the-new-passport-contract [accessed 21 October 2020]

6 www.thalesgroup.com/en/group/journalist/press-release/thales-completes-acquisition-gemalto-become-global-leader-digital [accessed 21 October 2020]

7 https://metro.co.uk/2020/02/22/new-brexit-blue-british-passports-actually-made-poland-12283240/ [accessed 21 October 2020]

8 https://cdn2.hubspot.net/hubfs/2752422/De%20La%20Rue%20Feb%202017/PDF/Half%20year%20results%202019/De%20La%20Rue%202019-20%20half%20year%20results%20statement%20FINAL.pdf p. 3 [accessed 21 October 2020]

9 https://cdn2.hubspot.net/hubfs/2752422/De%20La%20Rue%20Feb%202017/PDF/Half%20year%20results%202019/De%20La%20Rue%202019-20%20half%20year%20results%20statement%20FINAL.pdf p. 4 [accessed 21 October 2020]

10 www.delarue.com/media-center/de-la-rue-announces-sale-of-identity-solutions-business [accessed 21 October 2020]

11 www.theguardian.com/business/2019/nov/26/de-la-rue-warns-there-is-significant-doubt-about-its-future?CMP=Share_iOSApp_Other [accessed 11 August 2020]

12 www.forbes.com/sites/francescoppola/2020/01/30/why-is-a-company-that-prints-money-running-out-of-cash/#3c46095b3b5d [accessed 20 October 2020]

13 www.forbes.com/sites/francescoppola/2020/01/30/why-is-a-company-that-prints-money-running-out-of-cash/#3c46095b3b5d [accessed 20 October 2020]

14 www.forbes.com/sites/francescoppola/2020/01/30/why-is-a-company-that-prints-money-running-out-of-cash/#3c46095b3b5d [accessed 20 October 2020]

15 https://simplywall.st/stocks/gb/commercial-services/lse-dlar/de-la-rue-shares?blueprint=1308969&utm_medium=finance_user&utm_campaign=cta&utm_source=yahoo [accessed 20 October 2020]

16 www.delarue.com/media-center/turnaround-and-trading-update [accessed 21 October 2020]

17 www.delarue.com/media-center/turnaround-and-trading-update p. 6 [accessed 21 October 2020]

18 De La Rue 2019/20 annual report

19 www.chroniclelive.co.uk/news/north-east-news/jobs-risk-de-la-rue-18434883 [accessed 21 October 2020]

20 www.chroniclelive.co.uk/news/north-east-news/jobs-risk-de-la-rue-18434883 [accessed 21 October 2020]

References

Abell, D. F. (1980). *Defining the Business: The Starting Point of Strategic Planning*. Englewood Clifs, NJ: Prentice Hall.

Ackermann, F., & Eden, C. (2011). *Making Strategy: Mapping Out Strategic Success* (2nd ed.). London: Sage.

Adner, R., & Kapoor, R. (2010). Value creation in innovation ecosystems: How the structure of technological interdependence affects firm performance in new technology generations. *Strategic Management Journal, 31*(3), 306–333.

Amit, R., & Schoemaker, P. J. H. (1993). Strategic assets and organizational rent. *Strategic Management Journal, 14*, 33–46.

Anderson, E. W., Fornell, C., & Mazvancheryl, S. K. (2004, October). Customer satisfaction and shareholder value. *Journal of Marketing, 68*, 172–185.

Ansoff, H. I. (1965). *Corporate Strategy*. New York: McGraw Hill.

Ansoff, H. I. (1991). Critique of Henry Mintzberg's 'the design school': Reconsidering the basic premises of strategic management'. *Strategic Management Journal, 12*, 449–461.

Ansoff, H. I. (1994). Comment on Henry Mintzberg's rethinking strategic planning. *Long Range Planning, 27*(3), 31–32.

Arend, R. J., & Bromiley, P. (2009). Assessing the dynamic capabilities view: Spare change, everyone? *Strategic Organization, 7*(1), 75–90.

Baden-Fuller, C., & Stopford, J. M. (1994). *Rejuvenating the Mature Business*. Cambridge, MA: Harvard Business School Press.

Bagwell, P. S. (1955). The rivalry and working union of the South Eastern and London, Chatham and Dover Railways. *Journal of Transport History, 2*(2), 33–45.

Balogun, J., & Johnson, G. (2005). From intended strategies to unintended outcomes: The impact of change recipient sensemaking. *Organization Studies, 26*(11), 1573–1601.

Barksdale, H. C., & Harris, C. E. (1982). Portfolio analysis and the product life cycle. *Long Range Planning, 15*(6), 74–83.

Barney, J. (1986). Strategic factor markets: Expectations, luck, and business strategy. *Management Science, 32*(10).

Barney, J. (1991). Firm resources and sustained competitive advantage. *Journal of Management, 17*(1), 99–120.

Bartlett, C. A., & Ghoshal, S. (1992). *Transnational Management: Text, Cases and Readings in Cross-Border Management*. Homewood, IL: Irwin.

Becker, B. E., Huselid, M. A., Pickus, P. S., & Spratt, M. F. (1997). HR as a source of shareholder value: Research and recommendations. *Human Resource Management, 36*(1), 39–47.

Bengtsson, M., & Kock, S. (2000). "Coopetition" in business networks – to cooperate and compete simultaneously. *Industrial Marketing Management, 29*, 411–426.

Bennis, W., & Nanus, B. (1985). *Leaders: The Strategies for Taking Charge*. New York: Harper & Row.

Benson, J. K. (1977). Organizations: A dialectical view. *Administrative Science Quarterly, 22*, 1–21.

Berger, P. L., & Luckmann, T. (1966). *The Social Construction of Reality: A Treatise in the Sociology of Knowledge*. New York: Anchor Books.

Besharov, M. L., & Smith, W. K. (2014). Multiple institutional logics in organizations: Explaining their varied nature and implications. *Academy of Management Journal, 39*(2), 364–381.

Biggadike, E. R. (1981). The contributions of marketing to strategic management. *Academy of Management Review, 6*(4), 621–632.

Birkinshaw, J., Hood, N., & Jonsson, S. (1998). Building firm-specific advantages in multinational corporations: The role of subsidiary initiative. *Strategic Management Journal, 19*, 221–241.

Bottenberg, K., Tuschke, A., & Flickinger, M. (2016). Corporate governance between shareholder and stakeholder orientation: Lessons from Germany. *Journal of Management Inquiry,* Pre-published online. doi:10.1177/1056492616672942

Bower, J. L. (1970). *Managing the Resource Allocation Process*. Cambridge, MA: Harvard University Press.

Brandenburger, A. M., & Nalebuff, B. J. (1996). *Co-opetition: A Revolutionary Mindset that Combines Competition and Cooperation in the Marketplace*. Boston, MA: Harvard Business School Press.

Burgelman, R. A. (1983). A process model on internal corporate venturing in the diversified major firm. *Administrative Science Quarterly, 28*, 223–244.

Burrell, G., & Morgan, G. (1979). *Sociological Paradigms and Organizational Analysis*. London: Heinemann.

Burt, S., Johansson, U., & Thelander, Å. (2011). Standardized marketing strategies in retailing? IKEA's marketing strategies in Sweden, the UK and China. *Journal of Retailing and Consumer Services, 18*, 183–193.

Callon, M. (1998). *The Laws of the Markets*. Oxford: Basil Blackwell.

Campbell, A. (1987). Mission statements. *Long Range Planning, 30*(6), 931–932.

Chaffee, E. E. (1985). Three models of strategy. *Academy of Management Review, 10*(1), 89–98.

Chia, R. C. H., & Holt, R. (2009). *Strategy without Design: The Silent Efficacy of Indirect Action*. New York: Cambridge University Press.

Christensen, C. R., Andrews, K. R., & Bower, J. L. (1973). *Business Policy: Text and Cases* (3rd ed.). Homewood, IL: Richard D Irwin.

Christopher, M., & Ryals, L. (1999). Supply chain strategy: Its impact on shareholder value. *International Journal of Logistics Management, 10*(1), 1–10.

Clarkson, M. B. E. (1995). A stakeholder framework for analyzing and evaluating corporate social performance. *Academy of Management Review, 20*(1), 92–117.

Coase, R. H. (1937). The nature of the firm. *Economica, 4*(16), 386–405.

Cyert, R. L., & March, J. G. (1963). *A Behavioral Theory of the Firm.* Englewood Cliffs, NJ: Prentice Hall.

Das, T. K., & Teng, B.-S. (2000). A resource-based theory of strategic alliances. *Journal of Management, 26*(1), 31–61.

D'Aveni, R. (1994). *Hypercompetition: Managing the Dynamics of Strategic Manoeuvring.* New York: Free Press.

Day, G. S. (1981). Strategic market analysis and definition: An integrated approach. *Strategic Management Journal, 2*, 281–299.

Day, G. S. (1994). The capabilities of market-driven organizations. *Journal of Marketing, 58*, 37–52.

de Rond, M., & Thietart, R.-A. (2007). Choice, chance, and inevitability in strategy. *Strategic Management Journal, 28*, 535–551.

Dierickx, I., & Cool, K. (1989). Asset stock accumulation and sustainability of competitive advantage. *Management Science, 35*(12), 1504–1511.

DiMaggio, P. J. (1988). Interest and agency in institutional theory. In L. Zucker (Ed.), *Institutional Patterns and Organizations* (pp. 3–32). Cambridge, MA: Ballinger.

DiMaggio, P. J., & Powell, W. W. (1983). The iron cage revisited: Institutional isomorphism and collective rationality in organizational fields. *American Sociological Review, 48*(2), 147–160.

Donaldson, T., & Preston, L. E. (1995). The stakeholder theory of the corporation: Concepts, evidence, and implications. *Academy of Management Review, 20*(1), 65–91.

Dutton, J. E., Ashford, S. J., O'Neill, R. M., & Lawrence, K. A. (2001). Moves that matter: Issue selling and organizational change. *Academy of Management Journal, 44*(4), 716–736.

Easterby-Smith, M., Lyles, M., & Peteraf, M. A. (2009). Dynamic capability: Current debates and future directions. *British Journal of Management, 20*, S1–S8.

Eisenhardt, K. M. (1989). Agency theory: An assessment and review. *Academy of Management Review, 14*(1), 57–74.

Eisenhardt, K. M., & Martin, J. A. (2000). Dynamic capabilities: What are they? *Strategic Management Journal, 21*, 1105–1121.

Eisenhardt, K. M., & Zbaracki, M. J. (1992). Strategic decision making. *Strategic Management Journal, 13*, 17–37.

Elbanna, S. (2006). Strategic decision-making: Process perspectives. *International Journal of Management Reviews, 8*(1), 1–20.

Emerson, R. M. (1962). Power-dependence relations. *American Journal of Sociology, 27*(1), 31–41.

Etzioni, A. (1964). *Modern Organizations.* Englewood Cliffs, NJ: Prentice Hall.

Evans, S., & Tourish, D. (2016). Agency theory and performance appraisal: How bad theory damages learning and contributes to bad management practice. *Management Learning,* Pre-published Online. doi:10.1177/1350507616672736

Faulkner, D., & Bowman, C. (1992). Generic strategies and congruent organizational structures: Some suggestions. *European Management Journal, 10*(4), 494–499.

Fine, G. A. (1984). Negotiated orders and organizational cultures. *Annual Review of Sociology, 10*, 239–262.

Fleming, A. I. M., McKinstry, S., & Wallace, K. (2000). The decline and fall of the North British Locomotive Company, 1940–62: Mismanagement or institutional failure? *Business History, 42*(4), 67–90.

Ford, J. D., Ford, L. W., & D'Amelio, A. (2008). Resistence to change: The rest of the story. *Academy of Management Review, 33*(2), 382–377.

Freeman, R. E. (1984). *Strategic Management: A Stakeholder Approach.* Boston, MA: Pitman.

Freeman, R. E., & Reed, D. L. (1983). Stockholders and stakeholders: A new perspective on corporate governance. *California Management Review, 25*(3), 88–106.

Friedman, M. (1970, December 13). The social responsibility of business is to increase its profits. *New York Times Magazine.*

Frooman, J. (1999). Stakeholder influence strategies. *Academy of Management Review, 24*(2), 191–205.

Garud, R., Jain, S., & Kumaraswamy, A. (2002). Institutional entrepreneurship in the sponsorship of common technological standards: The case of Sun Microsystems and Java. *Academy of Management Journal, 45*(1), 196–214.

Gawer, A. (2014). Bridging differing perspectives on technological platforms: Toward an integrative framework. *Research Policy, 43*(7), 1239–1249.

Ghoshal, S. (2005). Bad management theories are destroying good management practices. *Academy of Management Learning & Education, 4*(1), 75–81.

Gioia, D. A., & Chittipeddi, K. (1991). Sensemaking and sensegiving in strategic change direction. *Strategic Management Journal, 12*, 433–448.

Goldblatt, H. (1999, November 8). Cisco's secrets. *Fortune,* 177–184.

Grant, R. M. (1991). The Resource-based theory of competitive advantage: Implications for strategy formulation. *California Management Review, 33*(3), 114–135.

Grant, R. M. (1996). Toward a knowledge-based theory of the firm. *Strategic Management Journal, 17*, 109–122.

Greenwood, R., & Hinings, C. R. (1988). Orgnizational design types, tracks and the dynamics of strategic change. *Organization Studies, 9*(3), 293–316.

Greenwood, R., Oliver, C., Sahlin, K., & Suddaby, R. (2008). Introduction. In R. Greenwood, C. Oliver, K. Sahlin, & R. Suddaby (Eds.), *The SAGE Handbook of Organizational Institutionalism* (pp. 1–46). Los Angeles, CA: Sage.

Grinyer, P. H., Mayes, D., & McKiernan, P. (1988). *Sharpbenders: The Secrets of Unleashing Corporate Potential.* Oxford: Basil Blackwell.

Gruca, T. S., & Rego, L. L. (2005, July). Customer satisfaction, cash flow and shareholder value. *Journal of Marketing, 69*, 115–130.

Hamel, G., & Prahalad, C. K. (1994). *Competing for the Future.* Boston, MA: Harvard Business School Press.

Hannah, D. P., & Eisenhardt, K. M. (2018). How firms navigate cooperation and competition in nascent ecosystems. *Strategic Management Journal*, *39*(8), 3163–3192.

Hargadon, A. B., & Douglas, Y. (2001). When innovations meet institutions: Edison and the design of the electric light. *Administrative Science Quarterly*, *46*, 476–501.

Haselhoff, F. (1977). *Ondernemingsstrategie, een dilemma: de moderne ondernemingsorganisatie in het spanningsveld van doelmatigheid, overleving en zingeving*. Alphen aan de Rijn: Samson.

Haveman, H. A., & Rao, H. (1997). Structuring a theory of moral sentiments: Institutional and organizational coevolution in the early thrift industry. *American Journal of Sociology*, *102*(6), 1606–1651.

Heinfeldt, J., & Curcio, R. (1997). Employee management strategy, stakeholder-agency theory, and the value of the firm. *Journal of Financial and Strategic Decisions*, *10*(1), 67–74.

Helfat, C. E., Finkelstein, S., Mitchell, W., Peteraf, M. A., Singh, H., Teece, D. J., & Winter, S. G. (2007). *Dynamic Capabilities: Understanding Strategic Change in Organizations*. Malden, MA: Blackwell.

Helfat, C. E., & Peteraf, M. A. (2009). Understanding dynamic capabilities: Progress along a developmental path. *Strategic Organization*, *7*(1), 91–102.

Henderson, B. (1984). *The Logic of Business Strategy*. Cambridge, MA: Ballinger.

Hickson, D. J., Butler, R. J., Cray, D., Mallory, G. R., & Wilson, D. C. (1986). *Top Decisions: Strategic Decision-Making in Organizations*. Oxford: Basil Blackwell.

Hill, C. W. L., & Jones, T. M. (1992). Stakeholder-agency theory. *Journal of Management Studies*, *29*(2), 131–154.

Hillman, A. J., & Keim, G. D. (2001). Shareholder value, stakeholder management, and social issues: What's the bottom line? *Strategic Management Journal*, *22*, 125–139.

Hinings, C. R., & Greenwood, R. (1988). *The Dynamics of Strategic Change*. Oxford: Basil Blackwell.

Hitt, M. A., & Ireland, R. D. (2000). The intersection of entrepreneurship and strategic management research. In D. L. Sexton & H. A. Landstrom (Eds.), *Handbook of Entrepreneurship* (pp. 45–63). Oxford: Basil Blackwell.

Hitt, M. A., Ireland, R. D., Camp, S. M., & Sexton, D. L. (2001). Guest editor's introduction to the special issue strategic entrepreneurship: Entrepreneurial strategies for wealth creation. *Strategic Management Journal*, *22*, 479–491.

Hodgkinson, G. P., Whittington, R., Johnson, G., & Schwarz, M. (2006). The role of strategy workshops in strategy development processes: Formality, communication, co-ordination and inclusion. *Long Range Planning*, *39*, 479–496.

Hofer, C. W. (1975). Toward a contingency theory of business strategy. *Academy of Management Review*, *18*(4), 784–810.

Hofer, C. W., & Schendel, D. E. (1978). *Strategy Formulation: Analytical Concepts*. Minneapolis and St Paul, MN: West Publishing.

Hood, C. (1991). A public management for all seasons? *Public Administration*, *69*, 3–19.

Hrebiniak, L. G. (2006). Obstacles to effective strategy implementation. *Organizational Dynamics*, *35*(1), 12–31.

Huff, A. S., & Reger, R. K. (1987). A review of strategic process research. *Journal of Management*, *13*(2), 211–236.

Hunt, S. D., & Lambe, C. J. (2000). Marketing's contribution to business strategy: market orientation, relationship marketing and resource-advantage theory. *International Journal of Management Reviews*, *2*(1), 17–43.

Hutzschenreuter, T., & Kleindienst, I. (2006). Strategy-process research: What have we learned and what is still to be explored. *Journal of Management*, *32*(5), 673–720.

Hypko, P., Tilebein, M., & Gleich, R. (2010). Benefits and uncertainties of performance-based contracting in manufacturing industries: An agency theory perspective. *Journal of Service Management*, *21*(4), 460–489.

Jacobides, M. G. (2019, September/October). In the ecosystem economy, what's your strategy? *Harvard Business Review*, 128–137.

Jacobides, M. G., Cennamo, C., & Gawer, A. (2018). Towards a theory of ecosystems. *Strategic Management Journal*, *39*, 2255–2276. doi:10.1002/smj.2904

Jarzabkowski, P. A., & Balogun, J. (2009). The practice and process of delivering integration through strategic planning. *Journal of Management Studies*, *46*(8), 1255–1288.

Jarzabkowski, P. A., Balogun, J., & Seidl, D. (2007). Strategizing: The challenges of a practice perspective. *Human Relations*, *60*(1), 5–27.

Jensen, M. C., & Meckling, W. H. (1976). Theory of the firm: Managerial behavior, agency costs and ownership structure. *Journal of Financial Economics*, *3*, 305–360.

Johnson, G. (1987). *Strategic Change and the Management Process*. Oxford: Basil Blackwell.

Johnson, G. (1988). Rethinking incrementalism. *Strategic Management Journal*, *9*, 75–91.

Johnson, G., Whittington, R., & Scholes, K. (2011). *Exploring Strategy: Text & Cases* (9th ed.). Harlow: Prentice Hall.

Kaplan, R. S., & Norton, D. P. (1992, January–February). The balanced scorecard: Measures that drive performance. *Harvard Business Review*, 71–79.

Kaplan, R. S., & Norton, D. P. (1996). *The Balanced Scorecard: Translating Strategy into Action* Boston, MA: Harvard Business School Press.

Kapoor, R. (2018). Ecosystems: Broadening the locus of value creation. *Journal of Organizational Design*, *7*(1), 1–16.

Kerr, S. (1975). On the folly of rewarding A, while hoping for B. *Academy of Management Journal*, *18*(4), 769–783.

Kiechel III, W. (1982, December 27). Corporate strategist under fire. *Fortune*, 34–39.

Kiechel III, W. (1984, May). Sniping at strategic planning. *Planning Review*, 8–11.

Kim, W. C., & Mauborgne, R. (2004). *Blue Ocean Strategy: How to Create Uncomtested Market Space and Make the Competition Irrelevant*. Cambridge, MA: Harvard Business School Press.

Kim, W. C., & Mauborgne, R. (2005). Value innovation: A leap into the blue ocean. *Journal of Business Strategy, 26*(4), 22–28.

Kogut, B., & Zander, U. (1992). Knowledge of the firm, combinative capabilities, and the replication of technology. *Organization Science, 3*(3), 383–397.

Komori, S. (2015). *Innovating Out of Crisis: How Fujifilm Survived (and Thrived) As Its Core Business Was Vanishing.* Berkeley, CA: Stone Bridge Press.

Kotler, P. (1976). *Marketing Management.* Englewood Cliffs, NJ: Prentice Hall.

Kraaijenbrink, J., Spender, J.-C., & Groen, A. J. (2010). The resource-based view: A review and assessment of its critiques. *Journal of Management, 36*(1), 349–372.

Lawrence, T. B. (1999). Institutional strategy. *Journal of Management, 25*(2), 161–188.

Lawrence, T. B., Leca, B., & Suddaby, R. (Eds.). (2009). *Institutional Work: Actors and Agency in Institutional Studies of Organizations.* Cambridge: Cambridge University Press.

Lawrence, T. B., & Suddaby, R. (2006). Institutions and institutional work. In S. R. Clegg, C. Hardy, & T. Lawrence (Eds.), *Handbook of Organization Studies* (2nd ed., pp. 215–255). London: Sage.

Learned, E. P., Christensen, C. R., Andrews, K., & Guth, W. D. (1965). *Business Policy: Text and Cases.* Homewood, IL: Richard D Irwin.

Leblebici, H., Salancik, G. R., Copay, A., & King, T. (1991). Institutional change and the transformation of interorganizational fields: An organizational history of the US radio broadcasting industry. *Administrative Science Quarterly, 36*, 333–363.

Lenz, R. T., & Lyles, M. (1985). Paralysis by analysis: Is your planning system becoming too rational? *Long Range Planning, 18*, 28–36.

Leonard-Barton, D. (1992). Core capabilities and core rigidities: A paradox in managing new product development. *Strategic Management Journal, 13*, 111–125.

Levitt, T. (1960, July/August). Marketing myopia. *Harvard Business Review*, 45–56.

Levitt, T. (1965, November/December). Exploit the product life cycle. *Harvard Business Review*, 81–94.

Levitt, T. (1983, May/June). The globalization of markets. *Harvard Business Review*, 92–102.

Lewin, K. (1945). The research center for group dynamics at Massachusetts Institute of Technology. *Sociometry, 8*, 126–135.

Logan, M. S. (2000). Using agency theory to design successful outsourcing relationships. *International Journal of Logistics Management, 11*(2), 21–32.

Lok, J., & Willmott, H. (2019). Embedded agency in institutional theory: Problem or paradox? *Academy of Management Review, 40*.

Lorsch, J. W. (1986). Strategic myopia: Culture as an invisible barrier to change. *California Management Review, 28*, 95–109.

Lounsbury, M. (2001). Institutional sources of practice variation: Staffing college and iniversity recycling programs. *Administrative Science Quarterly, 46*, 29–56.

MacKenzie, D. (2006). *An Engine, Not a Camera.* Cambridge, MA: MIT Press.

Mahoney, J. T., & Pandian, J. R. (1992). The resource-based view within the conversation of strategic management. *Strategic Management Journal, 13,* 363–380.

Mair, A. (1999). Learning from Honda. *Journal of Management Studies, 36*(1), 25–44.

Manatsa, P. R., & McLaren, T. S. (2008). Information sharing in a suppluy chain: Using agency theory to guide the design of incentives. *Supply Chain Forum: An International Journal, 9*(1), 18–26.

March, J. G. (1991). Exploration and exploitation in organizational learning. *Organization Science, 2*(2), 71–87.

Maritan, C. A., & Peteraf, M. A. (2011). Building a bridge between resource acquisition and resource accumulation. *Journal of Management, 37*(5), 1374–1389.

Maslow, A. H. (1943). A theory of human motivation. *Psychological Review, 50*(4), 370–396.

Mason, R. O., & Mitroff, I. I. (1981). *Challenging Strategic Planning Assumptions: Theory, Cases and Techniques.* New York: John Wiley & Sons.

Mellahi, K., Jackson, P., & Sparks, L. (2002). An exploratory study into failure in successful organizations: The case of Marks & Spencer. *British Journal of Management, 13,* 15–29.

Meyer, J. W., & Rowan, B. (1977). Institutionalized organizations: Formal structure as myth and ceremony. *American Journal of Sociology, 83*(2).

Meyerson, D., & Martin, J. (1987). Cultural change: An integration of three different views. *Journal of Management Studies, 24*(6), 623–647.

Mintzberg, H. (1973). *The Nature of Managerial Work.* Englewood Cliffs, NJ: Prentice Hall.

Mintzberg, H. (1987). The strategy concept I: Five Ps for strategy. *California Management Review, 30*(1), 11–24.

Mintzberg, H. (1990). The design school: Reconsidering the basic premises of strategic management. *Strategic Management Journal, 11,* 171–195.

Mintzberg, H. (1991). Learning 1, Planning 0: Reply to Igor Ansoff. *Strategic Management Journal, 12,* 463–466.

Mintzberg, H. (1994a). Rethinking strategic planning part I: Pitfalls and fallacies. *Long Range Planning, 27*(3), 12–21.

Mintzberg, H. (1994b). Rethinking strategic planning part II: New roles for planners. *Long Range Planning, 27*(3), 22–30.

Mintzberg, H., Ahlstrand, B., & Lampel, J. (1998). *Strategy Safari: A Guided Tour Through the Wilds of Strategic Management.* London: Prentice Hall.

Mintzberg, H., Pascale, R. T., Goold, M., & Rumelt, R. P. (1996). The "Honda effect" revisited. *California Management Review, 38*(4), 78–117.

Mintzberg, H., Raisinghani, D., & Théorêt, A. (1976). The structure of "unstructured" decision processes. *Administrative Science Quarterly, 21,* 246–275.

Mintzberg, H., & Waters, J. A. (1985). Of strategies, deliberate and emergent. *Strategic Management Journal, 6,* 257–272.

Mintzberg, H., Waters, J. A., Pettigrew, A. M., & Butler, R. J. (1990). Studying deciding: An exchange of views between Mintzberg and Waters, Pettigrew, and Butler. *Organization Studies, 11*(1), 1–16.

Mitchell, R. K., Agle, B. R., & Wood, D. J. (1997). Towards a theory of stakeholder identification and salience: Defining the principle of who and what really counts. *Academy of Management Review, 22*(4), 853–886.

Montgomery, C. A. (2008, January). Putting leadership back into strategy. *Harvard Business Review*, 54–60.

Moore, J. F. (1993, May–June). Predators and prey: A new ecology of competition. *Harvard Business Review*, 75–86.

Morgan, G. (1980). Paradigms, metaphors, and puzzle solving in organization theory. *Administrative Science Quarterly, 25*, 605–622.

Munir, K. A. (2005). The social construction of events: A study of institutional change in the photographic field. *Organization Studies, 26*(1), 93–112.

Munir, K. A., & Phillips, N. (2005). The birth of the 'Kodak moment': Institutional entrepreneurship and the adoption of new technologies. *Organization Studies, 26*(11), 1665–1687.

Narayanan, V. K., & Liam, F. (1982). The micro-politics of strategy formulation. *Academy of Management Review, 7*(1), 25–34.

Nelson, R. R., & Winter, S. G. (1982). *An Evolutionary Theory of Economic Change*. Cambridge, MA: Harvard University Press.

Noble, C. (1999). The eclectic roots of strategy implementation research. *Journal of Business Research, 45*, 119–134.

Oliver, C. (1991). Strategic responses to institutional processes. *Academy of Management Review, 16*(1), 145–179.

O'Reilly III, C. A., & Tushman, M. L. (2004, April). The ambidextrous organization. *Harvard Business Review*, 74–81.

Pascale, R. T. (1984). The real story behind Honda's success. *California Management Review, 26*(3), 47–72.

Penrose, E. (1959). *The Theory of the Growth of the Firm*. New York: Wiley.

Peteraf, M. A. (1993). The cornerstones of competitive advantage: A resource-based view. *Strategic Management Journal, 14*, 179–191.

Peteraf, M. A., & Barney, J. (2003). Unraveling the resource-based tangle. *Managerial and Decision Economics, 24*, 309–323.

Pettigrew, A. M. (1973). *The Politics of Organizational Decision Making*. London and Assen: Tavistock/Van Gorcum.

Pettigrew, A. M. (1985). *The Awakening Giant: Continuity and Change in ICI*. Oxford: Basil Blackwell.

Pettigrew, A. M. (1987). Context and action in the transformation of the firm. *Journal of Management Studies, 24*(6), 649–670.

Pettigrew, A. M. (1990). Longitudinal field research on change: Theory and practice. *Organization Science, 1*(3), 267–292.

Pettigrew, A. M., Thomas, H., & Whittington, R. (2002). Strategic management: The strengths and limitations of a field. In A. M. Pettigrew, H. Thomas, & R. Whittington (Eds.), *Handbook of Strategic Management* (pp. 3–29). London: Sage.

Pettigrew, A. M., & Whipp, R. (1991). *Managing Change for Competitive Success*. Oxford: Basil Blackwell.

Pettigrew, A. M., Woodman, R. W., & Cameron, K. S. (2001). Studying organizational change and development: Challenges for future research. *Academy of Management Journal, 44*(4), 697–713.

Pfeffer, J. (1981). *Power in Organizations*. Boston, MA: Pitman.

Pfeffer, J., & Salancik, G. R. (1978). *The External Control of Organizations: A Resource Dependence Perspective*. New York: Harper & Row.

Polanyi, M. (1967). *The Tacit Dimension*. Garden City, NY: Anchor Books.

Porac, J. F., Thomas, H., & Baden-Fuller, C. (1989). Competitive groups as cognitive communities: The case of Scottish knitwear manufacturers. *Journal of Management Studies, 26*(4).

Porter, M. E. (1980). *Competitive Strategy: Techniques for Analyzing Industries and Competitors*. New York: Free Press.

Porter, M. E. (1981). The contributions of industrial organization to strategic management. *Academy of Management Review, 6*(4), 609–620.

Porter, M. E. (1985). *Competitive Advantage: Creating and Sustaining Superior Performance*. New York: Free Press.

Porter, M. E. (Ed.) (1986). *Competition in Global Industries*. Boston, MA: Harvard Business School Press.

Porter, M. E. (1990). *The Competitive Advantage of Nations*. New York: Free Press.

Porter, M. E. (1991). Towards a dynamic theory of strategy. *Strategic Management Journal, 12*, 95–117.

Powell, W. W., & DiMaggio, P. J. (Eds.). (1991). *The New Institutionalism in Organizational Analysis*. Chicago, IL: Chicago University Press.

Prahalad, C. K., & Bettis, R. A. (1986). The dominant logic: A new linkage between diversity and performance. *Strategic Management Journal, 7*, 485–501.

Prahalad, C. K., & Hamel, G. (1990, May–June). The core competence of the corporation. *Harvard Business Review*, 79–91.

Priem, R. L., & Butler, J. E. (2001). Is the resource-based "view" a useful perspective for strategic management research? *Academy of Management Review, 26*(1), 22–44.

Quinn, J. B. (1980). *Strategies for Change: Logical Incrementalism*. Homewood, IL: Richard D Irwin.

Rappaport, A. (1986). *Creating Shareholder Value: The New Standard of Business Performance*. New York: Free Press.

Rappaport, A. (2006, September). Ten ways to create shareholder value. *Harvard Business Review, 84*, 66–77.

Reed, R., & DeFillippi, R. J. (1990). Causal ambiguity, barriers to imitation, and sustainable comeptitive advantage. *Academy of Management Review, 15*(1), 88–102.

Regnér, P. (2003). Strategy creation in the periphery: Inductive versus deductive strategy making. *Journal of Management Studies, 40*(1), 57–82.

Rockart, J. F. (1979, March/April). Chief executives define their own data needs. *Harvard Business Review*, 81–93.

Ross, S. A. (1973). The economic theory of agency: The principal's problem. *American Economic Review, 63*(2), 134–139.

Roth, K., & O'Donnell, S. (1996). Foreign subsidiary compensation strategy: An agency theory perspective. *Academy of Management Journal, 39*(3), 676–703.

Rumelt, R. P., Schendel, D. E., & Teece, D. J. (1991). Strategic management and economics. *Strategic Management Journal, 12*(Winter Special Issue), 5–29.

Rumelt, R. P., Schendel, D. E., & Teece, D. J. (Eds.). (1994). *Fundamental Issues in Strategy: A Research Agenda*. Boston, MA: Harvard Business School Press.

Samra-Fredericks. (2003). Strategizing as lived experience and strategists' everyday efforts to shape strategic direction. *Journal of Management Studies, 40*(1), 141–174.

Schein, E. H. (1985). *Organizational Culture and Leadership*. San Francisco, CA: Jossey-Bass.

Schein, E. H. (1992). *Organizational Culture and Leadership* (2nd ed.). San Francisco, CA: Jossey-Bass.

Schoenberg, R. (2003). Mergers and acquisitions: Motives, value creation, and implementation. In D. Faulkner & A. Campbell (Eds.), *The Oxford Handbook of Strategy* (Vol. 2, pp. 95–117). Oxford: Oxford University Press.

Schumpeter, J. A. (1934). *The Theory of Economic Development*. Cambridge, MA: Harvard University Press.

Schwenk, C. R. (1984). Cognitive simplification processes in strategic decision-making. *Strategic Management Journal, 5*, 111–128.

Scott, W. R. (1995). *Institutions and Organizations*. Thousand Oaks, CA: Sage.

Seo, M.-G., & Creed, W. E. D. (2002). Institutional contradictions, praxis, and institutional change: A dialectical perspective. *Academy of Management Review, 27*(2), 222–247.

Simon, H. A. (1957). *Models of Man: Social and Rational*. New York: John Wiley & Sons.

Sims, H. P., & Gioia, D. A. (Eds.). (1986). *The Thinking Organization*. San Francisco, CA: Jossey Bass.

Sminia, H. (1994). *Turning the Wheels of Change*. Groningen: Wolters-Noordhoff.

Sminia, H. (2003). The failure of the Sport7 TV-channel: Controversies in a business network. *Journal of Management Studies, 40*(7), 1621–1649.

Sminia, H. (2005). Strategy formation as layered discussion. *Scandinavian Journal of Management, 21*, 267–291.

Sminia, H. (2009). Process research in strategy formation: Theory, methodology and relevance. *International Journal of Management Reviews, 11*(1), 97–125.

Sminia, H. (2011). Institutional continuity and the Dutch construction industry fiddle. *Organization Studies, 32*(11), 1559–1585.

Sminia, H., Ates, A., Paton, S., & Smith, M. (2019). High value manufacturing: Capability, appropriation, and governance. *European Management Journal, 37*, 516–528.

Sminia, H., & de Rond, M. (2012). Context and action in the transformation of strategy scholarship. *Journal of Management Studies, 49*(7), 1329–1349.

Smircich, L., & Stubbart, C. (1985). Strategic management in an enacted world. *Academy of Management Review, 10*(4), 724–736.

Spender, J.-C. (1989). *Industry Recipes: An Enquiry into the Nature and Sources of Managerial Judgement*. Oxford: Basil Blackwell.

Stulz, R. M. (1999). Globalization, corporate finance, and the cost of capital. *Journal of Applied Corporate Finance, 12*(3), 8–25.

Sturgeon, T., Van Biesebroeck, J., & Gereffi, G. (2008). Value chains, networks and culsters: Reframing the global automotive industry. *Journal of Economic Geography, 8*, 297–321.

Suchman, M. C. (1995). Managing legitimacy: Strategic and institutional approaches. *Academy of Management Review*, *20*(3), 571–610.

Sydow, J., Schüssler, E., & Müller-Seitz, G. (2016). *Managing Interorganizational Relations: Debates and Cases*. London: Palgrave Macmillan.

Teece, D. J. (2010). Business models, business strategy and innovation. *Long Range Planning*, *43*, 172–194.

Teece, D. J., Pisano, G., & Shuen, A. (1997). Dynamic capabilities and strategic management. *Strategic Management Journal*, *18*, 509–533.

Thompson, A., Strickland III, A. J., & Gamble, J. (2013). *Crafting & Executing Strategy: Concepts and Readings* (19th ed.). New York: McGraw Hill.

Trompenaars, F., & Hampden-Turner, C. (2004). *Managing People Across Cultures*. Oxford: Capstone.

Tversky, A., & Kahneman, D. (1974). Judgement under uncertainty: Heuristics and biases. *Science*, *185*, 1124–1131.

Van de Ven, A. H. (1989). Nothing is quite so practical as a good theory. *Academy of Management Review*, *14*(4), 486–489.

Van de Ven, A. H., & Poole, M. S. (1995). Explaining development and change in organizations. *Academy of Management Review*, *20*(3), 510–540.

Van de Ven, A. H., & Sminia, H. (2012). Aligning process questions, perspectives, and explanations. In M. Schultz, S. Maguire, A. Langley, & H. Tsoukas (Eds.), *Constructing Identity in and Around Organizations* (pp. 306–319). Oxford: Oxford University Press.

Van der Heijden, K. (1996). *Scenarios: The Art of Strategic Conversation*. Chichester: Wiley.

Veldman, J., & Willmott, H. (2020). Performativity and convergence in comparative corporate governance. *Competition & Change*, *24*(5), 408–428.

Wareham, J., Fox, P. B., & Cano Giner, J. L. (2014). Technology ecosystem governance. *Organization Science*, *25*(4), 1195–1215.

Watson, T. J. (1994). *In Search of Management: Culture, Chaos & Control in Managerial Work*. London: Routledge.

Weick, K. E. (1989). Theory construction as disciplined imagination. *Academy of Management Review*, *14*(4), 516–531.

Wernerfelt, B. (1984). A resource-based view of the firm. *Strategic Management Journal*, *5*(2), 171–180.

Whipp, R. (1996). Creative deconstruction: Strategy and organizations. In S. R. Clegg, C. Hardy, & W. R. Nord (Eds.), *Handbook of Organization Studies* (pp. 261–275). London: Sage.

Whipp, R. (2003). Managing strategic change. In D. Faulkner & A. Campbell (Eds.), *The Oxford Handbook of Strategy* (pp. 729–758). Oxford: Oxford University Press.

Whittington, R. (1993). *What is Strategy – and Does it Matter?* London: Routledge.

Whittington, R. (2006). Completing the practice turn in strategy research. *Organization Studies*, *27*(5), 613–634.

Williamson, O. E. (1999). Strategy research: Governance and competitive perspectives. *Strategic Management Journal*, *20*(12), 1087–1108.

Wilson, D. C. (1982). Electricity and resistance: A case study of innovation and politics. *Organization Studies, 3*(2), 119–140.

Womack, J. P., Jones, D. T., & Roos, D. (1990). *The Machine That Changed The World*. New York: Rawson.

Wood, D. J. (1991). Corporate social performance revisited. *Academy of Management Review, 16*(4), 691–718.

Zajac, E. J., & Westphal, J. D. (2004). The social construction of market value: Institutionalization and learning perspectives on stock market reactions. *American Sociological Review, 69*(3), 433–457.

Index

Note: Page numbers in *italics* indicate a figure and page numbers in **bold** indicate a table on the corresponding page.

Milton Keynes UK
Ingram Content Group UK Ltd.
UKHW051950050923
428062UK00011B/82